Re-viewing Television History

RE-VIEWING TELEVISION HISTORY

Critical Issues in Television Historiography

Edited by

Helen Wheatley

Published in 2007 by I.B.Tauris & Co Ltd
6 Salem Road, London W2 4BU
175 Fifth Avenue, New York NY 10010
www.ibtauris.com

In the United States and Canada distributed by Palgrave Macmillan,
a division of St. Martin's Press, 175 Fifth Avenue, New York NY 10010

ISBN: 978 1 84511 188 5

A full CIP record for this book is available from the British Library
A full CIP record for this book is available from the Library of Congress

Library of Congress catalog card: available

Typeset in Goudy by Replika Press Pvt. Ltd., India
Printed and bound in Czech Republic by Finidr, s.r.o.

Contents

Acknowledgements   vii
List of Contributors   ix

Introduction: Re-viewing television histories   1
Helen Wheatley

Part One: Debating the Canon

1   Is it possible to construct a canon of television programmes?   15
    Immanent reading versus textual-historicism
    John Ellis

2   Citing the classics   27
    Constructing British television drama history in publishing and
    pedagogy
    Jonathan Bignell

3   Salvaging television's past: what guarantees survival?   40
    A discussion of the fates of two classic 1970s serials, *The Secret Garden*
    and *Clayhanger*
    Máire Messenger Davies

Part Two: Textual Histories

Introduction   53

4   Negotiating value and quality in television historiography   55
    Catherine Johnson

5   'A friendly style of presentation which the BBC had always
    found elusive'?   67
    The 1950s cinema programme and the construction of
    British television history
    Su Holmes

6   BBC English Regions Drama   82
    Second City Firsts
    Lez Cooke

Part Three: Production and Institutions

Introduction   97

7   Nostalgia as resistance   99
     The case of the Alexandra Palace Television Society and the BBC
     Emma Sandon

8   Shifting sentiments   113
     BBC Television, West Indian immigrants and cultural production
     Darrell Newton

9   Piecing together 'Mammon's Television'   127
     A case study in historical television research
     Jamie Medhurst

10   History on television   142
     Charisma, narrative and knowledge
     Erin Bell and Ann Gray

Part Four: Audiences

Introduction   157

11   Researching the viewing culture   159
     Television and the home, 1946–1960
     Tim O'Sullivan

12   Writing the history of television audiences   170
     The Coronation in the Mass-Observation Archive
     Henrik Örnebring

13   Teenagers and television drama in Britain, 1968–1982   184
     Rachel Moseley

Appendix: Directory of Key Research Resources for Television History
in the United Kingdom   199

Notes   203

Bibliography   219

Index   235

Acknowledgements

I would like to thank all the contributors to this collection for their hard work and patience in responding to my endless emails over this book's extended gestation period. The editing of this book has been an intellectually enriching process, thanks to the people whose work is collected here. I would also like to acknowledge the contribution made to my thinking about television history by students and colleagues at the University of Warwick, particularly the 'Film and Television' undergraduate class of 2006–7, and by Tom Steward, with whom I have had the pleasure to discuss the processes of television history at length.

This book was begun whilst I was working on the AHRC-funded research project 'Cultures of British Television Drama, 1960–82' at the University of Reading, alongside Jonathan Bignell, Lez Cooke, John Ellis and Stephen Lacey. Along with the rest of my colleagues at the University of Reading, and all the participants at the events that were organised around this project, these people provided a supportive and stimulating context for the genesis of this collection. My thanks must also go to the members of the Midlands Television Research Group and the Southern Broadcasting Histories Research Group for sharing their ideas about broadcasting history with clarity, generosity and insight.

As always, my friends and family have seen me through the sometimes difficult process of producing this book (particular thanks go to Amy and Tracey, and to Kees for putting up with my tantrums). I am extremely grateful to John Turner for producing fabulous cover images at the last minute. My friends Rachel Moseley and Helen Wood have offered unerring intellectual and emotional support throughout this project: you are both wonderful women and I don't know what I'd do without you! Finally, I would like to thank my mum, Merryll Wheatley, for everything – this book is dedicated to her.

This book was produced with the generous support of the Arts and Humanities Research Council and the University of Warwick's Humanities Research Fund.

List of Contributors

Erin Bell is Research Fellow at the University of Lincoln, on the AHRC 'Televising History 1995–2010' project. She is a historian and continues to publish on early modern gender and religious nonconformity.

Jonathan Bignell is Professor of Television and Film at the University of Reading, where he is Director of the Centre for Television Drama Studies. He works mainly on the history and theory of television drama, leading to many publications and collaborative research projects addressing aspects of this topic.

Lez Cooke is Research Associate in Television Drama at Manchester Metropolitan University. He has written books on *British Television Drama: A History* (2003) and *Troy Kennedy Martin* (2007) and a number of articles and book chapters on British television drama.

John Ellis is Professor of Media Arts at Royal Holloway, University of London and from 1982 to 1999 ran the independent TV production company Large Door Ltd. He is the author of *Visible Fictions* (Routledge, 1982), *Seeing Things* (I.B. Tauris, 2000), *TV FAQ* (I.B. Tauris, 2007) and, with Rosalind Coward, *Language and Materialism* (Routledge, 1977).

Ann Gray is Professor in Media and Cultural Studies at the University of Lincoln and is the director of the AHRC 'Televising History 1995–2010' project. She has published on gender and technology, audience research and research methods.

Su Holmes is Reader in Film and TV at the University of East Anglia. She is the author of *British TV and Film Culture in the 1950s: Coming to a TV Near You!* (Intellect, 2005) and co-editor of *Understanding Reality Television* (Routledge, 2004) and *Framing Celebrity Culture* (Routledge, 2006). She has published widely on 1950s British television, and contemporary popular television genres.

Catherine Johnson is a Lecturer in the Department of Media Arts, Royal Holloway, University of London. She has published on contemporary and historical British and US television drama and television branding, and is the author of *Telefantasy* (BFI, 2005) and co-editor (with Rob Turnock) of *ITV Cultures: Independent Television over Fifty Years* (Open University Press, 2005).

Jamie Medhurst is a Lecturer in Film and Television History at the University of Wales Aberystwyth, where he is also Deputy Dean of Arts. He teaches, researches and publishes in the areas of broadcasting history and television and national identity. He is currently working on books on the history of ITV in Wales and the history of the early years of BBC television.

Máire Messenger Davies is Professor of Media Studies and Director of the Centre for Media Research at the University of Ulster, Coleraine. She has research interests in the media and the young, and media policy, and is currently writing a book on *Star Trek* with Professor Roberta Pearson.

Rachel Moseley is Senior Lecturer in the Department of Film and Television Studies at the University of Warwick. She has published widely in the areas of film stardom, audiences, lifestyle and teen television and is currently working on histories of television for teenagers, and for women, in Britain.

Darrell Newton is an Assistant Professor of Mass Media at Salisbury University in the United States. He is currently working on several journal articles dealing with race, culture and BBC television. He is also completing two books on the history of BBC programming as related to West Indian immigration and the *Calling the West Indies* radio programme.

Henrik Örnebring is currently Axess Research Fellow in Comparative European Journalism at the Reuters Institute for the Study of Journalism, Oxford University. He was previously Senior Lecturer in Television Studies at Roehampton University.

Tim O'Sullivan is Head of Department of Media and Cultural Production in the Faculty of Humanities at De Montfort University, Leicester. He is currently researching the domestication of television in Britain from 1946 to 1960.

Emma Sandon lectures in film and television at Birkbeck College, University of London. She is currently writing a book on early television entertainment in Britain between 1936 and 1952. She has also published articles in the area of British colonial film and photography and co-edited a book on law and film.

Helen Wheatley is Lecturer in Film and Television Studies at the University of Warwick. She has published work on a range of popular television drama and factual entertainment in the UK, US and elsewhere, and is the author of *Gothic Television* (Manchester University Press, 2007).

Introduction: Re-viewing television histories

Helen Wheatley

> Over time, the most powerful versions of history are reconfirmed, they become sedimented down, pressed into new narratives and accounts. These always involve taken-for-granted assumptions which in turn shape the relationship of television's legislators, trainees, practitioners and historians in an imaginary past and an even more speculative future. (Branston, 1998: 51)

As the field of historical television studies continues to grow, this book seizes an opportunity both to reflect on the critical questions of historiography as it relates specifically to the study of television and to showcase some exciting new developments in the field. Moving beyond Graham Roberts and Philip M. Taylor's earlier collection on the subject of television and history, which quite rightly articulated its aims as 'legitimising the field of study and formulating the terms of debate within the field' (2001: 1), I want to argue that television history can now be seen as an already legitimate field of study in which 'the terms of debate' have been formulated, if not fully reflected on. The main aims of this book are, therefore, to explore and reflect on the process of television historiography via key historical case studies, reconsidering the calcification of historical narratives described above by Gill Branston. As Branston's argument suggests, there is a pressing need to challenge received notions of what television history is, or how one goes about 'doing it', since it has a direct impact on the kinds of television we might want, or need, to demand in the future. This book is therefore a timely and self-reflexive intervention in a growing debate about television historiography (see also Corner, 2003a, Bignell, 2005b, Jacobs, 2006b, and Lacey, 2006).

Growth in the area of historical television studies can easily be charted by looking at the number of new publications in the field, in the United Kingdom and beyond, or at the number of AHRC-funded research projects[1] and resource enhancement projects[2] begun in the last decade. One could also point towards the activities of specialist organisations and conferences on the subject of television and media history more broadly,[3] or at the proliferation of historical television research presented at large-scale conferences such as the Society for Cinema and

Media Studies in the United States or the Screen conference in the United Kingdom,[4] to see the expansion of this field. Indeed, it is not always clear where historical television research and other television scholarship begins and ends, as most, if not all, studies of television usually contain some historical contextualisation on a textual, industrial or sociocultural level. For example, key works of television theory such as Raymond Williams' seminal monograph *Television: Technology and Cultural Form* (1974), or more recently John Ellis's *Seeing Things: Television in the Age of Uncertainty* (2000a), can be seen as accounts that track the development of television as a medium, and are therefore deeply ensconced in television's specific history. Richard Johnson has said of Williams: 'Here is a not-historian who, however, worked in profoundly historical ways, with page on page of dense historical analysis, who plainly took account of temporality in his work all of the time' (2001: 263). Therefore, our key texts in the field have always placed television's history at the centre of any explanation of television as a medium.

There will inevitably be people who disagree with the notion of separating television history out as a distinct field of study; television history is often written as an integral part of broadcasting history (Scannell and Cardiff, 1991; Crisell, 2002), media history (Curran and Seaton, 1997; Dahl, 1994), communications history (Startt and Sloan, 1989) and cultural history (Johnson, 2001). To deal with the medium separately might be seen as deeply myopic. Within popular memory *and* academic histories, however, television is understood as being connected to a broader media history, but it is also seen as having a distinct history, or set of histories, of its own (see Jacobs, 2006b, for a discussion of this). We therefore turn towards television history, this specific aspect of broadcasting, media, communications and cultural history, in this collection.

It is not the intention of this collection to provide a comprehensive overview of, or offer the last word on, television history, either in the British context or beyond. This edited collection of long articles, rather than being a textbook of shorter chapters covering a broader range of subjects, provides in-depth case studies and new research, instead of a survey of the work already available. There are, in any event, a number of excellent textbook overviews of television history in the UK and US contexts already in existence (see Crisell, 2002, and Hilmes, 2003, for example). Additionally, then, I want to use this opportunity to push the field further into the analysis of what is too often assumed to be a 'contemporary' medium, and to do so in a self-reflexive way. It is also not the intention that this book acts as a history of the discipline; again, there are comprehensive accounts of this offered elsewhere (see Brunsdon, 1998, 2002, Corner, 1999, and Creeber, 2006). Rather, I hope that the chapters in this collection will offer a reflection on a series of critical issues in television historiography through a discussion of detailed case studies. Following the opening section, which reconsiders the canon of television history and the process of canonisation, each of the subsequent sections – Textual Histories, Production and Institutions, and Audiences – begins with a brief reflection on the key historiographic issues raised by each case study. John Corner has recently argued that '[i]t is easy to be suspicious of "case studies", but despite their hazards of unrepresentativeness, they have an imaginative and argumentative force that most historical writers find it hard to ignore if the material allows for their development' (2003a: 278). The authors of the articles collected here show that it is possible to explore key moments of historical change and the pressing issues of television historiography by looking at specific examples, thereby producing dynamic interventions that question the history and historiography of television more widely. These examples – the moments, texts, places and figures under scrutiny – cumulatively represent what Branston, drawing on Walter Benjamin's *Illuminations* (1973), sees as the 'flashes' of history (1998: 53), or what Johnson alternatively names 'raids' and 'spot checks' on history (2001: 279). They show that it is not always necessary to make great schematic sweeps in order to understand or interrogate television's history; it is sufficient that each chapter offers a 'flash' of illumination in the history and historiography of British television. Accordingly, the authors vividly bring into view a medium that has all too easily been regarded as ephemeral, transient or somehow beyond a historical materiality.

WHY *DO* TELEVISION HISTORY?

The production of this book was inspired partly by the experience of teaching television history, or, rather, by two questions that have recurred throughout my teaching career thus far: 'Why *do* television history?' and 'How can/should we do television history?'. Like some of the other contributors to this book (see Jonathan Bignell, John Ellis and Catherine Johnson, for example), my understanding of television historiography has been both enhanced and sometimes shaken by the experience of teaching and supervising research. When raising this issue at the end of the 'Cultures of British Television Drama' conference at the University of Reading in September 2005, it became clear to me that these were questions with which many other scholars of television history were grappling, and the former question in particular garnered a variety of interesting responses, all of which were variations on what Corner has called the 'utilitarian defence' of history (2003a: 275). To clarify Corner's point here, we might argue that understanding television's history offers us a clearer sense of television's present and future (as Branston, 1998, has also argued): 'An enriched sense of "then" produces, in its differences and commonalities combined, a stronger, imaginative and analytically energised sense of now' (Corner, 2003a: 275). In teaching television studies, then, an 'enriched' sense of television history helps to make sense of television's past as well as its current importance; its changing status within the global media economy; its ability to make a social impact, not just in its everyday ubiquitousness but also in relation to key media 'events'; and its aesthetic potential for producing programmes that are moving, entertaining, thought-provoking, even beautiful.

In effect, it helps to interrogate and underline the ways in which television might *matter*.

Considering television historically therefore unbalances television studies' 'frantically contemporary agenda' (Corner, 1999: 126), and the short-sightedness of a discipline that often claims so much for the new without rigorous investigation of the apparently 'old'. It appears that television studies sometimes inherits the industry's propensity for claiming 'the next big thing' or the 'never before seen', and historical television scholarship thus seeks to counter this tendency, offering a break to this present-ist momentum. As Corner reminds us, however, 'History's fascination and its value well exceed the utilitarian defence, despite the need to appeal to this for certain kinds of national funding' (2003a: 275). Thus we can also see history writing as a creative and imaginative process, as an artistic endeavour that sometimes manages to inform, educate, and even entertain at the same time.[5]

It is also becoming increasingly clear that one cannot separate television history out from broader social, cultural or political histories. As Jean Seaton has argued, drawing on the work of media historian Asa Briggs, '[Y]ou cannot bolt the media on as an optional extra to "proper" history – you can no longer do proper history without them, because they change everything' (2004: 143); or, as Briggs himself put it, '[T]o write the history of broadcasting in the twentieth century is in a sense to write the history of everything else' (1980: 5). Thus, as work in this collection demonstrates, such as Darrell Newton's essay on the BBC's representations of West Indian immigrants, or Jamie Medhurst's discussion of the development of Welsh commercial television, writing television history often means illuminating aspects of a country's socio-political life in parallel, given that these histories are intertwined and inextricable. A historiographic approach cannot, however, view television programmes simply as 'evidence' of social history without attending to the ways in which their images and representations are constructed according to specific production or reception contexts. This connection between the 'proper' history of the world 'out there' and television history, the world 'in there', suggests that there is a real need for engaged and informed analyses of the ways in which television documents and interprets – and often impacts on – a broader social history.

As other work on television historiography has pointed out, it is particularly poignant to be researching television history at the present time, when the medium is undergoing such radical change, marked by the diffusion of television production and broadcast (in a multichannel context), the convergence of television with other media forms, and a perceived threat to public service broadcasting in the United Kingdom and beyond. We might, however, counter this thought with the question 'When hasn't the medium been undergoing seismic changes in its institutional organisation, its technological possibilities, its predominant forms, styles and genres, and its relationship with its viewers?'. If we are truly at the end of the 'age of television' (see Roberts and Taylor, 2001, and Spigel and Olsson, 2004), however, perhaps it *is* time to reflect on what it is we are losing before it slips away. This is an adaptation of the utilitarian defence of television history, which is in danger of taking on a rather elegiac tone to suggest that we are simply looking back in order to mourn a loss or erect a historical monument to a bygone age. Nonetheless, if 'one of the functions of the writing of history is to counter the *inevitability* of the consequences of technological and aesthetic change, as well as to chart its course' (Lacey, 2006: 6; emphasis in original), then perhaps looking back at earlier broadcasting history to see how we have reached the current transformations in the industry is not simply a moment of elegy or nostalgia. For example, William Boddy's recent book (2004) about the ways in which successive media (including television) have been understood as *new* media historicises the concept of the 'new' and interrogates the relationship between technological change and cultural form without simply employing a teleological historiographic narrative that either mourns the loss of the old (cultural pessimism) or blindly celebrates the new (technological determinism and 'reinvention of the wheel' thinking). What Boddy's work shows us is that a discourse of 'newness' isn't necessarily a new phenomenon, counselling us to hold fire on our period of remembrance for the object in historical television studies.

HOW DO YOU *DO* TELEVISION HISTORY?

Whilst the question of *why* we do television history has been briefly introduced, if not wholly or satisfactorily answered, we now shift to the question of *how* we do television history. The collection as a whole presents us with a series of cues to questions of methodology, some of which are not typically central to reflection in the humanities; many of the case studies presented here also argue for the combination of historiographic methodologies in order to gain a more holistic picture of a moment, figure or issue in television history. As the study of historiography in the latter half of the twentieth century has more or less shown, the notion of a singular, objective, historical truth has been debunked by those who seek to interrogate the methods of historiographic interpretation. For example, E.H. Carr, in his now canonical study *What Is History?*, first published in 1961, argued that 'the belief in a hard core of historical facts existing objectively and independently of the interpretation of the historian is a preposterous fallacy' (Carr, 1990: 12). Similarly, Keith Jenkins writes: 'No matter how verifiable, how widely acceptable or checkable, history remains inevitably a personal construct, a manifestation of the historian's perspective as a "narrator"... The past that we "know" is always contingent upon our own views, our own "present"' (1991, 12). In contrast to historians such as G.R. Elton (1969), who believed in historiography as an objective search for an incontrovertible truth, Carr and others have thus questioned and examined the level of subjective interpretation at play in the processes of history writing. Furthermore, and more radically, the later postmodernist turn in historiography, responding to what was perceived by postmodern critics as the 'death of centres' and an incredulity towards the meta-narratives of history, prompted a destabilisation of the discipline, and a heated debate over the terms of history and the possibility for truth and objectivity. As Richard J. Evans puts it, '[H]istorians at the end of the twentieth century are haunted by a sense of [postmodern] gloom' (1997, 3).

The issues of truth, objectivity and the partiality of historical narratives are just as important in the consideration of how we go about researching and writing television history. The selectivity of the discipline operates at a number of levels: it is found in the decision to look either at those making television, at those viewing television or at television as a textual object (or a combination of these approaches), but also in which moments and eras, aspects, forms, genres or programmes one looks at in detail, and which one chooses to ignore. Jason Jacobs has argued that 'relevance is a matter of judgement, but this is not a subjective matter. The aspiration to objectivity and truth should be uppermost in the historian's mind even as he/she acknowledges that total objectivity is impossible to attain' (2006b: 111). The most visible case in point here is found in the radical work of feminist historians seeking to write a history of women's programming, viewing practices and female programme makers back into wider histories of television (see Leman, 1987, Spigel and Mann, 1992, and Haralovich and Rabinowitz, 1999, for example). Feminist histories have necessarily, therefore, illuminated the partiality of earlier histories of the medium, calling for an alternative and politicised focus for historical work, rescuing and even celebrating women's tastes and cultural competences, labour and creativity, in an otherwise typically male-centred account of the medium's history. This research still shows that partiality is unavoidable, given the extensiveness of television history; of course, the historian of television must sort through the artefacts of television history, according to their interpretation of interest and significance. Jacobs' proposal that this selection should be 'a matter of judgement' but not 'a subjective matter' suggests, however, that it is essential to reflect on this process of selection, to undertake it in a mindful, not mindless, way, and to consider what is missing from the histories produced through necessarily selective research, if we are to produce convincing and useful histories of television.

As several scholars have pointed out, in this collection and elsewhere (see Cooke, 2003, for example), in terms of its research resources (written archives, programmes for viewing, audience data, etc.) television history oscillates between having too much and too little data to cope with in any kind of systematic way. As the chapters in Part One of this collection, Debating the Canon, show, in the United Kingdom the archiving of early television programmes is, at best, scant and unrepresentative of what was actually shown on television in its earliest years; at worst, it is non-existent. At the present time, written institutional archives are extensive if you wish to study the BBC up to the 1970s, but virtually absent or inaccessible in all other cases. Later on in British television's history, the sheer volume of material available for study presents an entirely different, but no less difficult, problem for the historian. So the question of selectivity, both that which is enforced on historians by archiving practices beyond their control, and that which they must employ themselves in order to focus on a manageable research project, must be examined and questioned if we are to produce satisfactory histories of the medium. Of course, also related to this point about selectivity is the need to be self-reflexive about our contemporary positions as researchers and viewers in relation to material we are studying. As Carr observed, 'We can view the past, and achieve our understanding of the past, only through the eyes of the present. The historian is of his own age, and is bound by the conditions of human existence' (1990: 24). I will return to this issue below in discussing the dual problems of nostalgic and patronising approaches to television history.

Broadly, several key approaches to television history have developed in television studies in the UK and US contexts. Firstly, there have been histories of television as institution, in which meta-narratives of television's production, organisation and regulation have been foregrounded (e.g. Briggs, 1979; Barnouw, 1982; Sendall, 1982, 1983). Secondly, there are micro-histories of television production, or what Corner has called 'television as making' (2003a: 275), which focus on quotidian production cultures and examine production practices in relation to key periods or genres (e.g. Born, 2000; Cottle, 2004; Skutch, 1998). Thirdly, there are those histories that document television viewing in relation to social or political change, or to television's shifting meanings within everyday life (e.g. Meehan, 2003; Hallam, 2005b; Spigel, 2001; O'Sullivan, 1991). Fourthly, there have been a range of histories of television programming that illuminate issues of representation, form and aesthetics within a historical framework (e.g. Jacobs, 2000; Caughie, 2000; Johnson, 2005; Wheatley, 2006b). Finally, there is the rather neglected field of technological television history (see Winston, 1998), and studies that discuss television's promotion and marketing in the US (e.g. Boddy, 2004; McCarthy, 2001). There is certainly more work to do in this latter field, and, indeed, it is a shame that this collection does not offer more of this particular area of historical television studies (though the essays by Lez Cooke and Emma Sandon do discuss technological developments in the field of television *production*).

Organising this book around the headings for Parts Two to Four of Textual Histories, Production and Institutions, and Audiences, respectively, I had initially assumed that I would be able to offer key examples of different ways to approach each of these areas as objects of historical study. These headings do not actually hold fast, however – or, rather, they appear somewhat arbitrary in places – when looking at the *combination* of approaches that the contributors to the collection employ. If Rachel Moseley's study of teen television in the 1970s is an exploration of the institutional construction and regulation of the teen audience, it is also an elegant piece of textual analysis that analyses the programmes in question, looking at the textual mode of address directed towards a teenage viewership.

On the other hand, Su Holmes' textual history of film programmes in the 1950s also unpicks many of the historical commonplaces of institutional meta-histories of the BBC and ITV in the United Kingdom by looking at the example of a single genre. What this constant crossing over of foci and methods suggests, and what others concerned with television historiography have begun to argue for (see Roberts and Taylor, 2001, Corner, 2003a, Black, 2005 and Jacobs, 2006b), is a need for a multi-methodological approach to television historiography in order to produce a more rounded, holistic version of television history.[6] At a recent workshop on the question of the history of television for women, Ann Gray proposed that we conceptualise historical research methodologies as a kind of contingent mosaic, in which television historians draw together different strands of the production/text/viewer triumvirate according to the particular needs of the project.[7] Indeed, it has long been argued that we need to break down this triumvirate because of what it suggests about the distinctions between its elements, and because of its excessively linear account of the media process (see Moores, 1990). Gray's 'contingent mosaic' is a similar idea to Lynn Spigel and Denise Mann's notion of 'conjunctural histories' (1992: viii), and suggests that, whilst we might not want, or even be able, to look at television's production, textuality and reception simultaneously every time we approach the historical study of the medium, combining some of these approaches most of the time will prove more fruitful than not. Thinking beyond the disciplinary boundaries of 'television history', or 'broadcasting history', or even 'media history', might also bring the medium's history to light in new and interesting ways; as both Johnson (2001) and Spigel (2005) have argued, transdisciplinarity or interdisciplinarity also lie at the cutting edge of the field.

FOUR KEY PROBLEMS OF TELEVISION HISTORY: A BRITISH PERSPECTIVE

Before moving on to introduce the first essays in the book, I want to outline briefly what I see as four of the most significant problems or hurdles facing television historians, particularly in the UK context. These are:

- the 'problem' of national specificity;
- the (over-)privileging of institutional histories of television;
- the problem of nostalgia and the need to confront the connection between popular and academic histories of the medium; and
- the question of access to, and survival of, material that shapes our sense of television history.

To begin with the question of the national in television history, it will be clear to readers that the essays in this book are written about *British* television history, though not exclusively by British scholars, and that this not only has an impact on the histories that are being told here but also inflects the kinds of methodologies employed by contributors. Questions around public service broadcasting and quality television, explorations of the importance of the media in shaping and articulating viewers' cultural identities, examinations of the relationship between television and everyday life, and the connections between television and other art and media forms have abounded in British television studies, focusing almost exclusively on the production, broadcast and reception of a *national* television service. These concerns in turn constitute a particular form of television history, exemplified by the chapters in this collection. Our experience of television, however, is in fact unlikely to be based exclusively on the consumption of national television products, and our sense of 'television history' as casual viewers or scholars is likely to be inflected by our own national popular memory but infused with the impact of overseas imports. The broadcast of foreign television is a common practice in most countries, and the impact of foreign national television on other nations is likely to be felt in various ways and in relation to different geopolitical histories by programme makers, executives and other creative managers.[8] This fact, along with the desire to connect up nationalised 'pockets' of historical television scholarship more satisfactorily, have led to scholars calling for a reassessment of the national boundaries drawn up in television historiography, and for a move towards comparative international comparative histories (Dahl, 1994; Smith, 1998; Jacobs, 2006b). These are calls to be welcomed, if not ones that have been explicitly addressed in the construction of this book.

Of course, the question of access to research materials is a major shaping factor in the kinds of television historiography that get undertaken; in the British context, the relatively rich archive of institutional documents held at the BBC's Written Archives Centre (WAC) has arguably led to an uneven emphasis on this particular national institution and its policies and management structures, within broader histories of the medium. Needless to say, I am not suggesting that we abandon this important work on a globally significant public broadcaster, but that we

- supplement it with other, perhaps more obscure or more difficult to trace, institutional histories in the same national, or an international, context;[9]
- join institutional histories up with other forms of historiography (as this collection attempts to do); and
- interrogate the methods by which we approach and interpret this vitally important archive.[10]

In the field of institutional history there is still, perhaps, a good deal for the television historian to learn from history as an academic discipline, and from that Rankean spadework that encourages us to '[investigate] the provenance of documents, of enquiring about the motives of those who wrote them, the circumstances in which they were written, and the ways in which they relate to other documents on the same subject' (R.J. Evans, 1997: 19). Ultimately, then, the institutional history remains at the centre of British television studies at present, given that the questions of public service broadcasting in the UK, and the BBC's place as a publicly funded institution, remain such pressing issues.

Returning again to a 'utilitarian defence' of history raises the question of nostalgia in television historiography; it is, of course, as important to learn from the mistakes of television's past as it is to celebrate its victories, and imperative that we do not simply produce mournful or elegiac histories of television institutions, though slippage into this position is often found in discussions of television history, both from those who worked in the industry,[11] and also in sentimentalised discussions of past television programming. Carr raises the problem of those people who claim to 'love the past' and argues that 'to love the past may easily be an expression of the nostalgic romanticism of old men and old societies, a symptom of loss of faith and interest in the present or future' (1990: 25). Historian John Tosh qualifies this nostalgic position by relating it to the conditions of socio-historical change:

> [Nostalgia] works most strongly as a reaction to a sense of loss in the recent past, and it is therefore particularly characteristic of societies undergoing rapid change. Anticipation and optimism are never the only – or even the main – social response to progress. There is nearly always regret or alarm at the passing of old ways and familiar landmarks. A yearning backward glance offers consolation, an escape in the mind from a harsh reality. (2000a: 12)

On the other hand, viewing, or re-viewing or analysing television from the present frequently produces a reading of television's texts, and its production and viewing practices, as being quaint, or somewhat limited or rather odd in some way – a position that might be seen as the opposite of a nostalgic reading of television's past. In this collection, both Johnson and Ellis discuss this phenomenon in teaching television history to their students, albeit from different perspectives, and drawing different conclusions.

These dual problematic positions of the nostalgic or patronising reading of television history are, in part, created, or at least reinforced, via popular histories of the medium, particularly through the presentation of television's past on television itself. As Spigel has pointed out, when teaching television history, and when researching it ourselves, it is essential that we recognise and acknowledge the connection between popular history, or what she terms 'popular memory', and academic histories of television, given that they are so inextricably linked: 'Rather than deriding the popular and returning to a more "legitimate" historical/cultural canon… we need to examine the relationships between popular memory and professional history' (1995: 32–33). Thus Spigel urges us to ask 'to what extent is our "professional" historical text informed by these popular narratives?'. As I have argued elsewhere – for example, in relation to the history of British television drama – the rebroadcast of archival material has an enormous impact on the construction of historical commonplaces and the identification of programming trends, which often have little or no historical accuracy in relation to the broader picture of television broadcasting in a particular time or place (see Wheatley, 2007).

Of course, this also leads us on to the question of access to television's past, and specifically access to historical programming and the impact that this access has on the kinds of historical research that get undertaken. As Jason Jacobs has argued, 'The danger here is that television history gets reconstructed around what survives for viewing rather than what was actually shown' (2006b: 112). Máire Messenger Davies' analysis of the process of canonisation in this volume finds archival 'survival' at the centre of this process, unpicking the reasons for continued 'easy' access to canonised programming that are not necessarily based on notions of quality or historical significance/value. Whilst techniques have been developed in some areas of television studies (particularly in the field of historical television drama studies – see Jacobs, 2000) to critically reconstruct 'lost' programming using the written archive, it is important that we acknowledge the significance of the agenda of widening access to the programming that does survive, looking for ways to open up commercially run archives to the television historian, and connecting up the work of archivists and historians. I would also add, following the lead from Michele Hilmes (2003: vii), that archiving is a feminist issue, given the relative absence of texts and genres traditionally coded as feminine from publicly accessible archives, and that this is an absence that needs to be addressed by future historians.

The first three essays in this collection directly tackle many of the four 'problems' outlined above, in their discussion of the notion of a canon in television history. We begin here, taking the lead from Glen Creeber's suggestion that, 'if canon construction is inevitable, then [should we not]...talk about their construction and influence openly, discuss how and why they have been constructed and who has constructed them?' (2004: xv).[12] John Ellis's chapter opens the collection provocatively by critiquing the tradition of textual analysis in television historiography that he terms 'immanent reading', problematising the reinterpretation of historical texts through a modern optic. Relating this to the process of canonisation, and arguing that television is an essentially time-tied medium in which programmes are only temporarily meaningful, Ellis argues instead for a form of textual historicism that reinstates the importance of a text by referring it back to the context of its creation. Thus, he argues that a canon of television programmes has been problematically formed around immanent, ahistorical readings of texts thus far, and that this needs further qualification and historically situating analysis. Jonathan Bignell, on the other hand, offers an insightful overview of key histories of television drama, one of the most developed areas of historical television research in the United Kingdom and beyond. Bignell goes on to discuss the criteria for selecting and illuminating examples in teaching and publishing on television drama history, analysing the balance between the exceptional and the representative when focusing in on canonical moments within this history. Finally, in this section, Máire Messenger Davies offers us a case study of survival (or failure to survive) in relation to two literary adaptations,

The Secret Garden (BBC, 1975) and *Clayhanger* (ATV, 1976), and argues that the process of canonisation is particularly difficult in the case of television, given that so little of what was broadcast actually survives. Looking at the private ownership of historical television, Messenger Davies argues that the construction of the television canon might actually be working as a 'bottom-up' process, which nonetheless needs galvanising through institutional support and the further (re)distribution of copies of significant television programmes. Re-examining *Clayhanger* through access provided by this 'bottom-up' process of archiving and canonisation, Messenger Davies revisits arguments around quality (which are also addressed in the following chapter, by Catherine Johnson) and proposes that evaluative judgements in television historiography must be made within the historical context of its production.

It is hoped that the chapters that follow this opening section, and that raise similarly provocative questions about television historiography, will serve as useful case studies for the different ways in which television history can be approached: each essay will be introduced at the start of the relevant section, and the connections between them will be drawn out. If, as R.G. Collingwood argues, 'it is possible to be a quite good historian (though not an historian of the highest order) without… reflecting upon one's own historical thinking' (1994: 3), I also hope that the process of editing this collection will have made me a better historian, and that readers will find it the work collected here as illuminating and thought-provoking as I have.

PART ONE
Debating the Canon

1 Is it possible to construct a canon of television programmes?

Immanent reading versus textual-historicism

John Ellis

Any canon, or 'list of greats', discriminates. That is its purpose. A canon tells us what is important, what we need to know, and what it regards as having enduring value. Any good canon will also expose its biases and its underlying rationales. Now that television has become an object of study, it too is subjected to the activity of canon building, if only because lecturers and students choose to study and write about one programme, series or genre rather than another. A canon is implicit in every such choice. But TV presents a number of unusual difficulties in relation to the activity of canon building, as is clear to everyone who has been asked 'What are the 50 best or most important TV programmes?' (see Creeber, 2004). Elsewhere, I have examined the problems that such canon building faces in relation to the fiftieth anniversary of the avowedly populist channel ITV (Ellis, 2005). It is clear that one problem with such choices is that TV is more than simply the sum of its texts. It encompasses a shared viewing experience for millions of people. Even its texts are difficult to define and compare: how do you choose between *The Six O'Clock News* (BBC1, 1984–) and *Cathy Come Home* (BBC, 1966), between a vast series and a single influential programme, and between very different genres? This becomes even more difficult when another underlying principle of canon construction is added into the process: the criterion of 'lasting value'. When this is applied to TV, it highlights the contrast between two different interpretive procedures.

It seems that there are indeed two contrasting interpretive procedures in use in the emerging field of broadcasting or television studies. One studies texts in their historical context, tying meaning to the period in which the programme was made. The other centres itself on the texts and the potential meanings that

15

they carry, reinterpreting them through a modern optic. The tension between these approaches, the textual-historical and the immanent, is already beginning to emerge despite broadcast television's tiny historical span of a little more than a half-century. That this should be the case demonstrates a key feature of broadcasting as a medium: the intimate connections between its programmes and the moment of their intended broadcast. So tight is this connection between broadcast TV programmes and their moment of transmission that programmes very quickly become 'dated', for a number of different reasons. Nevertheless, it is still a shock to encounter the sheer otherness of programmes that, even to a viewer of my age, were once easy to engage with and transparent in their meanings.

The tension between textual-historicism and immanent reading as interpretive procedures is nothing unique.[1] Indeed, it is the tension between hermeneutics (understanding a text by relating it to its context) and exegesis (drawing out the immanent meaning of a text through understanding its own inner meaning). Examples of the contrast between these approaches can be drawn from the study of written texts, although I believe that the phenomenon of an intensely time-tied medium such as broadcasting raises some distinctive problems. To draw on a prominent example, textual-historicism is the province of a whole genre of writing about William Shakespeare, which seeks to trace how differing epochs have staged his texts (e.g. Wells, 1966; Schafer, 1998). This textual-historicism demonstrates that each century and culture has its own Shakespeare. Another form of textual-historicism will seek the roots of Shakespeare's inventions within the culture and events of his own times (e.g. Jardine, 1996). By contrast, an immanent reading of Shakespeare seeks to widen the possibilities of meaning, tracing the twists and turns of possible implication lying dormant in each phrase (e.g. Kermode, 2001).

The starkest example of immanent reading at work is offered by studies of the Bible. Since the Bible has been widely regarded as the nearest thing we have to the word of God, interpretations of it have generated actions, readings of it have changed the world. The Bible has provided rich material for immanent reading, since it contains many voices from differing periods and, in the New Testament, a series of different accounts of the life and works of Jesus. In the face of the Bible's rampant polysemy, textual-historical interpretation has remained a minority approach, apart from instances when history is drawn in to bolster one reading over another. A textual-historicist approach to the Bible would attempt to locate its constituent texts back into the periods and societies that produced them. Such an activity is regarded as suspect, however, since it reduces the polysemy of the texts, and, indeed, their subsequent cultural importance. As Francis Watson wrote when reviewing one such attempt:

> To locate the biblical world so exclusively in the distant past is to marginalize the texts' own claim to come from that past in order to address each subsequent present. This claim has generated rich and enduring interpretative traditions in both Christian and Jewish communities, for whom biblical texts continue

to mediate divine reality. In severing the Bible from the interpretative traditions it has generated, one simply destroys it. If the proposed 'historical contexts' prove surprisingly inhospitable to the biblical texts, this may suggest that one is looking for the biblical world in the wrong place. (Watson, 2003)[2]

Watson's position as a believer leads him to regard the biblical text not as a historically situated artefact but as a source of active guidance in successive present conjunctures. He believes that the biblical text internally claims to be the word of God seen through the eyes of men. As such, its words produce thought and action. Old meanings and source meanings don't matter: what matters is how it can be used in the present. At its weakest, Watson's argument leads to a position that there is no intrinsic meaning in the text at all, that everything lies in the beliefs of the beholder. At its strongest, however, his argument makes a case for a dynamic text that continues to be used and to be relevant, a text that renews itself with each interpretation. For the immanent reader, the Bible is that most valuable of creations: one that endures despite the centuries and the changes of habit and fashion. This leads to a position that sees the biblical text as beyond exhaustive interpretation, a totality that nevertheless resists total interpretation.

A religiously based defence of textual-historicism against Watson's criticism would emphasise the need to strip out that which distorts the word of God, the historically specific concerns that get in the way of what is being said. Or, again and more subtly, textual-historical study would show that the word of God is never clear but is always glimpsed through the historically and geographically specific. Textual-historicism can help the faithful to realise that many of the Bible's prohibitions and exhortations relate specifically to one place and moment, and should be adapted to suit other times and places rather than be adopted wholesale. Textual-historical interpretation can then be seen as reinforcing the importance of the text, drawing it away from wilful and partial interpretation, an activity that is sometimes known as 'heresy'.[3] Understandings of the Bible show very clearly the differences between an immanent reading and a textual-historical approach, and the strengths and weaknesses of each. Immanent reading privileges interpretation and the continuing vitality and relevance of the text. Textual-historicism seeks to orient that process of interpretation by referring the text back to the context of its creation. The Bible is a self-evidently historical text, composed of elements drawn from a long and fascinating process of collective writing. Yet what matters to most people is not its historically specific nature but what it says to them now, what they can get out of it and do with it. This is an enabling process. It has also created huge difficulties throughout the history of the Christian era, however. The Bible generates meanings that guide people's lives; but it also generates meanings that blight lives and produce conflict. This is particularly the case when readings of the Bible are not tempered by awareness of the historical nature of the text.

I am not about to argue that television programmes have the same status as the Bible. The greatest thing they have in common is that both are mandatory items in the hotel rooms of the Western world.[4] The Bible is a finite text that has a unique cultural status. Television is endless and everyday. Its programmes are the opposite of the biblical text, in that they contain no claims to any kind of pan-historical relevance. They claim relevance to their time only, and that time frame is often conceived as being extremely short. Nonetheless, the contrasting approaches to the biblical text that I have outlined can illuminate what is becoming the central problem of television studies as it develops. Immanent reading and textual-historicism will be as sharply opposed as they are in biblical studies because of the fundamental nature of the broadcast TV that has developed in the last 50 years.

Television technology has been developed as domestic[5] and constantly present.[6] This broadcast form of television has come to dominate our understanding of the medium. It emphasises the everyday. Television is always with its audience, constantly available, and watched an average of three hours a day.[7] Television programmes are made for a moment in time, which was originally a single transmission, after which the programme was often discarded. Some programmes (news, chat shows, etc.) are still made this way, but, increasingly, programmes (especially drama) are made for a commercial life of several years, which can encompass their sale as boxed sets of series as well as repeat viewings and syndication. The first moment of transmission, like the first release of a cinema film, remains the primary point of reference and the moment of definitive cultural impact.

Television programming is heavily time-tied. A sense of intimacy with the audience is generated by the use of references to a shared present moment, using terms such as 'here' and 'today', 'we' and 'you', 'is' rather than 'was'. Drama aims towards topicality, aspiring to becoming either a topic of conversation because of its issues, a common point of reference (as in 'Are you watching *Desperate Housewives?*') or a comforting feature of existence (as in *Heartbeat* or *Rosemary and Thyme*).[8]

The everydayness of TV presents real difficulties of interpretation for the historian. References are made to a common present moment, and relatively wide assumptions are made about shared assumptions regarding the conventions of human behaviour. Questions of taste and fashion, which are intensely time-tied, are frequently used to place characters and relate them to each other. Who in 50 years' time will be able to place the character of Gabrielle Solis (Eva Longoria) in *Desperate Housewives* as instantly as we do by her taste in clothing, home decor and vehicle? No dialogue is needed to set up a character whose stairway displays a series of portraits of herself in sub-Warhol primary colours, along with an expert copy in oils of a Titian *Madonna and Child* over the fireplace. Such issues of taste lose their meaning all too quickly. Older TV programmes tend to look simply 'quaint' to those too young to have lived the moment as the present. The references are lost on them unless the viewer has acquired some sense of fashion history. For those who lived through the period, the references remain clear, but another effect begins to develop: an odd sense of the period being 'older than I feel', of being more distant psychically than it is in literal years. Because such viewers now inhabit a different everyday reality with its own references and assumptions, a set of conflicting feelings begins to develop. An initial sense of nostalgia, an easy familiarity with the period, soon begins to pall. It gives way to a set of vague uneasinesses, a disbelief at the superficial ugliness of clothes, haircuts, furniture and decor, along with a vague discomfort at some of the working assumptions about the nature of life. All those jokes about strikes in programmes of the 1970s, all the unremarked-on smoking, are eloquent of the social and political changes that have taken place subsequently. As a result of both nostalgia and unease, the period feels further away in time and more strange than it ever was at the time.

So, even if you were there at the time, there is something about old TV that feels less comfortable, precisely because it was once so familiar and taken for granted. Old television programmes slip over a receding horizon of everydayness as common assumptions change. In addition, television has its own working assumptions, a sense of the contemporary of its own. Anyone trying to use old television as evidence of anything – even those who were 'there at the time' – therefore has to go through a phase of appreciating its status as within the history of television. He or she has to understand how the particular programme under consideration fitted within the overall universe of television available at that time. The meanings of a programme were (and are) altered by such considerations as these.

- Was this a 'popular' programme or an 'edge of the schedule' risk?
- How did it fit into the schedule and the market image of the channel for which it was made?
- What was the standard format of the programme and was this a typical programme for the series?
- Was this a typical programme for the format or genre, or an atypical or old-fashioned one?
- What was the reputation of the programme: what was it 'known for' (if indeed it was known for anything), and what expectations had been set up for it by pre-publicity?
- Was the acting style and dialogue perceived as 'clichéd', 'mannered', 'theatrical' or 'naturalistic'?
- What was the size of the budget for this programme and how did it compare with other contemporary productions?[9]
- How did the programme relate to the industrial and regulatory context of broadcasting at the time?

The older the TV material that is being considered, the clearer it becomes that television programmes are temporarily meaningful, and are designed to be so. TV programmes are designed for a particular moment, and care is taken that the language used in many pre-recorded programmes still gives the illusion that presenters are speaking directly to their viewers. Comedy is filled with contemporary references, and even drama assumes an often surprising level of common knowledge of the present in its audiences. Entertainment material is 'cross-sectional', dense with references to its time, sometimes to the point of being incomprehensible to subsequent generations. This is why the tension between immanent and textual-historicist approaches is central to the development of broadcasting and television studies. Historicist understandings would seem to be necessary in coming to terms with this phenomenon of the temporarily meaningful, both for those who were there at the time and those who are seeking to understand why a given TV text is as it is or meant what it was taken (explicitly or not) to mean.

A specific example will show how the nature of broadcast TV causes problems of interpretation quite acutely for a drama that is on its way to becoming a part of the canon. It is Alun Owen's 'Lena, O My Lena', an ITV play in ABC's *Armchair Theatre* series, directed by Ted Kotcheff and produced by Sydney Newman and shown on 25 September 1960. This programme survives from the period, whereas Owen's earlier and much-acclaimed 'No Trams to Lime Street' (ABC, 1959) does not. Thus it fulfils the first precondition for canonical treatment: it still exists. It has also been re-screened in the era of home video taping, so scholars have copies that can be studied: the second precondition. The programme is also felt to be of sufficient interest to have been discussed several times – in John Caughie's *Television Drama* (2000) and as a case study in Lez Cooke's *British Television Drama* (2003) – and it has a substantial entry on the British Film Institute's (BFI's) Screenonline website.[10] The programme is one of a series of remarkable experiments with live studio drama in the UK undertaken in the envelope of the *Armchair Theatre* series. It uses two spectacularly deep sets and composes action and camera movement within them. It was by no means the only such experiment, and it probably owes its survival to a technological experiment: it seems to have been an early example of the use of the new Ampex tape system to pre-record a live transmission.[11] The programme is, crucially, remarkable for its ease with a working-class setting, for its dynamic and startlingly naturalistic mise en scène and for its coherence and power as a drama.

Showing 'Lena, O My Lena' to third-year students yielded many problems of comprehension, however, because many misunderstood the central dynamic of the drama, which involves questions both of class and of gender conflict. The drama centres on Tom (Peter McEnery), a callow student from a working-class background who takes on a summer job in a warehouse. He starts a flirtation with Lena, a woman working in the small neighbouring factory (played by Billie Whitelaw). The wise foreman, Ted (Colin Blakely), tries to advise him against it. Lena uses Tom to taunt Glyn (Scott Forbes), her smouldering fiancé, who drives the warehouse delivery lorry. A huge variety of puzzled explanations were advanced for Lena's motivation. She was seen as substantially older than Tom because she appeared mature and 'in control', in contrast to Tom's apparent incompetence and his discomfort around his workmates. Nevertheless, this appeared to conflict with her desire for the dominating Glyn, whose jealousy she was seeking to provoke. Students began to question the characterisation, asking why Lena behaved as she did, and why she didn't simply leave the district if she hated it. They felt that the portrayal of Tom was embarrassing, and even inappropriate when he explains his attraction to Lena in terms of her being 'so real'. The drama had clearly affected these viewers, but the reasons why the characters act as they do were no longer clear; indeed, they were liable to misinterpretation. Tom was seen by one student as the victim of a systematic bullying campaign in which Lena was an active participant, if not the ringleader.

'Lena, O My Lena' shared a number of assumptions with its audience in 1960 that appear strange less than 50 years later. They relate to the nature of social class; the antagonistic nature of relations between men and women; and the social position of students. The class dimension of the play is crucial. It is set in a milieu that British film and TV were beginning to explore: the industrial working class of (particularly) northern England. This exploration gathered momentum just as its object of study began to disappear as a typical way of life, under the pressures of the decline of traditional industry, slum clearance and substantial immigration to such localities from the former colonies and elsewhere. In this working-class England, generations had lived and died with social horizons that were restricted though tolerably fulfilling. It is the kind of world that Henry Green portrayed in *Living* (1929), and Arthur Seaton tried to escape from in *Saturday Night and Sunday Morning* (Karel Reisz, 1960). Escape was not really an option for women such as Lena in that era. This is a working-class world in which small differentiations count for much. Ted's dry 'Oh yeah' when Tom reveals that his father is not a worker but a foreman reveals much about them both. It is a milieu where everyone knows everyone else's business, where 'Sunday is the worst day in the world. You can go out on Sunday and come back in everything sucked out of you by inquisitiveness in eyes in residential districts...' (Green, 1929: 189). To travel away from this milieu, as Green shows, is a major adventure, undertaken at considerable peril. It is also a milieu that, though confining, can find a place in the workforce for Derek (Patrick O'Connell), the 'simple lad'.

The particular problems of interpreting the class basis of 'Lena, O My Lena' were intensified by the portrayal of the outsider Tom as a student. For young people at university today, when participation is approaching 50 per cent of their generation, the pre-Robbins era of higher education of 1960 is indeed a distant era.[12] University education was an immense privilege for a small minority, supported as they were, for someone such as Tom, with a grant that would pay both fees and (at least) term-time living expenses. Tom, though, is in a special category, the working-class 'grammar school boy' who has made it across the class barriers to get to university. The plight of such individuals is well described by Richard Hoggart, one of their number, in his *Uses of Literacy* (1957). These boys were chosen for their academic abilities and felt profoundly ill at ease when they went to university, finding themselves in the company of people who took wealth and privilege as their right. Yet, by this stage in their lives, these grammar school boys were, as Tom is, equally uncomfortable with the people they had grown up with. Their success as grammar school boys required that they take on many of the prevalent cultural values of the middle and upper classes, seeing working-class lives as stunted and unfulfilling. This would particularly be the case for a student such as Tom, who appears to be studying English literature in the time of Leavisite values. It was against such values that Hoggart wrote *The Uses of Literacy* and Raymond Williams reformulated the concept of culture as 'a whole way of life' (Williams, 1984: 57–88; 1977: 11–20). Tom, however, is experiencing these conflicts, which is one of the reasons why the drama is so compelling, screened as it was just three years after Hoggart had identified the phenomenon.

The drama naturally assumes that its audience can place the characters in the class geography of contemporary Britain, and will be able to identify the dilemmas experienced by Tom. Both have disappeared, but have left sufficient cultural residues that contemporary students could find ways of understanding them. The third dimension of 'Lena, O My Lena' is less well charted, however. This is the dimension of 'sex antagonism', as it was identified in a groundbreaking piece of anthropological research carried out a few years later by Ann Whitehead and eventually published in 1976. Studying a rural community in Herefordshire, Whitehead identified the extent to which males and females acted as separate social groups, with a marked degree of antagonism between them. This is starkly borne out by the situation in 'Lena, O My Lena', where the small warehouse in which Tom works is an all-male workplace, and Lena's metal stamping factory is all-female. Whitehead describes the problems that this pervasive antagonism creates for the process of courtship, and the resulting nature of marriage as an uneasy truce directed towards survival. In Whitehead's village there are few social spaces for women; in Lena's city environment such spaces do exist, but sex antagonism is still the pervasive habit of mind, as many remarks and attitudes make clear. The idea of a non-sexualised friendship between a woman and a man is unimaginable in this context. This culture of sex antagonism is pervasive in television material of the 1950s and 1960s, but now appears quite strange. Whitehead's research was itself one of the founding texts of the feminism that brought about the end of this culture.

Students failed to understand the sexual dynamic between Lena, Tom and Glyn because the habits of sex antagonism portrayed were foreign to them; they failed to understand the limits of the working-class society assumed by the programme, or the privileged position of students in the period and the consequent resentment felt towards the grammar school boy, and his own confusions about his role. Several aberrant readings were produced as a result – or, more precisely, readings that could be supported by watching the text without having a supporting knowledge of its historical status. For a textual-historicist, such readings are simply wrong; for a scholar trained in the immanent reading approaches associated with literary study, however, they are not necessarily wrong at all. Even the most extreme immanent reader, however, would feel uneasy at taking such a position simply because the text is capable of generating such interpretations. Perhaps this is because the text is not a Shakespeare play, for which new interpretations come with each staging, but is a finished work, a particular staging of Owen's text by Kotcheff and the *Armchair Theatre* team. A considerable aspect of its importance lies in the innovative TV mise en scène and in the performance of the principal actors, especially Billie Whitelaw.

The pull of immanent reading is, nevertheless, a powerful one, both academically and in popular culture. Film studies are often tempted towards immanent reading, and the whole auteurist project could be understood in this way. The auteurist approach consists of treating films as free-standing texts that are then mined internally to discover common themes and tropes. Often this reveals ways of understanding film texts that simply were not available to anyone watching them, however intently, in the context of their original circulation. As Edward Buscombe (1973) writes of studies of John Ford's Hollywood films: 'There is no doubt that films such as *Donovan's Reef*, *Wings of Eagles* and especially *The Sun Shines Bright* (almost indecipherable to those unacquainted with Ford's work) do reveal a great deal of meaning when seen in the context of Ford's work as a whole.'[13] The same could be said of 'uninteresting' works by other Hollywood directors, such as Vincente Minelli's *On a Clear Day You Can See Forever*, which gain in meaning when seen in the context of other films credited to the same director. Auteurism is the immanent reading of a body of work usually identified under the label of the name of a particular director. An auteurist study will stand or fall on the quality and interest of the readings it offers of each text, especially readings that are not available through other routes of understanding that text. The approach is intellectually coherent and justifiable, and it remains the prime example of immanent reading in the area of audio-visual texts. Auteurism has not taken hold in broadcasting studies as yet, and there are a number of reasons why the terrain of TV is rather more hostile to it, although it has been used effectively on occasion both by creative artists such as Dennis Potter and those who study them.[14] These include an intellectual climate that currently avoids the more purely immanent reading procedures of auteurism (see Caughie, 1981, and Nowell-Smith, 2003).

There are also major differences, however, between film and TV texts themselves, and to understand why it is useful to contrast 'Lena, O My Lena' with the feature films of the period that dealt with similar themes. The films of the period present fewer difficulties of interpretation for groups of students. They are still easily accessible and understandable. There are several reasons for this, and to explore them is to understand why immanent reading here is a more viable activity than it is in the face of much TV production. Films such as *Room at the Top* (Jack Clayton, 1958), *Woman in a Dressing Gown* (J. Lee-Thompson, 1957), *Hell Drivers* (Cy Endfield, 1957) and *Saturday Night and Sunday Morning* are more explicit about their cultural assumptions. They had to be: they were constructed for an extended period of cinema release in the United Kingdom, and in the hopes at least of release in other markets, especially the United States. In such circumstances, it was a basic working hypothesis of the scriptwriting and mise en scène that such films could not make too many assumptions about what their audiences might know about the situation of the characters. Sometimes this makes the films over-explicit; at other times it leads to compromises in any project of fidelity to contemporary reality. Feature films were forced to universalise in order to ensure universal accessibility. Indeed, it was relatively common practice even in the 1930s for the commercial end of the UK film industry to submit UK scripts to the American censors in pre-production to reduce any problems on US release.[15] Domestic UK TV dramas of the early 1960s did not need to make such assumptions, and so provided a chance for writers to experiment with a form of realism that deliberately left loose ends and tried to share in the contemporary common assumptions of its defined audiences.

The classic feature film is a more explicit and self-defining text than is much TV drama. Faced with such texts, film studies as a discipline has felt more at ease with using immanent readings, seeking the inner psycho-dynamic of a text, or even possibilities of interpretation that would have been marginal at the time of the film's release. The use of immanent reading has also been made easier by the dominance of a single textual form, the feature film, both in film studies and in the institution of cinema itself. Yet even here the immanent reading can be wildly off-key, because these apparently self-contained texts also betray the impact of the everyday on the nature of the text. Any film of the classic cinema period had to work in order to claim and sustain its integrity when it faced audiences. This work is distinct from and in addition to the process of rendering the narrative universally intelligible. As I have attempted to demonstrate in relation to the classic British feature film, the mass cinema was often an unruly place to try to be an immanent reader. Other people in the same space profoundly affected the experience of film-going, sometimes enhancing the experience but all too often articulating conflicting interpretations based on boredom, or disbelief or 'excessive' credulity. Others were just using the warm, dark space for non-film-related activities. So the construction of each feature film and the whole cinema programme during the period of mass cinema seems to expend a lot of effort to 'create the mood', in trying to weld the audience together into a viewing collective, or at least to make sure that they sat down and shut up.[16]

Such mundane and everyday considerations rarely appear in the activity of film studies in relation to specific texts, because the form of the text is stable (an enclosed narrative fiction lasting about 90 minutes). Yet the feature film is a performative text, designed for a specific set of circumstances that are themselves beginning to be historically specific. The need to understand the work that its texts had to perform just to claim their place as a film (as it were) will be something that weighs more on film studies as the era of the mass cinema of the twentieth century begins to recede into memory. It is being replaced by many other ways of using feature films, and the form is responding, often by reducing its levels of universal address. Traditional mass cinema now requires explication where once it could be a cultural 'taken for granted'. TV is no different in this need, except that, as I hope my examples have shown, the considerations of the moment of broadcast seem to be more firmly and intimately embedded in the texts than is the moment of cinema performance in films, and so the impact of that moment cannot be so readily ignored.

The impact of the everyday on the fundamental nature of television texts makes it more difficult to create canons, or lists of 'must-see' programmes. Every age has its own canon of great texts, and one criterion for inclusion in any canon of classics is simply that a text should be amenable to use beyond the confines of the historical context in which it was generated. The idea of the canon is particularly attractive in relation to broadcast TV, as it both concentrates on specific texts (rather than structures or history) and creates a clear means of discriminating between the vast swathes of material that exist. We can see how attractive it has been for cinema, with top ten selections now a regular feature in magazines. But in the field of cinema the activity of canon building has been underpinned by the model of the feature film (about an hour and a half long; shown in cinemas), which has been remarkably durable, and means that radically different kinds of work can be seen in some way commensurable. It may well be that television studies cannot easily take an immanent reading turn, as has sometimes happened in film studies. There is less consistency of object in TV. If even a single drama such as 'Lena, O My Lena' poses problems because of its temporarily meaningful nature, then the long-form series presents even more problems for purely textualist approaches. They are simply too big to be encompassed by close reading techniques. Nevertheless, interpretation within television studies inevitably includes an element of reuse and reinterpretation of television programmes beyond the moment of first use for which they were made.

A canon has already begun to emerge in the popular culture of old television, through the release and recirculation of programmes on tape or digital versatile disc (DVD), the increasing number of broadcast repeats and the existence of nostalgia channels such as UK Gold. Some genres, such as situation comedy (sitcom), are more suited to this process than others. Within sitcom, there are some 'classics' that are already becoming canonical. *Hancock's Half Hour* (BBC, 1956–1960), *Steptoe and Son* (BBC, 1962–1974), *Dad's Army* (BBC, 1968–1970) and *The Good Life* (BBC, 1975–1978) are all re-screened and circulate on video, gaining a status separate from their historical moment of transmission. Another strand of comedy is less amenable to such treatment, however: *Till Death Do Us Part* (BBC, 1968–1975), *The Benny Hill Show* (BBC, 1955–1957, 1961, 1964–1966, 1968; ATV, 1967; Thames, 1969–1989), *That Was the Week that Was* (BBC, 1962–1963). This kind of comedy relates more to its immediate context. The on-screen arguments that made *Till Death Do Us Part* such compelling television at the time included the overt racism of Alf Garnett, stretching as far as a set-piece episode in a pub in which Alf argues with a workmate who proclaims himself to be a 'Paki Paddy', played by Spike Milligan. Richly evocative of then contemporary attitudes, this is scarcely something that would be marketable in the present conjuncture.

If popular culture is busy building a de facto canon of old television, so is academic discourse. The activity of reinterpreting texts in different contexts is a familiar habit of aesthetic discourses. The immanent reading approach tends to see the text as a system capable of generating meanings, of which the historically situated is just one. Indeed, one measure of the aesthetic value of a work is the degree to which it can generate successive phases of situated readings. This is the durability of Shakespeare. Once television studies as a discipline has found its Shakespeare, which is more or less inevitable, some television material, particularly fiction or drama (as UK TV tends to call it), can and will be submitted to immanent readings as well, if only as a response to the continuing dramatic power of the work, or to maintain its currency as a cultural object. This may turn out to be the case with the work of Dennis Potter, for instance.

In the end, an era will remember what it wants of itself. But what it memorialises may be seen in the future to be a symptom of particular social trends to the exclusion of others. The complexity and range of human activity necessarily means that a small fragment of it can be preserved, and, given our culture's lingering obsession with lasting cultural value, the temporarily meaningful texts will fare badly once they become mere historical curiosities. As a defence against such an inevitable process of loss, academic study can produce scoping studies, trying to rescue and define the broadcast context of material: a context that until recently broadcasting scholars have been able to assume is more or less a constant. Hence, a number of models and typologies of broadcasting history have begun to emerge, including my own tentative model of an era of scarcity, to which 'Lena, O My Lena' belongs; an era of availability, characterised by a multiplicity of scheduled services; and an emerging era of plenty, in which television-type material will be available in on-demand formats (see Ellis, 2000a, and Spigel and Olsson, 2004).

Television studies will need to combine a historical awareness with immanent reading approaches because of the specific problems of the everydayness of broadcasting and the phenomenon of the temporarily meaningful. The study of television has to deal with both the immanent and the historical impulses, and try to make sense of the friction that exists between them. This friction is felt most clearly in attempts to deal with the vast bulk of material that is television. It becomes an absolute problem as soon as anyone poses the inevitable question 'Why on earth was this (or wasn't this) a popular programme?'. To understand the popular in popular culture increasingly requires a perspective on the extra-textual. Fortunately, new forms of access will allow a more fragmentary, recombinatory and layered approach to this problem, allowing the text of 'Lena, O My Lena' to be laid alongside contemporaneous TV news material, complete schedules and listings and even, as archives open up, other programming. Applying the contemporary techniques of flicking from one item to another could be a fruitful way of mediating between textuality and intertextuality.

2 Citing the classics

Constructing British television drama history in publishing and pedagogy

Jonathan Bignell

This chapter addresses the theoretical and pragmatic issues attendant on the selection of programmes that delineate histories of British television, especially television drama. It focuses on the relationship between published television historiography and the formation of canons in the institutions of academic teaching and research. Beginning with a critical analysis of recent publications dealing with British television drama from the 1960s to the 1980s, the chapter moves towards a focus on the consequences of citing selected programmes as examples. This issue illuminates the tensions in historiography between presenting, explaining and narrating histories of British television drama for the different audiences of students, academic researchers and non-specialist readers that published work addresses. This tension is evident in the convergence and divergence of discourses that set in place a selection of programme examples as representatives of historical periods, tendencies or turning points in television drama, for there are two aims that shape these discourses. The first is the requirement to choose examples that will stand in for a broader grouping of programmes, and thus the choice of an example depends on its function as typical rather than exceptional. At the same time, however, the selection of an example makes it exceptional simply because it has been chosen from the wide but not infinite field of other possible examples. In this construction of a canon, those programmes privileged as examples become a series of relays that connect the historiographic discourse to an absent history that they represent. Critical discussion of this kind of canon is concerned with the accuracy of the representative history thus constructed, and the ways in which new research or theoretical insights might reshape that history, perhaps by questioning the example's representativeness or choosing alternative examples that fulfil the representative function more accurately.

A second historiographic discourse that is inhabited by the tensions inherent in the aims and audiences for work on television drama is the writing that uses programme examples as occasions for theoretical and methodological work. Here the example is not chosen for its representativeness but, instead, for its function as a resource that enables a theoretical or methodological insight to be concretised, worked through or tested. In this discourse, the example still has the function of a relay that leads to something else, but as a moment in an argument that begins from a conceptual problem, grounds it in an object of analysis and then returns to conceptual discussion, having bolstered its claim to truth and utility by application to a text. Each of these two kinds of discourse constructs canons, and do so by necessity. There is no possibility of avoiding the formation of canons inasmuch as the term refers to a privileged selection from a broader field, and the reiterative process by which subsequent work by other writers will necessarily engage with, refute, avoid or forget the canonical selections proposed by its antecedents. The extensiveness of television, broadcast on growing numbers of channels and now often for 24 hours a day, also means that selection is perhaps more challenging and equally inevitable as it is in media with longer histories, such as film. Therefore, this chapter does not constitute an argument against canons but, instead, an argument about the stakes and consequences of the process of canonisation.

THE STORIES SO FAR

Writing about British television drama is now sufficiently established to have its own history, and this section is a very brief commentary on books that have attained the status of landmarks and turning points in that history. These are some of the texts that are recommended to students studying television drama, and that writers contributing new work use as models, coordinates for positioning their own work or 'straw men' from which to differentiate themselves.[1] There are, therefore, two interacting processes of canonisation at work. One canon is the selection of programmes that persists or changes across the development of writing on television drama, and the other is the group of published studies that have been adopted for teaching purposes, or cited as reference points in research, thus mapping the field and representing its coordinates. These two kinds of canon interact, and to an extent legitimate each other. Publications on television drama implicitly select a canonised group of programmes, and those publications themselves become canonical partly because of the programmes they use to ground their critical insights. The early work in the field engaged with television drama through authorship, because methodologies for discriminating quality, political effectiveness and formal innovation could be exemplified in the single television play and the prime-time high-profile television serial, forms that already privileged authorship as both a differentiating brand and a guarantor of quality for broadcasters and reviewers. The essays in George Brandt's edited collection *British Television Drama* (1981) each address a different writer's work, analysing selected examples. These studies legitimated their criteria for selection by drawing on criteria already dominant in the study of literature and theatre drama, such as complexity, social engagement, originality or ambiguity. Unsurprisingly, the resulting selection of programmes consisted of dramas by established male writers of 'serious' television plays or serials. By 1990, however, John Tulloch's book *Television Drama*, significantly subtitled *Agency, Audience and Myth*, combined work on Trevor Griffiths' authorially branded television drama with empirical research on Australian viewers of popular drama such as *The Flying Doctors* (Crawford Productions, 1986–1991), and explicitly contested what Tulloch saw as Brandt's conservative, patriarchal and 'high-cultural' canon. Tulloch's work questioned the hierarchisation of drama into the 'serious' and 'popular', and signalled an interest in reception that became increasingly important to studies taking their methodological bearings from sociology and anthropology as much as from literary traditions. The selection of programme examples thus shifted from an implicit – and sometimes explicit – discrimination of quality in texts to the use of texts as locations for considering the competing claims of authorship, genre, institution and reception as agencies determining the cultural meanings of programme texts. The canon began to be not only a group of programmes but also a group of critical approaches, drawn mainly from cultural theory, that could be instantiated and developed for the analysis of television by means of their application to programmes.

The essays in Brandt's second collection, *British Television Drama in the 1980s* (1993), were organised around analyses of programmes, rather than writers, and placed some programmes in relation to genres such as sitcom and soap opera. Authors' names still featured in each essay's title, and Brandt (1993: 17) wondered whether the 'best' television drama of the 1980s was 'the golden glow of a setting sun', defending text-based evaluation against the redemptive readings of popular texts that granted centrality to the negotiation of meaning by real viewers or from hypothetical reading positions. Generic programmes such as *Yes, Minister* (BBC, 1980–1984), *Brookside* (Mersey TV, 1982–2003) and *Inspector Morse* (Zenith, 1987–2000) were implicitly canonised by their selection as examples of how such negotiations opened up the multiple significations of apparently conventional forms. This connected earlier criteria for quality with the new valuation of popular television as potentially resistant as well as hegemonic. By this point, the disputes about canonicity in television drama and the legitimation of canons by critical concepts such as authorship, genre or ideological stance had become sufficiently insistent and clear that Charlotte Brunsdon (1998) could undertake an important meta-critical analysis of academic publishing on this subject, illustrating it by reproducing the title pages of recent studies within her own article. Robin Nelson's *TV Drama in Transition* (1997) began with a demonstration of how critical emphases on authorship, the single play and a lament for the lost 'golden age' missed out on the increasing dominance of popular series drama in 1990s television, and also failed to account for audience response, the importance of genre as an organising principle of meaning, and postmodern questioning of evaluative methodologies of all kinds. Nelson's examples shifted the terrain of debate by including US drama series such as *NYPD Blue* (Bochco Productions/Fox, 1983–2005) along with the critical realist serial *Our Friends in the North* (BBC, 1996). The examples he cited did more than just show a transition in television from the location of quality in the authorial work and textual value of the British single play to the genre negotiations, narrative flexibility and self-consciousness of popular British drama and imported US series, however. The transition from authorship, social engagement and 'seriousness' to the valuation of audience pleasure and agency were not regarded as opposites, and *Our Friends in the North* was used to argue that critical realism, a mode seemingly derived from that authorial 'golden age' past, could offer its audience grounded recognition of television drama's relevance as a kind of pleasure.

Nelson's selection of *Our Friends in the North* was important as a way of connecting an earlier critical tradition with a current one, by means of a programme that drew on aspects of realism that belonged to earlier drama forms, and dealt with an ensemble of characters whose life histories were themselves mapped from the 1960s up to near the present. The re-evaluation of past drama in terms of more current methodologies, and the re-evaluation of past methodologies in relation to current programmes, motivated the collection of essays by television writers, producers and academics that I collaborated on (Bignell, Lacey and Macmurraugh-Kavanagh, 2000) at that time. The book brought together analyses of recent examples, such as dramas by the emergent writer Lynda La Plante and by the already canonised Dennis Potter, and contributions from 'golden age' writers and producers as well as those still working in the industry. Around the turn of the century, publication on British television drama historicised itself and its canons, and in 2000 John Caughie's work on aesthetic debates around naturalism, modernism, realism and authorship returned to 'serious' drama. He historicised discourses of seriousness and quality, and located them in specific cultural debates. In the same year Jason Jacobs' (2000) study of British television drama from 1936 to 1955 developed a self-consciously archaeological approach, reconstructing drama aesthetics from production notes, set designs and scripts because of the lack of archive footage to analyse in detail. For different reasons, studies of television drama were written with much greater reflexivity.

In the last few years the tensions in exemplarity have resulted in the co-presence of several different kinds of writing that deal in different ways with canonicity and exemplarity. Lez Cooke's history of British television drama (2003) is a chronological narrative that begins with the live productions of the 1930s and ends with the high-concept authored drama that attracted large audiences in the 1990s. By periodising drama into decades, Cooke (2003: 5) identifies 'broad tendencies in the historical development of British television drama', and also turning points that crystallise historical processes in key texts. Examples and narrative history are yoked together productively but in a necessary tension. The same tension inhabits Michele Hilmes' 2003 collection, which begins as Cooke's does with a debate about historiography. Hilmes' collection has two sections on programmes, but among these 53 pages there is only one essay (Wheatley, 2003) that grounds a historical account in an analysis of a British drama programme. Nonetheless, the widespread adoption of the publishing format of the 'grey box' in Hilmes' collection, now very common, concretises the tension between narrative and example. The separation of brief analyses of programmes on the page in a grey box both foregrounds the issue of citation and exemplarity but also conceals it, as a feature of the format, rather than facing it head-on as Cooke does. At the other end of this spectrum, Glen Creeber's (2004) selection of 50 key television programmes includes examples unframed by a historical narrative. In effect, these examples are all grey boxes without the surrounding historicising discourse. The story of the histories of British television drama is the story of how transitions in criteria for selection have changed from, crudely, the identification of landmark plays and serials that could compete with literature or theatre drama as artistic works, to the adoption of drama as a location for working through theories of ideology and agency, and finally the reflexive construction of histories and examples as formative of each other. Sue Thornham and Tony Purvis's recent book outlines its aims on the first page:

> The book outlines key approaches useful in the study of television drama, and explores the ways in which these approaches have been employed in television criticism over the past 30 years. Second, these theoretical and critical approaches are considered in relation to specific case studies… Finally, both television drama texts and the critical perspectives used to explore them are contextualized in terms of the changing identities, histories and discourses which have structured television's drama output and which inform how audiences and critics have read television dramas. (2005: viii)

While different publications negotiate these canonising aims in different ways, and with greater or lesser awareness of their contradictions, publishing about British television drama has become canonical enough to develop meta-historical discourses.

ACCESS, EXAMPLES AND PEDAGOGY

My brief account of academic books about television drama began with publications appearing in the 1980s, largely because this leads to a further issue that concerns access to programmes and the possibility of working with a stable and accessible object of analysis. Until the early 1980s, and the spread of the domestic video cassette recorder (VCR), there was no ready means for non-professionals to record or play back television programmes. As Helen Wheatley (2005) has explained in a recent essay on *Upstairs Downstairs* (London Weekend TV,

1971–1975), for example, early work on this and other series discussed them as industrial rather than aesthetic objects of study precisely because of a lack of access to the programme for repeat viewing. This meant that studies of television drama had to resort to some combination of four strange procedures to discuss it. To analyse the aesthetics of programmes, by addressing their visual and aural components, narrative form and generic characteristics, it was often necessary to describe shots and sequences in detail. As well as loading down the resulting student essay, article or chapter with lengthy passages of information, the translation of these issues into written language necessarily segues from description to interpretation, and often unconsciously. An alternative to this activity, or a supplement to it, was the occasional use of sequences of still images reproduced in the text, for example in some of the essays in the journal *Screen Education*'s special issue (1976) on *The Sweeney* (Euston Films, 1975–1978). Here, too, the activity of selection had to negotiate the problems of representativeness and exceptionalness that I have been discussing in the context of canon formation as a whole, but on the reduced scale of the selection of stills that marked key images, turning points or representative shot compositions. A third procedure was to write or teach about television drama by referring to a written script. The consequence of this choice was that it pushed the subject towards dramas that had acquired sufficient profile or valuation to be selected by publishers as a plausibly commercial venture. So David Mercer's publication of collected television plays (1967) or the script of Jeremy Sandford's *Cathy Come Home* (BBC, 1967) found a place in critical writing and television teaching partly by default, because they were available, or because they had been pre-selected as significant by the gatekeepers of the print medium. This reinforced the focus of analysis on the authorial contribution of the writer, rather as writing and teaching about theatre drama as literature (as opposed to performance) tended to do. The final alternative for publishing and pedagogy in the field of television drama studies was to follow the theoretical and methodological directions of cultural, sociological or institutional approaches, which addressed issues such as the representations of gender, violence or social class, and the role of television as a product of and negotiation with the ideologies of media culture. This pedagogical approach drew more commonly on generic serial and series drama than the authored play, leading, for example, to the important collections of essays produced by the BFI, such as the volume on *Coronation Street* (Granada TV, 1960–) (Dyer et al., 1981).

With the arrival of videotape for recording current programmes, and subsequently the retail sale of videotapes of a small selection of earlier programmes, the emphases of the field were transformed. Until this moment it was necessary, for example, to agree with a group of students that they would all watch the same programme as preparation for a class, assuming that all of them had access to a television set in a hall of residence, shared house or a university building open to them after normal working hours. It should also be briefly noted that a very small number of television dramas could be hired on 16mm film from the BFI, and when videotape became common this library of holdings began to include taped copies of programmes that could be sent by courier for screening and then returned the next day. When television was taught in university departments that also taught film, these arrangements could be assimilated relatively easily, since the requisite administration, technical support, equipment and hire budget already existed. But the BFI's catalogue of available copies, *Films on Offer*, held many fewer examples of television drama than cinema films, and in itself constituted an informal and unsystematic canon of programmes. The situation is now somewhat different because of the legacy of programmes recorded on university staff's VCRs over the last 20 years. Access problems are now much more confined to programmes that have not been repeated in broadcast form since then, are lost or were not preserved by their makers, or have not been released in commercial videotape or DVD form.[2] This still leaves the problem that academic researchers are sometimes able to access programmes for specialist study (in the BFI's National Film and Television Archive, for example) that cannot be copied, distributed or screened for educational use. The very broadening of the range of recorded and retail-distributed television of the past has two unfortunate consequences: that the desire to see the reduced but still enormous variety of inaccessible programmes becomes greater as access becomes less of a restriction; and that the separation between a research canon and teachable canon persists despite the redrawing of its boundaries.

As well as this problem of access to programme examples, the issue of citing the classics of television drama is shaped by the subject's canonised learning outcomes, among which the skills of close analysis, knowledge of historical and cultural contexts that programmes illuminate and to which they belong, and programmes' relationships with discourses of critical theory are key components. A very large number of students study television in British higher education (HE), whether as a free-standing subject or as part of a course on media, communications or cultural studies at undergraduate level, with yet more students taking A levels at school or in further education (FE). Almost all universities teach courses on which academic books about television history could be used as course texts. There are about 500 institutions in the United Kingdom offering media courses of all kinds, awarding about 250 honours degrees with the word 'media' in their title. Of these, nearly 60 offer named modules in television studies. Books that suit this market have very large potential sales in Britain and are occasionally relevant to similarly large markets in the United States and Australia, where there are shared traditions of television teaching and research, and some shared experience of programming because of the international distribution and co-production of television drama. In comparison with the amount of material available in film studies, the field of writing in television studies is still relatively limited, and thus a small number of texts have become staple in university library collections. It was a selection from this corpus that was discussed above in relation to its activities of selection and canonisation. In further education there are about 200

British institutions that offer courses as part of Advanced GNVQ (General National Vocational Qualification), A level or BTEC (Business and Technology Education Council) studies and use television course texts. Television studies as a subject forms about a half of the work covered in media courses at school AS level, and more than a half at A2. While practical courses are significant at this level, the syllabus requires practical work to address the issues and debates in critical modules, so there is also relevance for critical textbooks in the practical components of courses, though the importance of television history to courses that aim to teach the skills and creative thinking required in television production varies greatly. Introductory books that bridge the teaching of professional competencies and critical methodologies are, understandably, concerned largely with the present and the immediate future (e.g. Bignell and Orlebar, 2005). The emphases in much current research in the field on textual analysis and institutional contexts match closely the divisions of topic and methodology adopted in FE and HE qualifications. Tutors at all levels recommend some of the books discussed above as further reading to more advanced students, and may use copyright-cleared extracts from them in some class teaching. It would seem, therefore, that the canon of television drama and the history of television are of widespread interest.

Books dealing with television drama in a historically informed way are not likely to be required reading at FE level or the first year of undergraduate degree courses, however, because their intellectual level and specific focus on television histories are thought to be too specialised by publishers aiming, for economic reasons, at volume sales.[3] Instead, course texts surveying critical approaches and discussing a wide range of genres, usually with a strongly contemporary rather than historical focus, are increasingly used to introduce the study of television. Since the majority of students using books as part of courses are likely to be between 17 and 25 years of age, a desire to engage their own experience of the programme examples discussed means that these examples tend to be chosen from the decade preceding the book's publication. When discussing histories of television drama, and thus implicitly constructing its canon, older programmes tend to be those that have been discussed before, thus reinforcing canonicity by summarising, questioning or developing what are considered to be key insights by earlier academics. Interacting with this is a tendency to discuss examples that are likely to have been collected or made available for retail, or are being repeated because of their continuing popularity. Keith Selby and Ron Cowdery's *How to Study Television* (1995), for instance, uses case studies of the contemporary continuing soap *Neighbours* (Grundy TV, 1985–) and the readily available and canonised *Fawlty Towers* (BBC, 1975–1979), among others. My own contribution in this area (Bignell, 2004) attempts to signal television history and the process of canonisation as a topic for discussion by devoting a chapter to the issue, but is also constrained by its function and market to occupy itself mainly with programmes of the last decade.

Because of this context, the opportunities for specialised work on the histories of television drama, and the histories of its criticism and theorisation, are rather limited. In seeking to introduce new emphases and topics of study into the field, academic writers are required to engage with the current orthodoxy even if they seek to argue against it. The major differences between courses of study are in their focus on one or two of the following areas: the analytical study of television programmes as texts, the television industry as institution and its production practices and organisation, television in contemporary culture and the sociological study of audiences, and television history and developments in broadcasting policy. So, when setting up 'The Television Series' of academic books with Manchester University Press in 2000, fellow series editor Sarah Cardwell and I sought to demonstrate how the books we intended to commission would connect with but differ from the existing traditions in pedagogy and research. The central aim of the series is to provide clear, comprehensive analysis of the work of key screenwriters, directors and producers for British television.[4] Each volume outlines the body of work of a single creative figure (or a long-established team), provides a critical study of his or her significant work, and foregrounds original sources such as interviews and archival historiography. The tensions between discourses that I outlined above in relation to publication in the field persist here, since each volume has to negotiate its own balance between authorship, programme examples, institutional contexts, and the legacies of criticism and theory of television. The Series is itself an instance of the negotiation between programme examples and narrative histories of television drama, with the added inflection of the placement of programmes in the professional career of their creator, thus linking life history to television history. The tension between agency and the structures of genre, institution and cultural contexts reappears in the self-conscious return to authorship via the critical discourses of recent pedagogy, in which programmes function as the ground through which cultural theories and theories of television are explored.

The risk of the Series is that the viability of any individual volume depends largely on whether it can demonstrate its subject's connection with programme examples that are either already canonical or can be argued into the canon, and the publication of some volumes as paperbacks and some only as hardbacks has been driven by the publisher's estimation of market appeal in these terms. The canon has partial stability and identity inasmuch as it is a locus of pedagogical activity, and as a result of that it works as a key definer of the market for commercial publication. In summer 2005 the BFI was preparing to launch its 'TV Classics' series, running in parallel with its existing series on cinema, 'Film Classics' and 'Modern Classics'. Market research for the new series involved questionnaires that exactly reproduced the tensions in the economy of television publication that I have been outlining. They requested suggestions for programmes to be the subject of series volumes, offering a long list of programmes to choose from. The list covered drama much more than other forms, and named series and

serial titles rather than anthologies or single plays, for example. Key questions
for the publisher included whether such books could be used as required course
reading for students, whether programmes were important as representatives of
a larger critical issue or historical moment, and whether the availability of video
or DVD recordings should constrain the choice of programmes to be written about.
The initiation of such new ventures is certainly to be welcomed, though the
interdependent political economies of research, teaching, publishing and access
continue to take their established forms.

STEPPING TO ONE SIDE

This final section considers how the citation of classics might be sidestepped,
but the paradox of the kind of work discussed here is, of course, that its effect
might be to shift the boundaries of the canon such that the television histories
it reworks or discovers will themselves become canonical. Nevertheless, the cases
outlined here attempt to forestall this iterative problem while necessarily
succumbing to it in some respects. The first case is the research project 'Cultures
of British Television Drama 1960–1982', devised by Stephen Lacey and me, to
which this chapter and this book are contributions (see the acknowledgement
below). The outline of the project attempted to avoid specifying any programmes
at all as objects of analysis, a move designed to sidestep issues of canonicity at
the same time as providing new ways of conceptualising them. The project
addressed British television drama as a culture rather than a canon of programmes,
consisting of television institutions and their cultures as they were constituted
by the people working in them and in turn affecting those people. Sidestepping
'serious' drama, the project addressed popular drama forms and especially those
that had not been highlighted in previous academic histories, such as fantasy and
horror drama, comedy and science fiction. Rather than the predominantly national
focus of studies of television drama as public service broadcasting, the project
investigated regionality in television production and representation. The meta-
theoretical reflections on selection, canonicity and exemplarity were at stake in
the project's address to popular drama genres and how distinctions between the
forms of popular British television drama and canonised flagship drama were
dependent on institutional forces and conflicts within and between television
institutions, including the regional organisation of production, changes in policy
and regulation, and the quotidian detail of production practices. The project
worked on how a canonical body of texts and received histories have been
established in studies of British television drama, evaluating this process and
questioning its methodologies, theoretical assumptions and exclusions, as this
chapter has done.

Because it was funded by the Arts and Humanities Research Council the project
did not have to be tailored solely to the demands of the pedagogical economy

described above, and many of its results were directed to academic journals rather than commercial publications. This relative freedom was constrained by three factors, however. First, the design of the project had to appeal to the expert constituency of evaluators from within British academia, and therefore demonstrate both originality and connection to the existing strands of research outlined in the first section of this chapter. Second, the results of the research were published in academic journals aimed at a similar constituency and thus with similar constraints, and also in some commercial publications subject to the market restrictions outlined in the second section of this chapter. Third, the achievability of the project within a three-year time span required the adoption of a relatively limited focus, and therefore only a limited contribution could be made to the potentially huge research issues described above. In each of these ways, the project worked to supplement, in a deconstructive sense, the canons of programmes and publication. It added to those canons, but also redirected them, refracted them or displaced them.

Similar difficulties attend studies that address the absence of developed work on television institutions' production practices, and especially those of Britain's commercial broadcasters. Problems of access to archives, the less frequent or systematic rebroadcast of drama programmes in comparison to the BBC, and the sheer complexity of writing the history of networking arrangements have made writing about them more difficult. Nevertheless, the 50th anniversary of ITV's start-up in 1955 has led to greater interest in its history and the recognition of a market for studies of its output. Some recent publications, such as Cathy Johnson and Rob Turnock's collection of essays (2005), match the agenda for multifocal approaches to television history that I think are now required, and the explicit problems of historiography posed by addressing ITV as an institution, programme producer and cultural phenomenon can be interestingly handled in relation to drama. For example, television scholars have been quick to contribute much-needed work on ITV in the supposed 'golden age' of about 1955 to 1975 to redress the emphasis on BBC output in almost all the books discussed in the first section of this chapter. One productive response to a lack of access to production archives in ITV companies is to make links with the television industry professionals whose recollection of working in television drama can correct, or at least modify, some of the preconceptions that have been accepted in earlier studies.[5]

For example, it is easy to import into historical studies of ITV drama the contemporary preconception that audience ratings and the maximisation of audiences for financial gain and competitive advantage vis-à-vis the BBC were motivating forces for the producers of programmes. While this was the case with serials and series in which a format could be altered during a long run of production (as with *The Avengers* (ABC TV, 1961–1969)), one of the producers of *Armchair Theatre* (ABC TV/Thames, 1956–1973), Leonard White, remarked: 'The only two people I ever used to get any feeling from, or any sort of response in relation

to whether they liked it or didn't was when I got trapped in the barber's chair...
when I would hear chapter and verse, and I couldn't remove myself of course,
and the person that fuelled my car whenever I used to have to go in the line-up
in the garage to get some petrol.'[6] As Wheatley (2004) has shown, *Armchair Theatre*
had a highly organised production system whereby writers and producers were
grouped into teams, and as well as the canonised 'kitchen sink' dramas featuring
working-class characters and everyday subjects there was a preponderance of work
that contrasts with this, such as generic thrillers, mystery stories or comedies. On
the one hand, this suggests that the canonisation of the former kind of drama,
exemplified in academic work by 'Lena, O My Lena' (ABC, 1960), has omitted
to understand *Armchair Theatre* plays as products as well as texts, and collectively
produced texts rather than parts of an author's oeuvre. On the other hand,
however, it suggests that the acceptance in earlier studies that there was a division
between 'serious' and 'popular' drama in the production culture of ITV is wrong,
not because 'serious' drama was also a product but because 'popular' drama was
taken just as seriously (Wheatley, 2004, 2007). Canonicity, citation and
exemplarity in existing work on television drama have neglected relationships
between 'serious' and 'popular' generic television drama, which should be studied
interdependently as part of a single television culture.

Despite the presence of work that historicises the conception of the popular
as a relational construct developing alongside shifting conceptions of quality
(Bignell and Lacey, 2005), studies of popular television drama that address the
histories of aesthetic forms have been restricted to analyses of programmes in
genres and forms that allow for the rediscovery of unconventional expressive
techniques rather than the historicisation of relatively conventional ones. Even
so, different kinds of canonisation of science fiction and fantasy programmes occur
in relation to the different readerships for recent work, and there is an increasing
tendency to address mixed readerships, with consequent mixed effects on the
vigour of television scholarship. There is a long tradition of British science fiction
production going back to the beginnings of television broadcasting, but
monographs and edited collections on British science fiction programmes are few.
John Tulloch and Manuel Alvarado's (1983) study of *Doctor Who* (BBC,
1963–1989) pursued a similar agenda around agency, ideology and textual analysis
to Tulloch's 1990 book discussed in the first section of this chapter, but was also
widely read by enthusiasts of the programme. In recent years, academic writers'
strategy of addressing a mixed readership of academics, students and fans with
work on science fiction drama has been remarkably successful. Some examples
include books by Toby Miller (1997), Chris Gregory (1997), James Chapman
(2002) and Jonathan Bignell and Andrew O'Day (2004). Work on science fiction
drama has thus sidestepped to some extent the economic restrictions on commercial
academic publishing for a student readership outlined in the second section of
this chapter, and thus re-inflected the canon inasmuch as it is constituted by the
programmes that become the subjects of academic studies. This matches the

argument, made above, that the distinctions between 'serious' drama and generic popular forms are artificially created by the processes of historiography and canonisation, and parallels the deconstruction of that opposition in the deconstruction of the opposition between categories of reader.

Opportunities for new historiographical scholarship on television drama in the field of television science fiction and fantasy seem likely to emerge as a result of this happy conjunction between different readerships and the different agendas of television historians and television enthusiasts. For example, there is as yet no book on the science fiction anthology *Out of This World* (ABC , 1962), produced by Leonard White between seasons one and two of *The Avengers* in 1962, though recently a volume on *Out of the Unknown* (Ward, 2004) joined the many detailed studies produced by television enthusiasts on television science fiction and fantasy drama. The first episode of *Out of This World*, 'Dumb Waiter' (1962), was produced for *Armchair Theatre*, but ABC's head of drama, Sydney Newman, had the play transferred to begin the anthology series instead. The series was created by Irene Shubik, the chief story editor for ABC Television, was introduced by the 75-year-old Boris Karloff and consisted of adaptations of stories by writers such as Isaac Asimov, Philip K. Dick and John Wyndham. Some of its productions were aesthetically experimental, designed, for example, by the immigrant avant-garde designer Voytek. These little-known and inaccessible dramas offer opportunities to consider the development of science fiction as a television genre, the relations between high-profile drama anthologies such as *Armchair Theatre* and these generic programmes, and the role of visual aesthetics for studio drama (see Wheatley, 2004) that have been unrecognised as forms of experimentation within popular forms. Histories of British television will be unable to sidestep completely the citation of the classics and the negotiation of relationships with existing canons, but there are many interesting opportunities to bring historiographic narratives, programme examples, production cultures, generic relationships and readerships for new work into productive and deconstructive conjunctions.

ACKNOWLEDGEMENT

This chapter is one of the outcomes of the research project 'Cultures of British Television Drama, 1960–1982', funded by the AHRC. Research was undertaken between 2002 and 2005 by Lez Cooke and Helen Wheatley, and the project was managed by Jonathan Bignell, John Ellis and Stephen Lacey, at the University of Reading, Royal Holloway, University of London, and Manchester Metropolitan University.

3 Salvaging television's past: what guarantees survival?

A discussion of the fates of two classic 1970s serials, The Secret Garden *and* Clayhanger

Máire Messenger Davies

> The lost cannot be recovered; but let us save what remains: not by vaults and locks which fence them from the public eye and use, in consigning them to the waste of time, but by such a multiplication of copies, as shall place them beyond the reach of accident. (Thomas Jefferson, quoted in Eisenstein, 1993)

Thomas Jefferson was talking about the written laws of Virginia in the eighteenth century, copies of which were few and in danger of disappearing, until the reproduction technology of printing came to the rescue. His warning emphasised two vital functions of what Walter Benjamin and his Frankfurt School colleagues – wrongly, in my opinion – denigrated as 'mechanical reproduction' (1973). The first function of mass reproduction is survival: the more copies there are, in more hands, the greater the chance that records will survive. And secondly – Jefferson's main point – a multiplicity of copies in a variety of hands is necessary for the democratic health of society. The cordoning off of a society's records – which includes cultural artefacts – with 'vaults and locks' offends against the democratic right of citizens to know their own culture and their history.[1]

This chapter deals particularly with TV survival in a physical sense, and some of the issues for scholarly research that arise out of the physical survival, or lack of it, of television programmes. Survival is here discussed as an essential (but sometimes neglected) ingredient of canonicity. The chapter compares two pieces of television drama from the 1970s, both costume drama, both literary adaptations, chosen firstly because they provide a clear and contrasting illustration of some of the issues involved in TV survival that I want to address, and secondly – to make the point more emphatically – because I happen to have had access to copies of them, one with ease, the other with considerable difficulty.

One of these TV dramas has 'survived' – that is, it is still commercially available in video and DVD form: this is the BBC's 1975 adaptation of Frances Hodgson Burnett's 1911 children's classic *The Secret Garden*, with a non-celebrity cast and produced for an unsung part of the BBC's 1970s output, the children's afternoon schedule.[2] One can still buy copies of this version from the BBC, and online as well. The other adaptation has proved very difficult to reconstruct in a complete form, and is not available commercially: ATV's prestigious 26-part 1976 adaptation of Arnold Bennett's *Clayhanger* trilogy, set in the nineteenth-century Staffordshire potteries, with a starry cast (Peter McEnery, Janet Suzman, Harry Andrews, Denis Quilley), and an eminent producer (Stella Richman), adapter (Douglas Livingstone) and director (John Davies). The entry on the Internet Movie Database (IMDb) website has no links, and no comments, and – as mentioned – there are no commercial versions to buy. Unlike its contemporary, *The Secret Garden*, it is not accessible to the public in any form.

An increasing number of scholars and citizens share these concerns about the disappearance of our television heritage: access to broadcasting archives was the topic of a seminar at the University of Westminster in September 2003 called 'Sound and Vision: the History of the BBC', at which the BBC archive and questions of ownership and access were debated intensively. Concern has arisen because much British (and international) television drama has never been kept, let alone properly archived and catalogued, and has either vanished altogether, or – as is the case with *Clayhanger*, as we shall see – has fortuitously survived in private ownership, thus emphasising Thomas Jefferson's point about the value of copies in 'a multiplicity of hands'. Given the fact that so many key texts from even the relatively recent past have disappeared (see, for example, Lez Cooke in this collection on the BBC's half-hour play series *Second City Firsts* (1972–1978), of which only 29 out of 73 survive), how can we either establish a television canon, or fully debate the terms upon which any particular piece of work should belong to this canon?

From comparing my two broadcast texts, one 'unlocked' and in circulation, the other apparently gone for good, it becomes apparent that sheer physical survival is a key prerequisite of any discussion of canonicity. Such survival may well be a fluke, a matter of chance, rather than the result of any deliberate critical decision to place a particular cultural value on a cultural product. The 'classic canon' of Greek theatre consists simply of the very few live, one-off performances that happened to be preserved in written form, and didn't get overwritten in medieval monasteries or lost at the Reformation. Survival may also derive from less haphazard factors, such as the personal meanings and usefulness that a text has for some individuals. Such meanings, I propose, are an important aspect of creating a canon, which is sometimes seen – wrongly, again, in my opinion – as an elitist top-down way of preserving bourgeois cultural values. Canonicity – the establishing of the value, and hence the preservation, of an artefact – is also the prerogative of Jefferson's 'multiplicity of hands' and Benjamin's 'masses'.

When individuals value a text, whether written, filmed or broadcast, they want
to own and conserve their own copies, as in the case of the two videotapes I used
for this essay (and they are videotapes, not DVDs – another survival issue, since
video is rapidly becoming obsolete). The importance of the viewer as
collector/archivist has begun to be recognised within academic television studies,
for instance by Uma Dinsmore (1998) and Ann Gray (1997a). Like every other
media studies lecturer and teacher I know, my copies of television teaching texts,
such as *The Secret Garden*, are part of a large personal collection, some programmes
copied off air, some copied for me through the ERA (Educational Recording Act)
system at work for use in my job, some bought commercially (all, incidentally,
creating a major problem of storage and cataloguing around my house). The copy
of *Clayhanger* that I am referring to does not actually belong to me. I borrowed
it from the Arnold Bennett Society and it is one of three copies of 18 surviving
episodes kept by the society's archivist, Keith Poynton, in *his* home and loaned
out to society members for the price of postage and packing. Thus, in the case
of broadcasting, once the technology – video, and more recently, recordable DVD
– had been invented that permitted personal copying, some broadcast material
has indeed survived in a multiplicity of hands. The public usefulness of this can
be seen by the fact that the publicly funded broadcasting institution, the BBC,
was able to replace two lost episodes of *Dad's Army* in its archives, by appealing
to viewers, who donated private copies.

CLASSIC SERIALS AND LITERARY ADAPTATION ON TELEVISION: THE CASE OF CLAYHANGER

Clayhanger (ATV, 1976) is of particular interest in this regard. The study of the
adaptation is hampered by the fact that the series is not in the public domain,
yet the survival of such copies as have reached the public domain – for instance,
in screenings at the Arnold Bennett conferences at Staffordshire University in
2004 and 2006 – has shown how Bennett's status as an important regional
novelist, and ATV's status as an important regional drama producer, come together
in interesting ways. The Arnold Bennett Society *Clayhanger* tapes illustrate a
number of points about the necessity of 'private hands' in preserving TV heritage.
As an adaptation of a literary classic, set in the late Victorian era, *Clayhanger*
was an important regional drama, heralded in the *TV Times* with a special colour
brochure about the production and its setting in the Staffordshire potteries, a
precious copy of which was shown to me by the former chair of the society, John
Potter. *Clayhanger* also belonged to a genre that was a staple of the public service
broadcasting tradition at that time: costume drama – a genre that has been
commercially valuable and has provided continuing earnings both from overseas
co-production and from video and DVD commercial sales. As Helen Wheatley
(2005) further points out in an essay on LWT's *Upstairs Downstairs*, *Clayhanger*

was set in an era, the Edwardian, that was particularly fashionable in the 1970s, not only in dramas such as *Upstairs Downstairs* and its spin-offs but also in lifestyle and fashion. Nonetheless, *Clayhanger*, despite being enormously prestigious and expensive at the time of its production (1975–1976), is a series that did not achieve posthumous revival in new and profitable formats, unlike, for example, the BBC's 1980 *Pride and Prejudice*, still available on video and DVD.[3]

The company that now holds the rights to the televised *Clayhanger*, and the only full set of episodes, is Carlton International. The progress of this text from its ownership by the Midlands-based ATV, which produced it, to ownership by a bigger Midlands-based production company – Central, which had nothing to do with producing it – that was then taken over by London-based Carlton, via Polygram, which is a publisher/broadcaster rather than a producer, is a case study in the contemporary economics of television. This process shows a move away from a system of regional productions of texts of local cultural and historical interest (as Bennett's 'Five Towns' were for ATV) towards a concern with maximising profits for shareholders in a global market, with the public's access to their own cultural, historical and local products becoming less and less of a consideration.

The way in which the Arnold Bennett Society came to own nearly a full set of *Clayhanger* tapes illustrates the truth of Jefferson's championing of 'a multiplicity of hands' in ownership. The surviving set of *Clayhanger* tapes in the hands of the Society has been pieced together entirely from private individuals' personal copies of it. The particular tape discussed below, episode 26, is one of 18 out of the 26 episodes of the series now owned by them. These copies were acquired partly from a member in Ireland who, after commercial videotape became available for private recording, was able to record some of the episodes when *Clayhanger* was broadcast in Ireland in the 1980s. The rest came, after an appeal in the Society's newsletter, from the private collection of the leading actor, Peter McEnery, who allowed the Society to make copies of the episodes he owned. The official National Film and Television Archive at the BFI has only one episode, which cannot be borrowed. National Museum of Photography, Film, and Television at Bradford also has just one episode. The programme's owners, currently Carlton International, although they have a complete set, do not answer queries from the public – including scholars – about it, so the whole series still cannot be seen; it remains in the 'locks and vaults' of a multinational corporation.

The survival in the public domain of one 1970s TV drama, *The Secret Garden* (not a very prestigious production at the time), and not the other, *Clayhanger* (a very prestigious production at the time), raises questions about what constitutes the conditions for entering the 'canon'. And what exactly *is* a canon in broadcasting? I want to explore the following possible answers:

- the bottom-up process of canonisation: the role of the 'multiplicity of hands';
- their institutional provenance;
- the differing generic nature of the texts; and
- the qualities of the texts and whether they 'deserve' to survive.

THE BOTTOM-UP PROCESS OF CANONISATION

There are a number of reasons why someone might want to create a TV canon – that is, to have access to copies of material from television's past and to preserve, discuss and celebrate them. There are institutional reasons, such as the BBC's remit as a public service broadcaster to keep its records. There are commercial reasons – an increasing market for old television material, which DVD technology and the new, multi-channel digital TV world have made more possible. There are historical reasons, and the important question of public record, as policy makers, academics and BBC archivists pointed out at the Westminster seminar. First, though, I want to discuss the bottom-up process whereby television drama is preserved and celebrated by private individuals. Individuals such as myself, and many other teachers and scholars, have two reasons for wanting to track down and preserve TV texts: the first is personal, for our own use; the second is professional, for teaching and research purposes.

I wanted to get hold of copies of ATV's *Clayhanger*, primarily for personal reasons. I loved the book by Arnold Bennett, published in 1911 – the same year as *The Secret Garden*, which is wholly coincidental, but interesting. I became a fan of Bennett, eventually joining the Arnold Bennett Society partly because Bennett himself, despite being one of the most famous and successful authors of his time, is not currently in the English literature canon, at least in terms of being a component of English literature courses. Given the quality of a book such as *Clayhanger* (and of his masterpiece, *The Old Wives' Tale*), many critics believe that the canon is where he should be. The former chair of the Arnold Bennett Society, John Potter, told me about the difficulty of getting copies of the TV series. Even the Society then (in 1998) had a copy of only one episode. This became a challenge; I became determined to track down this series, especially as I was then collaborating on a project about the digitising of some of the BFI's archive with academics, archivists and computer scientists at the University of Glamorgan.

My desire to view this adaptation raises issues of reception and pleasure in the study and teaching of television adaptations. What is the special charm of viewing filmed adaptations of loved texts? What are the specific pleasures of seeing characters we have 'met' in literary fiction, embodied on the screen? Even when the characters seem miscast, and the adaptation takes extensive liberties with the original, noting these differences and discussing them with fellow enthusiasts are an important part of the pleasures of viewing and reviewing, and a major reason why people want to own their own copies. This desire will not abate: it is why we like to have our own copies of books (which a flourishing market exists to satisfy, and which may expand even further if books are digitised), and also of feature films. For the same reasons, there needs to be a similar market for copies of noteworthy (for whatever reason) television drama. It is not enough for canonicity that copies are available only in institutional settings – libraries, archives, closed websites.

My other 1970s TV literary adaptation, the BBC's *The Secret Garden*, has been more fortunate than *Clayhanger* in this regard: you can still buy it. This is also a loved text, which I and my children enjoyed both in print and television form; unlike *Clayhanger*, we (I and my then six- and four-year-old children) saw *The Secret Garden* adaptation when it was broadcast as a weekly children's drama on BBC1, and we also bought the TV-linked printed text, with a still from the production on the cover. This tape has come to feature in this essay by a different route – a more standard route for canonical texts. For many years I taught about TV adaptation of children's fiction in a class called 'The Culture of Childhood', and *The Secret Garden* is a good teaching text. Being a good teaching text is another way – perhaps the only way – for non-blockbuster texts, whether print or television, to survive institutionally, as distinct from the haphazard process of survival involved in private collections.

The Secret Garden is a particularly good text for teaching and research. It exists in a number of formats: many printed editions, from lavishly illustrated glossy hardbacks to cheap paperbacks – it has never been out of print; there are several films, the most recent being Agnieszka Holland's 1993 Hollywood version; audiotape versions (for instance, Miranda Richardson's reading in a Hamlyn 'Books on Tape' edition, published by the Octopus Group in 1988); a Broadway stage musical; and several television adaptations both in the United States and the United Kingdom, including the BBC's 1975 version. As mentioned earlier, you can still buy the BBC *Secret Garden* and rent it from video stores. It is in university libraries. It is in the public domain. The television *Clayhanger* is not. Why not?

INSTITUTIONAL SUPPORT

The first reason for the canonical survival and circulation of *The Secret Garden*, unlike *Clayhanger*, is institutional. *The Secret Garden* was fortunate to have been produced by the national public service broadcaster, the BBC, which means, as pointed out at the Westminster seminar, that it has been looked after in a proper, highly professional archive with continuity going back to the origins of the BBC in the 1920s. It has also been made available for sale to the public by the BBC's commercial arm, BBC Worldwide.

Clayhanger, by contrast, despite its much more lavish production values and promotion at the time, was produced by the Midlands commercial ITV company ATV, which no longer exists; the company archive was taken over first by Central, which was then taken over by Carlton, then Polygram, and finally – and currently – Carlton International, where the sole surviving full set of the series that anybody knows about languishes at present.

GENERIC DIFFERENCES

The second reason for the difference in the fates of the two series, I suggest, is generic. As a children's production, *The Secret Garden* has particular qualities that make it more 'recyclable' than adult programming. Despite much contemporary sociological debate about the social constructedness of childhood (see James and Prout, 1990, for example), the fact remains that certain elements of children's storytelling have recognisable universal qualities that can appeal across cultures and generations. The children in *The Secret Garden* may seem to have nothing in common with contemporary children; the book was written before the First World War, about rich ten-year-olds living in a big country house with lots of servants. Yet the story has never been out of print, partly because of its undoubted literary quality, but also because it has durable fairy-tale elements: the abandoned child (as in *Hansel and Gretel*); the ugly duckling (Mary Lennox, the heroine, is initially 'thin and sour'); the child as saviour/hero; the reversal of fortune '*Cinderella*' plot (an interesting and ironic inversion of this plot, since the children in *The Secret Garden* are rich but dysfunctional to start with); and, of course, the empowering 'magic' (a term used repeatedly in the book) of the natural world. The story also has a still contemporary regional and psychological realism, which make it continuingly relevant to new generations of children. This BBC version of *The Secret Garden*, made in 1975 – prior to MTV, prior to the multichannel world of specialised children's channels, prior to the internet and computer games, prior to DVD and even video – still survives in the market place.

Thus, another way of ensuring the kind of survival that leads to a place in the broadcasting canon is generic status, in this case as 'children's'. Other differences follow from *The Secret Garden's* generic status. Its survival enables it to be taught about, as in my course. It is still sold as a children's book to the general public, as well as to scholars. It's written about by widely read critics such as Alison Lurie (1990). It circulates widely in public discourse – it is almost impossible for anyone to write about children's culture without invoking Burnett's 'garden' metaphor for childhood.[4] Parents remember it fondly from childhood. It has websites. *Clayhanger* has none of these things. Bennett as an author is out of favour, so the book, which is in fact still in print, like *The Secret Garden*, does not support the TV text in the same way the popular children's text does that. Neither is there any fond parental memory to hand it on from one generation to the next.

THE QUESTION OF QUALITY

When it comes down to deciding what should go in the canon, however, surely we have to address the question – as a member of the audience put it at the Westminster seminar – 'Is it any good?'.[5] Certainly, there are extra-textual institutional and generic reasons why some material survives and continues to be used and enjoyed, and other material does not. Nevertheless, the question of whether a TV text 'deserves' to survive (apart from simply as a matter of record) does need to be addressed.

When I began work on this essay, I wanted to make a simplistic and easy distinction between my two texts by saying *The Secret Garden* is good television, whereas *Clayhanger*, while having a number of virtues, is not. As work progressed, this judgement changed: this raises the issue of viewing context in making canonical value judgements, and also of having the whole text, as well as having as much as possible of its context, fully available to us. Issues of cultural value have always been debated contentiously in television studies, from John Hartley's *The Politics of Pictures* (1992) to Jason Mittell's throwing down the quality gauntlet in the online journal *Flow* (2006) and demanding to be able to say that television drama, such as *Lost* (2004–, Touchstone/Bad Robot productions, for ABC/Disney), is 'good'.[6] While Hartley, and others, make valuable political and educational points about the inconsistency of cultural values that elevate literature and denigrate television, Mittell demands that television scholarship should pay more detailed attention to actual television texts and forms in making value judgements. His article praises *Lost's* narrative complexity and ingenuity – and his attempt to evaluate a television drama by close textual, narrative analysis generated some hostile responses.

It is, of course, essential to pay attention to content and format; but viewing *context* is particularly necessary with episodic television, which is viewed over time, from one week to the next, and which is contemporaneous with people's daily lives and other media experiences (see Scannell, 1996, for a useful discussion of this point), although, with facilities such as Sky Plus and TiVo, and DVD packages, weekly viewing is now not the only means of keeping up with serialised narratives.[7] I thought that *Clayhanger* was 'bad' television out of context, on the basis of having seen only one and a half episodes – the one episode owned by the BFI, and half of another one owned by the Arnold Bennett Society. These episodes (the half-one from the middle of the series, in which Janet Suzman and Denis Quilley have a seemingly endless dialogue in a railway carriage, and the other, the 26th and last, consisting largely of a monologue from Peter McEnery as the series hero, Edwin Clayhanger) I found almost unwatchable. They seemed stagey and undramatic, with too much monologue, both internal and external, no physical action and very little in the way of inventive production techniques. They were also somewhat baffling with respect to what exactly was supposed to be going on, even though I knew the book and its sequels very well.

For example, in this final episode there is a scene with Peter McEnery, as the middle-aged Edwin, walking around the 'town' – the studio set – after a row with his wife Hilda, and angrily reminiscing aloud about his marriage and her 'impossibility' and strangeness. It is a voice-over monologue lasting several minutes. There is very little editing and no opportunity is taken actually to show filmed flashbacks of the incidents Edwin is referring to. It could be a theatrical stage performance, and at first viewing I found it dull and undramatic, especially in the context of its position as the climax of the original trilogy of novels. Andrew Lincoln's introduction to the 1989 Penguin edition persuasively makes the link between the story of the Clayhanger family and the huge social and political changes overtaking the Staffordshire potteries in the nineteenth century, and he points out the effectiveness of Edwin's naivety as a narrative device. Because everything, from the plumbing in his new house to the desperation of starving workers on strike, appears fresh and interesting to him, Bennett can explain in great detail, through Edwin's eyes, the social and physical impact of these changes. The technique chosen to translate this naive point of view in the TV series, however, was primarily the undramatic and unvisual one of the voice-over monologue – and for me, as a 'fan' of the book, the technique failed to reproduce the quality of the original.

When I had seen all 18 of the available episodes, I revised my opinion of the style and function of this final episode, voice-over and all. It seemed to me that the 26 episodes of the TV *Clayhanger* were made with reference to what was then, and even now, in the digital multi-channel age, is still, the major popular television dramatic form: the soap opera. *Clayhanger* needed to be seen in the context of a period when audiences watching *Coronation Street* (Granada TV, 1960–) and *Z Cars* (BBC, 1962–1978) and their successors were counted in tens of millions: it was a regional as well as a historical drama, showing the slow unfolding of the story of a family and its community over 20 years in the life of the novel and over 26 weeks – half a year – in the life of the series. Once I had got hold of the 18 episodes and had begun to 'read' the series more like a soap opera (although I couldn't do it week by week, as original viewers had), I began to apply different criteria from those I would have used had it been a mini-series (six episodes) or a single play. At the time, Clive James (1976) criticised the rather mundane representation of the minutiae of the Clayhangers' lives – the mealtimes, the petty marital quarrels, the new furniture. In soaps, however, these mundane things become interesting, because, diegetically, they are interesting to the characters – people we have come to know and care about through long familiarity. Nevertheless, I suspect that the combination of soap opera and period costume drama – a form that, as Charlotte Brunsdon (1997) points out, usually has upper-class taste values, not lower middle-class ones – may not have had universal appeal to the 1970s audience. The contemporary and more successful *Upstairs Downstairs* could be said to have got the formula right by showing us the upper classes (an aristocratic family) and the working classes (their servants), but not the tradesmen; upper and lower echelons seem usually to generate more dynamic dramatic material than does the bourgeoisie, and *Clayhanger* is emphatically about the bourgeoisie.

Nevertheless, after seeing the earlier episodes, the final episode of *Clayhanger* appeared to me as something very different from the climax of a standard six-episode TV costume drama such as *Pride and Prejudice* (such as the BBC's productions in 1958, 1967 and 1980). The episode, which I originally thought was not working dramatically because nothing happened in it, is a deliberately extended reflection on all that has gone before – analogous to the episode-long two-handers that we have sometimes seen in *EastEnders* (BBC, 1985–) between characters such as Den and Angie and Dot and Ethel. The luxury of hearing an extensive review of the action from only one voice, or two voices, is permitted in the soap form because we already know the character and his or her history. Having the space to hear his views and feelings about what has happened over the last few months is part of the pleasure for the experienced regular viewer.

In recognising the soap-like quality of this dramatisation, as distinct from trying to compare it with mini-series such as *Middlemarch* (BBC, 1994) or *Oliver Twist* (ITV, 1999), I have also gained new respect for the adaptation – which illustrates the variability and the importance of context and repeated viewings in judgements about quality. Initially, when I had only seen one or two episodes, I found them unbearably literal. As a reader very familiar with the original texts, I found the adaptation's tendency to transcribe to the letter every scene of dialogue, every 'stage direction' given by the author in the original novels, tedious. Having now seen the whole thing, thanks to the archaeological efforts of the Arnold Bennett Society's Irish members and a helpful actor, it seems to me that Douglas Livingstone and his directors were attempting a quite sophisticated translation of the early twentieth-century realism of the author's style into the equivalent televisual/cinematic form: the soap opera. The soap opera is the nearest thing to Bennett's documentary realism of literary style in television terms. One could almost infer that the adaptation was deliberately measured and apparently old-fashioned, as Bennett himself, in his arguments with Virginia Woolf and D. H. Lawrence, and his loyalty to his French realist models such as Emile Zola and Guy de Maupassant, pretended to be (he liked to call himself a 'has-been', in contrast with the 'highbrows').

INTRINSIC QUALITY: TELEVISUALITY

Having made all due allowance for context and format, however, I still find *The Secret Garden* a better piece of televisual work than *Clayhanger*, for a number of reasons. I want to select just one: what Robert Giddings proposes is the primary requirement of screen adaptations of literary texts: '[T]he translation of what the novelist imagined and wrote in words into moving pictures and sound...finding the appropriate equivalent, the right style or tone, in which to recast the original' (2000: 32). In discussing canonical virtues, it is necessary to identify aspects of interesting television work that appear to be specific to the medium. In *The Secret Garden*, this is the televisual translation of the episode in which Mary, the bratty, lonely heroine, learns to skip, after a young servant, Martha, gives her a skipping rope. In the BBC version, made specifically for children, the significance of this sequence is given great emphasis. Mary's grudging acceptance of the other girl's gift and her lengthy and irritable struggle to master the skill of skipping are faithfully, almost boringly, reproduced. Most significantly, Mary's accomplishment of the skill is acquired in a real garden; the learning to skip sequence was one of the few scenes in the TV programme shot on film, not in the studio, but on location. By making sure that this scene was given its full length, and was shot outdoors in a natural setting, the production values heightened the significance that Burnett intended. As Mary struggles with and eventually masters the rope, so she is drawn into the liberating spaces of the garden, until eventually she finds the key to the Secret Garden. The underlying message (not, of course, literally explicit to a child audience) is made clear: Mary cannot develop healthily into a young woman, by exploring the garden, until she has first mastered the skills of being a child. This treatment is precisely faithful to the original text, both to the narrative, and to the underlying psychology and symbolism of the story (it is virtually eliminated in the 1993 feature film, aimed at an adult/family audience: see Davies, 2001). In this case, literal translation was a virtue, working in favour of the story's imagery and themes.

Even with allowances for context, my view is that, on the whole, *Clayhanger* fails Giddings' test. In *Clayhanger*, most of the time, the literal translation of Bennett's dialogue and stage directions seems to me unimaginative, and misses the atmosphere, poetry and symbolism of the original – criticisms that were made by reviewers at the time. In one scene, however, Livingstone and his director appear to have said 'Enough of literal fidelity, and painstaking realism; we're going to take the opportunity to solve an adaptation problem by doing something that only film or television can do'. In other words, they decided to translate a literary quality of the text into a primarily televisual one, and, in so doing, they jettisoned literal fidelity to the written text.

One of the most powerful and important sections of the book occurs very early in it, in the form of a 'flashback': the dreadful tale of Darius Clayhanger's (the hero's bullying father's) childhood. In the novel, the information we are given about Darius's experience as a seven-year-old in the 1840s working on a pot bank, and later being sent to the workhouse with his family, is known only to the reader and to the writer. It becomes an important ironic device throughout the novel; we, the readers, know why Darius is so bullyingly desperate that his business will survive and that his son Edwin should continue in it (instead of fulfilling his ambition to become an architect); the characters in the novel do not know, and never know. This ironic subtext runs throughout the account of the relationship between the novel's diffident hero, Edwin, and his dominating father, Darius, and is one source of the novel's considerable emotional power. Its undercurrent also lends power to the developing attraction between Edwin and Hilda, when she shows 'divine mercifulness' in rescuing the aged Sunday school teacher, Mr Shushions, from being bullied. This moment is 'one of the epochal things' of

Edwin's experience, but only we, the readers, are aware of just how epochal it really is: we know that Mr Shushions had saved the child Darius from the workhouse, and Hilda's 'lovely' gesture is, for us, an echo of this act of compassionate rescue.

How, then, to translate this powerful material into television? The solution chosen by Livingstone, and his director, John Davies, was adventurous in a way that the literal style of the rest of the adaptation was not. Instead of giving us this backstory at the beginning, as Bennett did, it is withheld until episode 12, halfway through. We see it in the form of visualised flashbacks when Darius visits the town workhouse, having heard that the man who rescued his own family from the workhouse, the old Sunday school teacher, Mr Shushions, is dying there. This, as Bennett says, is the most unimaginably distressing thing that could have happened to him. Edwin and his other children and relatives never find out why Darius breaks down and never recovers after Shushions' death in the workhouse – but we know why.

The scene illustrating this is strikingly similar in format to the clip of Edwin's angry walk through the 'town', but differs fundamentally in its use of the audio-visual medium. In this scene, the grief-stricken Darius walks through Bursley, and every building recalls an incident from his early life. Fading from close-ups of Darius's face to scenes of his childhood, the opportunity is taken to *show* us as viewers, not just tell us, what this childhood was like. First, we see the child Darius working with other children on a pot bank, naked from the waist up, grimy, sweaty, pounding clay, staggering with heavy loads against the backdrop of the roaring flames of the kiln. The novel's allusions to the profanity and dissoluteness of adult life on the pot bank are visualised here; these visualisations are not just emotionally and politically disturbing, in the way that Bennett meant them to be, they are also aesthetically and dramatically appropriate in making the point in televisual form that the author made in literary form, about the roots of Darius's personality. The adaptation here breaks free of literalness and the soap-like conventions of TV realism, and delays the information about Darius's childhood until a later stage in the story than it occupied in the original novel. In so doing, televisual techniques, such as flashbacks, close-ups, multiple disembodied voice-overs and music, as well as the viewer/reader's so far limited knowledge, can be utilised. It is a break away from the plodding realism of most of this 'faithful' adaptation, and thus makes better use of the television medium.

Despite the shortcomings I've mentioned (some hotly contested by members of the Arnold Bennett Society, who, unlike me, faithfully watched the whole series when it was originally broadcast), the televised *Clayhanger* should be seen as an important TV production historically, not least because it contains some of the finest performances its leading actors gave, Harry Andrews as Darius and Denholm Elliott as Tertius Ingpen in particular. These actors deserve to have the high-quality work that they did in this series preserved. The production also deserves further study because of its role in ATV's history and demise, and in the continuing vicissitudes of costume drama as a staple of TV schedules. *Clayhanger* did not do well either critically or in the ratings, and the next two major costume series made by a commercial company, Granada, were both more contemporary and a lot shorter: *Brideshead Revisited* (1981) and *Jewel in the Crown* (1984), at 11 and 12 hours respectively.

For all these reasons, it is important in any discussion of canonicity – whether in terms of history, public record, institution, public access or quality – that the physical and institutional barriers to survival are addressed before emphatic critical judgements are made about hierarchies of cultural value. The reasons for keeping, or discarding, copies of some material but not others also need to be more transparent – particularly when that material, as in the case of the BBC's archive, in a sense 'belongs' to the public, who paid for it through the licence fee. This brings us back to the democratic point made by Thomas Jefferson. Jefferson championed the 'multiplicity of hands' and the ownership of the 'masses' because he wanted to ensure that the foundations of civic justice and legal rights in his state were generally known and conserved. To this socio-political point, we can add the further cultural point that members of the public also play a part in establishing the aesthetic and social values of cultural products. As in the case of the *Clayhanger* fan in Ireland: the simple expedient of making sure that a loved text survived on video meant that it could then become available for critical public scrutiny, through the – again by chance – contact of this viewer with the Arnold Bennett Society. Literary societies are a semi-formal way in which texts can be preserved; at least through their archives and newsletters, which are lodged with the copyright libraries, information that forgotten texts still exist can be made available to wider publics. It was only through this circuitous route that the television series *Clayhanger* was brought to the attention of new viewers, then to some scholars, and now, perhaps, eventually to other cultural commentators who knew nothing about it. Only at the end of this process can it begin to find its place in a television 'canon'.

PART TWO
Textual Histories

INTRODUCTION

> We can experience the televisual past almost as directly as [earlier viewers] experienced the televisual present. Although we can never go back, it is perhaps the nearest we can ever get to a time machine. (Jacobs, 2006b: 114)

Following on from the debates about the canon of television history in the previous section of this collection, Catherine Johnson makes a persuasive argument for the role of evaluative criticism in television historiography. She acknowledges that this form of criticism has become rather unfashionable in recent writing on UK and US television, but proposes that it is essential to reinstate this work within the critical agenda. Drawing on her own research into the telefantasy genre, Johnson argues that evaluative judgements of television programming must be historically situated in relation to questions of theme, style, genre, technology and socio-historical context. She therefore urges us to embrace, rather than ignore, questions of creativity, artistry and excellence in television historiography, whilst simultaneously interrogating these categories.

Su Holmes' chapter on the 1950s cinema programme offers us a case study that debunks many of the commonplaces of institutional television history in the United Kingdom. She combines close textual analysis of key programmes with research in the written archives, to reassess the institutional character of the BBC and ITV in this period by focusing on a single, previously neglected, genre. Looking past the focus on television drama that characterises much of the historical writing on this period, Holmes' research shows the importance of popular factual entertainment in broader histories of the medium. This chapter also demonstrates that it is possible to employ historiographic techniques developed for the study of early television drama (see Jacobs, 2000), such as the critical reconstruction of programming (drawing on programme files, scripts and press reviews to re-envisage 'lost programming'), to broaden our knowledge and understanding of the form and presentational style of other early television.

A history of regional drama, and specifically the *Second City Firsts* anthology series produced by the BBC's English Regions Drama Unit at Pebble Mill in Birmingham, is offered by Lez Cooke in the last chapter of this section. Cooke's painstaking research on this series combines close analysis of the dramas in question with production research in the archives and original interviews with key personnel involved in the production of these programmes. In this chapter he charts the early work of many of the foremost writers, directors and producers of television drama in Britain, offering a picture of diversity and creativity in response to the remit to produce *regionality* in television drama. Employing this particular methodology, Cooke is able to fill in the gaps of an only partially archived series, making a strong case for its significance in the field of historical television drama studies, and connecting an analysis of television form and style with a vivid account of production practices and technological developments at the BBC during the 1970s.

The essays included in this section thus all approach television history from a 'textual perspective', given that television programmes, and the issues raised by the study of them, are at the centre of each chapter. Each chapter in this section moves beyond over-simplistic readings of historical television either as constituting a lost golden age or as a collection of quaint, old-fashioned or aesthetically impoverished programming. Each author also elucidates the connections and disjunctions between television's textual history and its textual present, albeit in markedly different ways.

4 Negotiating value and quality in television historiography

Catherine Johnson

In the last ten years there has been a renewed call within television studies for academics to engage in evaluative criticism of television programmes, yet this call has been primarily addressed towards contemporary television. Christine Geraghty (in line with Charlotte Brunsdon, 1997) argues that evaluative criticism of television programmes in research and teaching would enable scholars to contribute more directly to public and policy debates (2003: 36), and would 'encourage a critical audience that might demand quality television in whatever its forms' from broadcasters (2003: 37). Hence, for Geraghty, one of the functions of evaluative criticism is to inform contemporary and future television policy and production. While Jason Jacobs is not opposed to Geraghty's arguments, he is more particularly concerned with the importance of evaluation as a means of demonstrating the possibilities for 'artistic accomplishment' in television, a medium often characterised as one of relay and communication, rather than as an art form in its own right (2001: 427). For Jacobs, the need for such work has become particularly pressing since the mid-1990s, with the emergence of programmes that 'begin to demand criteria that have to account for their excellence' (2001: 432). Jacobs is arguing, therefore, that there has been a recent rise in television programmes that particularly demand and reward detailed evaluative criticism.

In both instances, however, history cannot be avoided altogether. While public and policy debates about the quality of television are focused on improving current and future provision, historical comparison is often mobilised, particularly in claims about the decline of certain genres (such as the recent claims that documentary television production in the United Kingdom has been 'dumbed down'). These debates draw on historical comparison, and in order to engage with them we need to able to compare television programming from different eras. Meanwhile, Jacobs' argument that certain television programmes from the mid-1990s demand aesthetic evaluation also draws on historical comparison. While

55

Jacobs accepts that 'there are clear examples of excellence' prior to the mid-1990s, he does argue that 'the historical development of television's dramatic efforts has reached a point where issues of excellence are pressing to an extent that has not been before' (2001: 432). Both Geraghty's and Jacobs' arguments, in different ways, imply the need for evaluative criticism that extends beyond the contemporary moment and for research that evaluates the quality (or 'excellence', in Jacobs' (2001) terms) of historical television programmes. This chapter is concerned with asking what role evaluations of quality might play in the writing of television's history and how we might go about this task. To what extent should television historians be engaged in the kinds of evaluative and critical practices proposed by Geraghty and Jacobs? How might critical evaluation contribute in particular to text-based histories of television?

EVALUATION AND HISTORIOGRAPHY

Evaluations and critical judgements have certainly not been absent from historical studies of television, and have emerged most prominently in the identification of historical golden ages and in the construction of canons.[1] The identification of a particular period in television's history as a golden age explicitly combines history (in that it is an attempt to understand the past) with evaluation (in that it is based on value judgements about the programming of the past). In the United States, the golden age has traditionally been located in the 1950s with live television dramas that had strong associations with the theatre (see Sturcken, 1990, Boddy, 1993, and Barr, 1997). In the United Kingdom, the golden age has been positioned in the 1960s and 1970s; a period in which the funding structures and ideological values of public service television were seen to provide the space for aesthetic innovation and socio-political purpose in television. In more recent historical work, however, the identification of a particular period as a golden age has fallen under some suspicion. The privileging of social realism in defining the 1960s as a golden age of British television has been understood to limit historical exploration of this period by marginalising other forms of television, such as the action-adventure series (Chapman, 2002), fantasy (Johnson, 2005) and commercial television (Johnson and Turnock, 2005).[2] It is notable that the contributions in Michele Hilmes' recent edited collection, *The Television History Book* (2003), acknowledge and examine the construction of certain periods in television's history as golden ages but largely refrain from evaluating the programmes and periods they refer to (see, for example, those by Jamie Medhurst and Jane Feuer).[3] Yet the problem with the construction of golden ages is not that it introduces evaluation into historiography but that this evaluation stems from a small number of programmes. As a result, any golden age is inevitably a generalisation that not only offers a limited understanding of a particular period but also potentially marginalises the study of other areas of television's history.

The construction of canons of the programmes that are deemed the most important in television's history has also been criticised for its tendency to limit understanding of the past by perpetuating certain values, and hence certain versions of the past. As Glen Creeber argues, however, canons are also an inevitable part of the way in which knowledge is organised (2004: xv), and avoiding evaluative comparisons and judgements 'may disable us from examining or discussing a number or group of texts in any detail at all' (2004: xv). As a consequence, Creeber argues that, rather than trying to avoid canon construction, academics should openly discuss and debate their construction. Creeber practises what he preaches by listing the selection criteria for the programmes included in his edited collection of *Fifty Key Television Programmes*. These selection criteria include popularity and familiarity, diversity of genres and historical periods, availability, and the demands of publishers. Nonetheless, as Jacobs points out, artistic quality is absent from this list. Indeed, Creeber concludes explicitly by stating of the programmes selected, 'We do not pretend that these are the "greatest" television programmes of all time' (2004: xvii).

Jacobs sees Creeber's avoidance of 'artistic or creative excellence' (2006a: 27) in the selection criteria for *Fifty Key Television Programmes* as evidence of a broader disciplinary anxiety about the role of criticism within television studies, and of a fear that it leads to 'the imposition of judgement from a position of privilege' (2006a: 27).[4] It is just as likely, however, that Creeber's anxiety about including an evaluation of the 'greatest' television programmes in his selection criteria may *also* arise from the particular demands of writing history. Anxieties about the role of judgements of artistic quality in media historiography are not new, and are articulated particularly clearly in Robert C. Allen and Douglas Gomery's seminal book *Film History* (1985). The book explores a number of different approaches to the study of film history, including a chapter on 'Aesthetic Film History'. Allen and Gomery argue that the dominant form of film history has been the history of film as an art form, exemplified by the 'masterpiece tradition' that dominated in the 1960s (1985: 67). Drawing on Gerald Mast and Andrew Sarris, they define the masterpiece tradition as an approach to film history that is primarily concerned with identifying and evaluating the 'significant works of the cinema art' (Mast, quoted in Allen and Gomery, 1985: 67–68) in which contextual economic, technological and cultural factors are of secondary importance. As such, Allen and Gomery argue that the masterpiece tradition is less concerned with historical context than with a film's 'enduring values as a work of art', and tends to privilege a small number of films by cinematic auteurs whose artistic vision can be clearly delineated (1985: 71–73). Allen and Gomery go on to critique this approach for assuming that the meanings of a work of art are timeless, for limiting the subject matter of history and for holding aesthetic aspects of cinema separate from other contextual factors, such as economics (1985: 74–76). Ultimately, for Allen and Gomery (drawing on Edward Buscombe) the primary focus on aesthetic evaluation in the masterpiece tradition inhibits examination of other factors that shape the history of cinema, resulting in 'a brand of film history that is not very *historical* – that is merely film criticism and aesthetic evaluation applied to films in chronological order' (1985: 76). Drawing on the developments offered by semiotics, they argue for a redefinition of aesthetic film history 'that lays aside matters of taste and evaluation' and explores 'the history of film as a signifying practice' (1985: 79).[5]

In many ways, Allen and Gomery's critique of the masterpiece tradition in film history, and Creeber's anxiety about the inclusion of artistic quality as a criterion of selection in canon construction, seem entirely valid. Certainly, to take an approach to film or television history that included only those texts considered 'great works of art' would diminish and limit the range and possibility of historical scholarship. Nevertheless, my contention is that historians should be engaging in evaluations of the quality of old television programmes, and that there should be a debate about how this takes place. To do so I want to unpick some of the implications of Allen and Gomery's arguments, looking first at the association of aesthetic evaluation with taste, and second at the implication that aesthetic criticism is simply 'not very historical'.

EVALUATION, TASTE AND HISTORICAL IMPORTANCE

In their critique of the masterpiece tradition, Allen and Gomery implicitly link aesthetic evaluation with taste and subjectivity when they argue for a new approach to aesthetic film history 'that lays aside matters of taste and evaluation' (1985: 79). Yet the articulation of critical judgements about television programmes need not equate to the simple expression of taste or subjective opinion, but can be constructed as a rational argument. As Jacobs argues,

> The subjective basis of casual judgement is undeniable, but our judgements are not necessarily restricted to our immediate subjective response. As soon as we begin to reflect on that response, to think about it, to articulate it in conversation (with ourselves and others) and in our writing, we necessarily begin to impose an objective structure on it. (2001: 431)

Evaluative judgements, therefore, can be articulated as arguments that can be rationalised and justified. This challenges not only the association of evaluation with subjectivity but also the understanding of evaluation as the imposition of timeless criteria. Once evaluation is understood as a rational argument, it must also be understood as an argument that is open to debate and open to challenge. Hence, evaluation is also necessarily *contingent*. This accounts for the ways in which the evaluation of certain works might change over time, and enables programmes that have previously been dismissed to be re-evaluated. As such, the act of evaluation can be understood as both rational and contingent, challenging

Allen and Gomery's association of evaluation with taste and with the imposition of timeless criteria onto works of art.[6]

Recognising the contingency of evaluative judgements allows us to examine the ways in which such arguments are formed and structured. As Barbara Herrnstein Smith argues in her illuminating discussion of literary value,

> If we recognize that literary value is 'relative' in the sense of *contingent* (that is, a changing function of multiple variables) rather than *subjective* (that is, personally whimsical, locked into the consciousness of individual subjects and/or without interest or value for other people), then we may begin to investigate the dynamics of that relativity. (1988: 11, emphasis in original)

Herrnstein Smith goes on to argue that any explicit value judgement of a particular work can be broken down as '(a) articulating an estimate of how well that work will serve certain implicitly defined functions (b) for a specific implicitly defined audience, (c) who are conceived of as experiencing the work under certain implicitly defined conditions' (1988: 13). Hence, an evaluation of a particular work, such as a television programme, asserts how well that work performs a particular function. The act of evaluation, therefore, stems from an interpretative engagement with a particular programme in order to assess what the programme is trying to achieve and how well it achieves it. Noël Carroll (2000) argues (in relation to film) that making such assessments of function necessarily involves placing the text into a category that will shape the criteria of assessment. To put it crudely, we could judge a comedy on its ability to make us laugh, but this would be an inappropriate criterion of evaluation for a current affairs programme. One of the difficulties for television studies, however, as Geraghty (2003) points out, is that television programmes are more diverse and potentially much harder to categorise than film (see also Brunsdon, 1997, and Jacobs, 2001). There is less consensus about the appropriate categories for television programmes, and complications may arise from programmes that could be situated in a number of different categories. Furthermore, the criteria associated with particular categories may be open to debate and cannot be understood to exist prior to the programme itself; rather, 'judgemental criteria have to be worked out in relation to specific instances, at least as a starting point' (Jacobs, 2001: 430).

All the same, this process is further complicated in relation to television history when the distance of time can affect the ways in which programmes are categorised, interpreted and evaluated. For example, a programme originally billed as a thriller may have subsequently come to be understood as an early example of a science fiction drama (as is the case with the *Quatermass* (BBC, 1953, 1955, 1958–1959) serials discussed below), a categorisation that might change the terms within which it is evaluated. In addition, any assessment of what a programme is trying to achieve will be shaped by the broader historiographic context within which it is analysed. As will be discussed below, a programme that appears to be badly paced and poorly executed to contemporary eyes may well be understood as innovative when placed within its context of production and reception.[7] Here, historical reviews from the initial moment of transmission can be useful in offering an insight into the ways in which a programme was historically received and evaluated. This critical context can help to challenge our initial subjective response to an old television programme and provide part of the interpretative context through which we evaluate its function. In addition, examining the ways in which our current evaluations coincide with or differ from historical evaluations of the same programmes can allow us to study the historical shifts in evaluative discourse, and critique the assumptions of contemporary evaluative criteria. Ultimately, engaging in evaluations of historical television programmes demands an assessment of the function of a particular programme that must stem from an exploration of the historical context within which the programme was produced, transmitted and received. Far from being 'not very historical' (Allen and Gomery, 1985: 76), such work is precisely concerned with exploring and illuminating the past, and examining its relationship to the present.

Furthermore, while Allen and Gomery call for film historians to lay aside 'taste and evaluation' (1985: 79), all historical research has to make selections about what to study from the vast expanse of history, and such selections involve the mobilisation of judgements and evaluations. Such judgements appear primarily as an argument for the 'historical importance' of a particular aspect or area from the past. In relation to text-based histories, certain programmes may be judged to be of particular historical importance because they are revealing of the sociocultural context of the period in which they were produced. For example, certain programmes might be particularly useful for examining the construction and representation of gender, race, nationhood or politics. Other programmes might reveal the impact of the development of new technologies, or a significant shift in a particular genre or programme form. Any argument for historical importance will take the same form as the articulation of an explicit value judgement outlined by Herrnstein Smith above. For example, in her article on the 1970s television costume drama, Helen Wheatley (2005) makes a claim for the historical importance of the largely overlooked series *Upstairs Downstairs* (LWT, 1971–1975) by arguing that it uses the studio space to explore important social issues concerning women's rights that were dominant in the 1970s. As such, Wheatley argues that the series serves an important historical function in revealing and complicating our understanding of the visual pleasures of studio drama and the ways in which television explored the women's movement of the 1970s. This argument is made for scholars and students who are understood to have encountered the programme in relation to existing histories of television drama in which *Upstairs Downstairs*, and studio drama more broadly, have been sidelined as lacking historical interest (2005: 145). It is apparent here that the claim for historical importance takes the same rational form as Herrnstein Smith's breakdown of the articulation of a judgement of value. A claim for the historical importance of a television programme is the judgement of how well that particular text performs a particular function for a particular audience understood as experiencing the work under certain conditions.

Evaluations of historical importance need not involve judgements of the artistic quality of the work under consideration.[8] Yet I want to question the extent to which judgements of artistic quality can easily be separated out from other criteria of historical importance. To do so I want to return to Glen Creeber's criteria of selection for his edited collection *Fifty Key Television Programmes*. Creeber's first criterion of selection is 'Be extremely popular with audiences and widely recognizable to potential readers' (2004: xvi). This is explained as the need to select programmes that readers of the book will be familiar with. It may not always be possible, however, to make a judgement about the popularity of a particular programme without engaging with evaluations of artistic quality, and these may shape both which programmes are selected and how they are written about. For example, is a particular selected programme popular and familiar to readers because it has been broadly critically acclaimed (such as *Cathy Come Home* (BBC, 1966) or *The Singing Detective* (BBC, 1986)) or because it received a large audience but is widely critically derided (such as *Dallas* (CBS, 1978–1991) or *Big Brother* (Endemol, 1999–)? Whether we are studying programmes that have been generally regarded as the best of their kind, or whether we are attempting to argue for the historical importance of programmes that have been dismissed as of poor quality, all programmes exist within regimes of value and quality. When undertaking historical research it is important to acknowledge the extent to which the values associated with the programmes that we study have had an impact on our historical research. One way to do this is to reveal and challenge the terms under which a programme has previously been evaluated. Wheatley's (2005) article is an excellent example of this approach. For instance, she argues that part of the reason for the dismissal of *Upstairs Downstairs* stems from the reading of studio drama as 'clumsy, dated, and inexpressive' (2005: 145), particularly in comparison with the wide vistas and visual excesses of filmed television costume dramas. Wheatley refutes this evaluation by demonstrating the ways in which the studio space can make expressive use of mise en scène to display period detail and to 'worry at' issues surrounding women's role in society.

Wheatley's argument is not explicitly concerned with evaluating the artistic quality of *Upstairs Downstairs*. Nevertheless, it does not avoid issues of artistic quality altogether, and it is possible to read the assertion of *Upstairs Downstairs*' 'expressive' use of the mise en scène of the studio as both a reason for its historical importance and an indicator of its artistic quality. The point here, which I want to go on to develop, is that evaluations of the quality of artistic expression in television programmes need not be opposed to the historiographic aims of understanding and interpreting the past, and that such evaluations may have a valuable role to play in the writing of text-based histories of television.

AESTHETIC EVALUATION AND THE FUNCTION OF HISTORY

To illustrate how critical evaluation might contribute to the writing of history, I want to begin with the example of the *Quatermass* television serials that were transmitted live by the BBC in the 1950s.[9] The serials were billed as thrillers and, broadly, concerned the threat of an alien invasion, which is discovered and eventually thwarted by the brilliant scientist Professor Quatermass. When I screen the second *Quatermass* serial, *Quatermass II* (BBC, 1955), to my third-year students as part of a course on television history they complain that it is slow, boring and, sometimes, unintentionally comical.[10] They do not respond to all early television in this way, however. By contrast, my students consistently find the 1965 documentary-drama *Up the Junction* (BBC, 1965) to be engaging, moving and fresh. We could take this difference in response as an indicator of a difference in aesthetic value – maybe *Up the Junction* is simply a better drama than *Quatermass II*? I want to argue against this: that the difference my students perceive is not an aesthetic one but one of style, theme and context. Put simply, *Up the Junction* uses a style of filming and a mode of storytelling that my students are already familiar with, and that is more broadly valued within the discipline and in British culture.[11] Its concerns with revealing and critiquing social problems, and its use of discontinuity in its structure and editing, are valued within the academy and associated with discourses of high culture and art. It was directed by Ken Loach, a director who now works in cinema and continues to produce films that are culturally valued, evidenced by the Palme d'Or that his most recent film, *The Wind that Shakes the Barley* (2006), has won at Cannes.[12] In contrast, *Quatermass II* employs a style and mode of storytelling designed to exploit its live studio transmission. As recording technologies have since largely replaced live television drama, this is a form and style of television drama with which my students are unfamiliar.[13] Its narratives of alien invasion have associations with the genres of science fiction and horror, genres that have been more widely dismissed and ridiculed than the social realism of *Up the Junction*. It was written by Nigel Kneale and directed by Rudolph Cartier, two men who are considered as pivotal to the history of British television, but who are largely unknown to all but the most ardent and historically aware undergraduate student.[14]

These categorical differences of theme, style, genre, technology and context all impact on the ways in which my students 'see', and hence evaluate, *Quatermass II* and *Up the Junction*. To be able to evaluate *Quatermass II* critically my students need to begin by understanding the serial's context of production. This was the aim of my monograph *Telefantasy* (2005), which explored the history of science fiction and fantasy television in the United Kingdom and United States. It argued that, while histories of the aesthetics of science fiction and fantasy television had tended to dismiss pre-1980s television as lacking visual complexity,[15] in fact television dramas that represented the fantastic were particularly valuable for demonstrating how well television drama could be used to display visual style and spectacle. To demonstrate this, the book selected a number of programmes as case studies and situated an analysis of their representation of the fantastic in relation to their particular historical context of production and critical reception. The case study of the *Quatermass* serials examined the programmes in relation to the technological and production context of the 1950s and the debates at that time about the aesthetics of television. This provided a context for an analysis and evaluation of the ways in which the serials used the studio, the liveness of the drama, filmed inserts, and the representation of the fantastic to explore the expressive and visual possibilities of television. To challenge previous understandings of (particularly pre-1980s) television drama as lacking complex visual style and spectacle, the book argued not simply that these programmes demonstrated expressive visual style but that they used it successfully and effectively. This evaluation depended on an examination of the context of production and had a clear historiographic purpose: to challenge previous understandings of television drama, and to provide a new understanding of the different periods studied and of the historical development of television drama. Despite this, however, the evaluative judgements of *Telefantasy* remain largely implicit. This was the consequence of a misplaced anxiety during its writing that such judgements were inappropriate in historical research. One of the intentions of this chapter is to encourage historians to be less reticent in making such evaluations explicit in television historiography, by demonstrating that such evaluations do not run counter to the aims of history.

John Caughie is much more explicit in his use of evaluation in his monograph on 'serious' television drama, *Television Drama: Realism, Modernism and British Culture* (2000). In examining a particular strand of legitimate and culturally valued television, Caughie is particularly concerned with issues of aesthetics and evaluation. Part of the intention of *Television Drama* is to argue that 'serious' television deserves to be evaluated as serious (without the scare quotes), and to do so Caughie situates the development of this form of television drama in relation to a broader history of the social, cultural, political and aesthetic development of modernism and realism in British cultural history. In doing so, Caughie constructs a definition of serious television that is at once descriptive, evaluative and historical, demonstrating the ways in which evaluation can be central to (and inseparable from) the writing of television's history.

CONCLUSION

In this chapter I have argued that any evaluation is an assessment of how well a particular text performs a particular function within a particular context. This may be an evaluation of historical importance, of artistic creativity or of quality, yet in each case a more detailed set of criteria will emerge from the particular instance at hand. For example, while both *Telefantasy* and Caughie's *Television*

Drama are concerned with arguing for the aesthetic and historical importance of certain television dramas, the nature of the evaluation differs in each case. While both are concerned with the artistic creativity and quality of the works studied, it is a different form of artistry and quality stemming from the different kinds of programmes under examination. Furthermore, in each case the examination of artistry and creativity is inseparable from the broader historiographic concerns at hand. Hence, Caughie is particularly concerned with works whose artistic quality demonstrates and complicates our understanding of the development of realism and modernism in British television culture. By contrast, *Telefantasy* is concerned with programmes whose quality lies in their ability to demonstrate how well television could be used for visual spectacle and display.

One of the difficulties in writing about evaluation is that the terms 'aesthetics', 'creativity', 'importance' and 'quality' tend to get used interchangeably, making the nature of the debate somewhat obtuse. In some ways this is unavoidable. For example, I have demonstrated here that an argument for historical importance may inevitably need to deal with evaluations of quality or artistry. By the same token, however, making explicit evaluations of old television programmes would force the historian or student to unpack and explain what he/she means by 'artistic creativity', 'historical importance', 'quality', and so on.

In particular, there is a need for further examination of what we mean by 'artistic creativity' in relation to television. It is perhaps unsurprising that the two examples provided here of the kind of work that I am advocating are concerned with television drama, since television's dramatic forms accord most closely with the more established aesthetic debates from film and literary studies. For example, while aesthetic evaluation of literary fiction has a long history, it would be far more unusual to assess the artistic creativity of a newspaper, despite the creativity involved in journalistic writing and newspaper design. Hence, the artistry involved in the production of television fiction is arguably more apparent and open to evaluative analysis than the artistry involved in the production of news, televised sport, a live cookery programme, quiz shows or a televised concert. Yet that does not mean that such television programmes are not open to aesthetic criticism. Surely it *is* possible to make a judgement about the quality of the coverage of a sporting event or a news item. Clearly, one of the issues here is not that artistic creativity is absent in these forms of programming but, rather, that the nature of this creativity is different from that in a drama.[16] Part of the value of making aesthetic judgements about these programmes would be to begin to tease out the nature of this difference.

Over and above this, there is also a need for further critical debate about the relationship between artistic creativity and quality, and, more specifically, what we mean by 'quality' when evaluating television, and specifically historical television. Certainly, I would not want to argue for an approach to television history that examined only those programmes considered to be of good quality. Yet avoiding evaluations of quality limits the potential of television historiography and makes implicit those judgements that might shape the writing of television's history. Indeed, the avoidance of evaluations of quality becomes particularly problematic for studies of popular television. Much of the work on popular television has eschewed aesthetic evaluation 'in order to allow it to concentrate on something else, on the workings of language and ideology' (Caughie, 2000: 22). Programming forms such as light entertainment and studio drama, and other forms of what might be termed 'bread and butter' television (including what Frances Bonner, 2003, usefully terms 'ordinary television'), are ones that conflict most overtly and strongly with the contemporary dominant criteria of aesthetic value. At present vast swathes of the most ubiquitous television programmes remain under-explored. While some of the recent work on different forms of reality television and factual entertainment has started to challenge this (see, for example, Hill, 2004, and Holmes and Jermyn, 2004), bar a few exceptions, their historical precedents are largely overlooked in television studies.[17] I would like to conjecture that one of the reasons why these areas have been relatively neglected in histories of television is precisely because it is hard to write about such generally derided (or, at least, not critically applauded) programmes without engaging with questions of quality. This makes them potentially difficult historical subjects, because aesthetic evaluation has been seen as problematic in television historiography.

Work that attempted to counter this by asking *how* we might evaluate the quality of such popular forms of television would provide a valuable historical tool, not simply for what it can tell us about the past but also for what it can reveal about the present. In his recent inaugural lecture as Professor of History at Royal Holloway, University of London (2006) Justin Champion argued that one of history's most valuable functions is providing 'new ways of seeing' that could encourage (or even force) us to look and think in different ways about the present. For television history, which is concerned with both the recent past and with a ubiquitous social and cultural form, these new ways of seeing are invaluable. History can help us to see the very familiar and everyday medium of television afresh, in new and surprising ways. As such, history can also provide us with a means to challenge the ways in which we think about television in the present. Evaluating the quality of old television programmes, therefore, can provide new ways of 'seeing' the current debates about quality television, and new ways of evaluating the range of television's output. As Charlotte Brunsdon (1997) has argued, television has always sat rather problematically in relation to conventional criteria of aesthetic value, making aesthetic evaluation difficult and even more necessary for television studies. Engaging in evaluations of the quality of old television programmes, and particularly those programmes that have traditionally been derided, could therefore offer one way of challenging the dominant criteria for evaluating the quality of contemporary television, as well as complicating and making explicit the implicit evaluations that have shaped the writing of television's history.

There are a further set of historiographic problems here, which have been beyond the scope of this chapter, related to the archive availability of historical television programmes, and the extent to which evaluative judgements in previous archiving policies have affected the audio-visual and paper records that we now have. Although Jason Jacobs (2000) and Su Holmes (2005) have demonstrated the effectiveness of using paper archives where audio-visual records do not exist, the possibilities for aesthetic evaluation will clearly be limited by the material held in the archives. Nevertheless, Jacobs has argued that criticism is important because it 'is a way of articulating why television programmes matter to us and the nature of that significance' (2001: 431). One of the ways in which old television programmes matter to us in the present is their ability to demonstrate the different range of qualities through which we might evaluate television, and, as such, their ability to offer us new ways of seeing and thinking about what we consider to be quality television in the past, in the present, and in the future.

5 'A friendly style of presentation which the BBC had always found elusive'?

The 1950s cinema programme and the construction of British television history

Su Holmes

In the late 1950s Viewer Research Reports on the BBC's cinema programme *Picture Parade* (1956–1962) often asked viewers to comment under the heading of 'Presentation'. The reports repeatedly note how the audience had 'nothing but praise for the delightfully informal [and]…extremely pleasant and friendly manner' of the presenters, Peter Haigh and Derek Bond.[1] In fact, they were 'most agreeable personalities whom it was a pleasure to meet each week', representing some of 'the most charming comperes we have on TV'.[2] In terms of television history, these statements could be seen as interesting for a range of different reasons – the reception of early modes of televisual address; offering comments on two popular television presenters of the time; or even suggesting the kinds of questions asked by the BBC when conducting audience research. These statements are particularly intriguing, however, when placed alongside a broader history of British television in the 1950s that pivots on institutional and cultural *differences* between the BBC and its commercial rival, ITV. Usually supported by the assertion that ITV 'provided a lively counter to the stuffiness of the BBC' (Stokes, 1999: 34), it now seems widely accepted that 'ITV forged a friendly style of presentation which the BBC had always found elusive' (Black, 1972: 116). As Bernard Sendall explains, the ITV presenters 'set up a personal relationship with the viewer', while the BBC's were largely 'mouthpieces for the Corporation' (1982: 325). The question I want to raise here is encapsulated by the contradictory relationship that structures the sources above. What do we do when a particular text or genre doesn't seem to 'fit' the conventional assumptions that circulate in institutional histories? What issues does this raise about the construction of television history, or, more specifically, the relationship between 'broadcasting history' and 'television history' – if the latter is defined as the historical study of television texts, aesthetics and forms? I want to suggest here that these questions are *central* to debates about the critical and methodological construction of television history, and the questions we should ask when approaching this field.

In terms of focus, however, it is also significant here that (particularly at the level of aesthetic form) the history of early British television has largely been mapped through the development of drama (Jacobs, 2000; Caughie, 2000). Replicating the wider imbalance that structures the study of television genres (see Bonner, 2003), this then marginalises a large proportion of television output – particularly that represented by studio-based entertainment programming. Here, I want to draw upon wider archival research into the television cinema series *Current Release* (BBC, 1952–1953), *Picture Parade* and *Film Fanfare* (ABC, 1956–1957), which, despite their huge popularity in the 1950s, have remained largely invisible in both British television and cinema history (see Holmes, 2005). Much like today, the cinema programme in the 1950s was a studio-based, presenter-led genre that previewed the latest film releases, interviewed stars and directors, and took us behind the scenes of film production. Unlike today, however, it occupied a unique position in the developing relations between the media. The roles of cinema and television (as media industries and cultural forms, but, crucially, as sites of screen entertainment) effectively came together at this time in such a way that is unique to this decade. Television's growing status as a mass medium developed throughout these years, and, although this certainly hastened the cinema's decline, the cinema remained a central part of cultural consciousness and experience for much of the 1950s. This created a context in which the media temporarily shared a status as forms of 'mass' *screen entertainment*, something that is often overlooked in conventional perspectives of their relations at this time, but that comes out strongly in the programmes themselves.

BROADCASTING IT: CONSTRUCTING TELEVISION HISTORY

In *The Intimate Screen: Early British Television Drama* (2000), Jason Jacobs describes the need to consider a relationship between the 'macro-overview of broadcasting history' and the more local analyses of specific genres or texts (2000: 9). In focusing on the institutional history of the BBC, interventions such as Asa Briggs' *The History of Broadcasting in the United Kingdom* (volumes 1–5) have offered an influential model of such a 'macro-overview' which, by its very nature, has excluded a detailed analysis of the programmes themselves (Jacobs, 2000: 8). Following the increase in interest in television history since the early 1990s, scholars have often attempted to combine these perspectives (e.g. Corner, 1991b; Thumim, 2002), although this has involved drawing on 'macro' narratives in order to contextualise the background to more specific studies. As a result, the issue of chronological development is important here. The wider institutional narratives of broadcast history pre-existed archival interest in programme forms, and this has encouraged their appropriation as a 'backdrop' that can help to contextualise studies of programmes, genres and audiences. This is in many ways a practical necessity, yet my point is that, despite the increasingly self-reflexive attitude that shapes the construction of media history (as well as the concurrent questioning of 'grand' meta-narratives and paradigms), the potentially *complex* relationship at work here has witnessed little debate. Unless we are to ignore the institutional contexts in which television programmes are conceived, developed and produced, however, it is a question that *any* generic study must at some point confront. While my interest here is in the specificities of the British television system in the mid-1950s, this is also true of any national context (which will have its own institutional narratives and histories).

This also has a particular significance in relation to the 1950s given that so little of the programming has survived, particularly in the years leading up to 1955. The notion that much of television's past inhabits a 'dim pre-history', from which many programmes have not survived (Caughie, 2000: 9), has made the institutional histories seem all the more impenetrable. Even with programming from the mid- to late 1950s, access to surviving editions of many programmes is still limited. Indeed, the utter *certainty* of the contrasts drawn between the BBC and ITV in this period – not simply at an institutional level but in terms of textual address – is quite remarkable in this respect. Given the availability of existing evidence, my reconstruction of the BBC's *Current Release* and *Picture Parade* is based primarily on the programme files, scripts and press reviews. Both programmes were broadcast live, but in the case of *Picture Parade* there is also limited access to existing telefilmed editions. Editions of both shows were telefilmed quite regularly in the 1950s (apparently just for the BBC's own purposes), but archiving was patchy and sporadic. Those that do exist are then not usually made available for research purposes. At the same time, the BBC's Written Archives Centre provides an extraordinarily detailed range of material, providing a unique entry into the development and circulation of a particular programme culture. As Jacqueline Kavanagh observes, the 'programmes tell us what was said and shown: the written archives may help to tell us how and why' (Kavanagh, 1999: 81). In the case of the cinema programme, this material offers access to the 'world' of an entire programme culture, its everyday routines, practices and rhythms. Jacobs describes a similar approach to early television drama as the 'reconstitution or reconstruction...of "ghost texts"...that do not exist in their original audio-visual form but exist instead as shadows, dispersed and refracted amongst buried files, bad memories, a flotsam of fragments' (2000: 14).

This raises the issue of comparative access to sources when it comes to considering the BBC and ITV. It is certainly somewhat frustrating to be able to access the smallest details about the production of a programme, such as what time they had sandwiches in the rehearsal for the BBC's *Current Release*, but then never actually to see it play out on the screen. The balance of evidence is completely the reverse where ITV is concerned. In contrast to the BBC, existing editions of ABC's *Film Fanfare* and ATV's *Movie Magazine* (1955–1956) are relatively plentiful, while (aside from press reviews and the film trade press) the written material is non-existent. This is particularly so when it comes to contextualising the institutional production of the programmes, and the debates and factors that may have shaped this process. This disparity in terms of audio-visual evidence arises partly from the fact that ITV made greater use of filmed material in the 1950s (and its archival practices may also have been shaped by commercial imperatives).[3] *Film Fanfare* was broadcast live only for a few weeks, and many of the filmed editions have survived. Unlike the BBC, though, ITV did not perceive itself as having any particular institutional, historical or cultural responsibility to retain the written traces of its existence – thereby creating an absence that poses a much greater challenge for research. The point here is that, in addressing a possible comparison between the channels, the question of how to 'reconstruct' the programmes must also confront the issue of sources, and the *different* forms of access these may offer.

To contextualise the significance of these programmes in film and television history briefly, a key point is that they question certain assumptions made about the relations between British cinema and television in the 1950s. Unlike the American context, where it is now understood that Hollywood and broadcasting operated in a symbiotic relationship from the 1920s (see Hilmes, 1990, and Anderson, 1994), existing work on the British context has continued to emphasise the hostility between the media – based largely on the protracted debates surrounding the sale of feature films to television (see Buscombe, 1991). This was only *one* sphere of negotiation, however, given that cinema programmes kept the film industry and television in near-constant interaction throughout the 1950s. Furthermore, while undoubtedly providing evidence of a longer historical trajectory in which television has increasingly functioned to domesticate film culture, there is something special, unique and particularly revealing about the cultural significance of the cinema programme in the 1950s (the genre in the contemporary context can hardly be conceived of as 'appointment viewing'). As noted in the introduction, the roles of cinema and television as sites of 'mass' screen entertainment briefly overlapped in the 1950s – creating the cultural and institutional centrality of the cinema programme. Particularly after the advent of a second channel in 1955, it is not surprising that television coverage of the cinema became a key site in the competition for audiences. It was part of a shared, and still everyday, culture that defined the existence of the cinema in such a way that differentiates it from today. By the end of the decade the institutional, industrial and cultural contexts that had fostered this interaction had changed (particularly, of course, where the cinema was concerned), bringing what I suggest is the 'golden age' of the cinema programme to an end (see Holmes, 2005).

Given my argument that this early period can effectively be conceived as 1952–1962, spanning the emergence of the BBC's *Current Release* and the end of *Picture Parade*, it also traces a crucial period of institutional change for British television, and its wider expansion as a mass medium. While it is fair to suggest that 'commercial television promised greater choice of viewing, an expansion of the market, and a new optimism about popular broadcasting' (Stokes, 1999: 33), it is difficult to disentangle this from the extent to which 'a substantial myth has grown up, based on a picture of the energetic...showbiz visionaries [of ITV] elbowing aside the complacent bureaucrats of the BBC' (Black, 1972: 109) – a 'myth' to which Black's study contributes. Certain histories have emphasised the BBC's refusal to acknowledge the economic and cultural realities of this change, suggesting, for example, that 'the BBC continued to prepare its schedule as though the competitor did not exist' (Black, 1972: 134), or that the ITV companies 'awaited the BBC's counter-blow, and were puzzled when it did not arrive' (Sendall, 1982: 112). Yet Andrew Crisell emphasises how the BBC had a more nuanced approach when he argues that

> [u]nder the Director General Sir Ian Jacob the policy was partly to compete with ITV, to match like with like, but true to its old public service philosophy of providing a range and catering for minorities, the BBC also tried to offer contrast by scheduling some of its more serious output at peak viewing hours. (1997: 88)

As the competing natures of *Picture Parade* and *Film Fanfare* will suggest, by the mid-1950s the cinema programme provided a clear example of an attempt to match 'like with like', while there were also discernible differences between the series. My comparison of the programmes considers their approach towards film culture, as well as notions of presentational style and audience address. Following the conventional institutional narratives, we would somehow expect the BBC to offer a more 'worthy' and didactic approach to the cinema (entrenched within more formal modes of address), as opposed to the presumably more populist and commercial attitude of ITV (driven by entertainment). The nature of their differences, however, and the factors that shaped them, demand consideration within a more complex framework than this seems to suggest. In order to make this comparison, it is necessary to contextualise the historical relationship between British broadcasting and film culture.

'TEACHING THE PUBLIC HOW TO LOOK AT FILMS'?: THE BBC AND FILM CULTURE

Despite the emphasis on the BBC's elitist disdain for the commercial cinema (Briggs, 1979; Buscombe, 1991), coverage of film culture was an integral part of the radio service from the late 1920s, whether in the form of reviews, talks or magazine programmes. It is difficult to describe the Corporation as having one single approach to the cinema, as the institutional correspondence reveals a range of different attitudes, which shifted across different programmes and periods. Furthermore, the relationship between film culture and the concept of public service is highly complex. Partly because of the historically elusive nature of public service (see Scannell, 1990), and partly because of the difficulty in pinning it down in relation to particular programme forms, it is not simple to describe the ways in which film programming fulfilled this remit. Indeed, whether on radio or television, all film review features could be broadly conceived within the context of 'public service', given that they were originally conceived as helping the 'interested listener' select the films he or she wished to see.[4] Nevertheless, it is broadly possible to suggest that there was an intention at the BBC, in keeping with an ethos of public service, to improve the audiences' critical appreciation of film.

In 1936, for example, the BBC emphasised that 'the most hopeful line of approach [was] the teaching of the public how to look at films, to recognise the special quality and habits of various producers'.[5] Despite the cinema's status as the most popular mass medium of its day, it is clear that – from the very start – the BBC believed in conceptualising film as an 'art'. It is also important to emphasise that film critics associated with a serious critical literature on the cinema (such as C. A. Lejeune, Roger Manvell, Dilys Powell, Basil Wright and Arthur Vesselo) broadcast regularly on BBC radio. In fact, in examining the files at the BBC's Written Archives Centre, it is notable just how seriously film could be taken by the Corporation at this time (as well as how articulate certain staff members were in discussing this sphere). It is important to stress, however, that there was also a strong emphasis on the *popular* culture of the cinema – stars, quizzes and studio news – on a number of different levels. This was particularly so from the 1940s onwards, when the restructuring of the BBC's radio service represented what Paddy Scannell and David Cardiff describe as 'a redefinition of [the BBC's]…relationship [with] its audience, or rather its acceptance of the audience with different tastes and needs' (1981: 41). In the post-war period BBC radio was restructured with the advent of the Home, Light and Third Programmes (see Crisell, 1997), with the Third Programme offering the somewhat highbrow approach. The Controller of Talks was keen to develop the Third Programme's coverage of film at this time and would repeatedly insist that the Corporation had 'significantly underestimated the amount of serious interest in the cinema today'.[6] Nonetheless, while the Third Programme did occasionally cover film-related topics (such as 'Cinema and the unconscious', 'Shakespeare and the cinema' and 'The British quota system'), he was abruptly informed by the controller of the Third Programme that

> [t]he major interest is in the popular film and in the cinema star… I know there are those who are seriously interested in 'the film' and there are some films which are worth while taking seriously, but I believe the former number is very small, and the latter are rare occurrences.[7]

While these dialogues clearly emphasise two quite different perspectives on what 'film culture' actually was (and how it should be dealt with by the BBC), it is also suggestive in indicating a potential shift in the BBC's approach. Essentially, this appeared to put the focus more squarely on entertainment, in line with the popular interest referred to above, and the advent of film magazines such as *Filmtime* (Home, 1948–1949), *Movie-go-Round* (Light, 1956–) and *Picture Parade* (Light, 1949) in the late 1940s and 1950s epitomised this shift.

Certainly, as the title of *Current Release* suggests, the cinema programme on television in the 1950s was largely focused on popular film culture and previews of the latest films. Nevertheless, from the BBC's perspective at least, there remained a perpetual *tension* where the relationship between the cinema programme and public service was concerned. In broad terms, this can be conceived as a struggle between the balance of programme material and promotion, mapped across the differing investments of the BBC and the film industry. The film industry obviously approached the series as advertising, which, in itself, was technically a violation of the BBC's official charter. As such, the film industry resisted any real scope for *criticism* of the films. This was something that, from the BBC's point of view, served only to exacerbate the problem of advertising where the genre was concerned, and freedom of criticism also had a long discursive history in relation to public service.[8] But the Corporation repeatedly explained to the film companies how it hoped to produce something that 'would be of interest and enlightenment to viewers' and did not wish the public to 'criticize the BBC, alleging that it had made a deal with the film industry to help exploit its films'.[9] For example, presented by the amiable John Fitzgerald on a fortnightly basis, *Current Release* was primarily organised around previews of four to five new films, with occasional interviews with film stars. It also included, however, sections intended to elucidate how editing, or sound dubbing worked (illustrated in the 'cutting room'), or items in which directors occasionally explained artistic or technical elements in film construction. According to the producer, this was explicitly conceived by the Corporation as 'the BBC end of the programme, [which]...should have a high interest appeal to viewers and not merely be a flabby framework' for the promotion of current films.[10] With such elements often received by the film industry with a mixture of bemusement and dislike, the balance of the cinema programme remained a constant area of struggle in the developing relations between the BBC and the film interests.

While the issue of advertising (which was effectively intrinsic to the genre) remained an acute concern for the Corporation, there was less evidence of the bid to educate viewers or to raise their critical appreciation of film as the 1950s progressed. Beginning in 1956, in both the BBC's *Picture Parade* and ABC's *Film Fanfare*, the emphasis was clearly on new releases, but, even more centrally, their *stars*. As film star appearances on television became conventionalised (see Holmes, 2001a), there were as many interviews as previews, with such glamour apparently conceived as a key weapon in the bid to attract audiences. This in itself indicates how the advent of competition had reshaped the contours of the genre. In general terms, when ITV emerged film programming (including profile features) seemed to proliferate, and, as suggested below, it is not insignificant that certain programme contractors had direct economic links with the film industry. Equally, this period saw a much greater formalisation of relations with the film industry where these programmes were concerned – how, for example, meetings about the programmes were planned, and how requests for excerpts and star interviews were to be organised.

The weekly parallel existence of *Picture Parade* and *Film Fanfare* is borne out in their conception and development. Particularly given the cessation of a regular review series after the end of *Current Release* in 1952, it seems no coincidence that the BBC's *Picture Parade* emerged when it did. Weeks before ITV's *Film Fanfare* began, the BBC's Cecil Madden informed Cecil McGivern that

> I learned that Howard Thomas [managing director of ABC TV] has notified ATV that he plans a one hour film magazine on Sundays, 3–4 pm, and that in return he will network *Sunday Night at the London Palladium* and perhaps others. It means that [*Movie Magazine*] ...on ATV will have to move. This is the hour I wanted for...*Picture Parade*.[11]

Film Fanfare was initially a Sunday afternoon programme and later became a Saturday night feature screened at 10 p.m., while *Picture Parade* was ultimately screened at 9:15 p.m. on Mondays. Yet the specific detail of their scheduling is not as important as the sense that they were clearly understood, in their general planning, development and conception, as *competing* series from the start. In their launching of a cinema programme at this time, it seems clear that the Corporation did not intend to be beaten in an area it had pioneered. It is within the field of their competing existence, then, that we also need to recognise their potential differences. The key issue is *how* these differences might be conceived, and (in questioning the unsatisfying broad strokes of the institutional narratives) the ways in which they might be contextualised and explained.

The advent of competition clearly altered the institutional relations between the film industry and television. British film companies, such as the Associated British Picture Corporation (ABPC) and Granada, submitted successful bids for ITV network franchises, becoming programme contractors in 1956. It is ABPC that is particularly important here, given that ABC TV produced *Film Fanfare*. The Associated British Picture Corporation was one of the most powerful organisations in the British film industry from the late 1920s to the late 1970s (Porter, 2000: 152). This power emerged from the fact that, like the Rank Organization, ABPC was a vertically integrated company that not only produced films at Elstree studios but also owned the distribution outfit Associated British Pathé and the well-known ABC cinema chain. In 1955 ABC TV was added to the corporate empire, and *Film Fanfare* suggests ways in which these various media interests could interact and coalesce. In fact, the managing director of ABPC,

Howard Thomas, was repeatedly quoted in the press as saying that ABPC had moved into television to 'boost cinema admissions'.[12] Although this was clearly in part a bid to appease the complaints of the film industry, which had concerns about the company moving into the enemy camp, it does suggest an awareness of the possibilities of using television to promote the cinema (at a time when admissions were now beginning to see a more alarming and spiralling slump). *Film Fanfare* was effectively able to promote ABPC's films, their stable of stars and the wider releases on the ABC cinema chain – and viewers were given an opportunity in the programme to 'win tickets to their local ABC cinema'. While this economic bias was implicit in the programme, however, ABC operated under the same advertising strictures as the BBC when it came to programme material – the parameters of which had been tested by the controversy surrounding the advertising magazine, or 'admag'. This genre deliberately blurred the boundaries between promotion and programme material, and, after considerable debate, the form was later outlawed by the Pilkington Committee in 1962, when it was decided that it broke the terms of the Television Act (see Sendall, 1982: 213). While both channels operated under the same strictures here, it was nevertheless the case that the cinema programme necessarily occupied a rather ambiguous space in this respect. In operating as a form of consumer guide, it was intrinsically promotional. In fact, it was often dismissed by critics as a form of 'plug TV' – a popular phrase also associated with the advent of ITV, and particularly the early confusion surrounding the relations between advertising and programme content (Holmes, 2005: 54). Equally, it seems too simple to conceive of this institutional context as neatly constructing a 'public service' versus 'commercial' dichotomy where the BBC's and ITV's relations with film culture were concerned. This is not least because, as discussed, the BBC's coverage of film had already undergone a series of redefinitions.

WITH A FANFARE AND PARADE: COMPETING FILM CULTURES

In terms of their general programme content, *Picture Parade* and *Film Fanfare* included many of the items that we continue to recognise in the genre today: the mixture of previews, interviews, film 'gossip' and 'behind-the-scenes' footage of films in production. Their historical specificity means, however, that they look quite different from contemporary examples, not simply in terms of the more obvious significance of an 'early' television aesthetic but in terms of their imaging of, and conception of, film culture. Central here was television's *attitude* towards the cinema, its utter deference and excitement, the 'excessive' celebration of its glamour, importance and charm.

First, in both programmes there was a bid to create the impression that the series emerged from inside the film industry. The sets of *Picture Parade* included a cinema foyer (complete with doorman), a film 'office' (with female secretary)[13] and a projection room. Similarly, the more spacious set of *Film Fanfare* simulated the spaces of a cinema (where the excerpts were previewed), an office (adorned with portraits of film stars) and several 'studio' areas, where we were given the impression that film production might commence at any minute. These spaces included the technological apparatus of filmmaking – cameras, arc lights, booms and set scaffolding. In both programmes, the camera would sometimes cut to a presenter 'caught' on the telephone, being told that a star had arrived in reception, for example, in such a way as to suggest that these were actual *operational* spaces dealing with the hustle and bustle of film. While it is true that ABC's *Film Fanfare*, with its frequent visits to the ABPC studios, constructed a closer discursive relationship with the British film industry, both programmes blurred the boundaries between cinema and television on a number of different levels.

As explained at the start of this article, the BBC's *Picture Parade* was presented by the popular TV presenter Peter Haigh and the British film actor Derek Bond. In comparison, *Film Fanfare* was based around a larger range of presenters, including the popular TV presenter MacDonald Hobley, John Fitzgerald, 'roving reporter' John Parsons and Peter Noble (a well-known show business journalist and author of several books on the film industry), as well as Canadian film actors Peter Arne and Paul Carpenter. In both programmes, this use of film actors was perhaps intended to contribute to the discursive impression of an 'inside' perspective on film culture. *Picture Parade* and *Film Fanfare* both placed the emphasis firmly on contemporary mainstream films and their stars, but this was contextualised in different ways by surrounding magazine material. For example, as its title implies, *Film Fanfare* was based within the context of a 'show', with the presence of an orchestra functioning to facilitate this. Many existing editions begin with a high-angle shot of an orchestra, staggered on platforms, as the words 'Film Fanfare' appear in fancy script accompanied by stirring orchestral music. The camera then tracks down to meet the orchestra at eye level, and in certain editions we see an enormous studio arc light on a platform that is directed at the musicians by a technician. It is then switched on with an audible 'click' as the orchestra leaps into action – conducted by the film composer Muir Mathieson. This not only gives the impression that we are witnessing part of the production process but also foregrounds the *staging* of the programme, and the construction of the orchestra (with their suits and bow ties) as a spectacle. Indeed, the opening of *Film Fanfare* seems to invoke the grandeur of the theatrical rather than the cinematic, in which a concert orchestra is brought to the home. With its orchestral framing and aspirations to the theatrical, it is the ITV programme that in fact gives the impression of a rather middle-class formality. In fact, in comparison, the BBC's *Picture Parade* begins with the presenters aiming to give the impression that they are chatting 'casually' in the office as the title credits roll down. Furthermore, when *Film Fanfare* moved from Sunday afternoon to Saturday night the presenters adopted formal evening attire, whereas, in the BBC series, Haigh and Bond were seen in 'casual' suits and ties. While not an uncommon sight on 1950s television (indicative of the more formal dress codes of the time), formal evening appearance also draws on very middle-class codes of conduct: if 'guests' are welcomed into the home in the evening, they wear evening attire.

The orchestra was there not simply to play the grand title music: it had a much wider role in the programme. Viewers were encouraged to send in requests, asking the orchestra to play the music from their favourite films. It is also notable here that the film material was interspersed with items in which songs were performed from past or present films, often by British film actors and actresses. While, from a retrospective point of view, this may appear to be a rather eclectic and fragmented mix of items (with the presenters simply stating 'Now let's take time out for a song...' or 'Let's enjoy a dance with music from Dave Shand's band...'), it can perhaps be situated within the context of ITV's greater success with variety programming at this time (see Sendall, 1982). It also raises issues about methodological approaches to television genre from a historical perspective. While Jane Feuer (1992) points to the need to consider the development of television genres within the context of the medium's wider flow (to which she attributes their greater tendency for generic hybridity), this wider context is particularly important in trying to 'reconstruct' programmes and genres from the past; *Film Fanfare*'s structure appears far less strange and eclectic when situated within the context of ITV's surrounding programme culture.

Film Fanfare certainly made an attempt to emphasise that there was more to the series than 'simply' the promotion of contemporary films (as the items about film music indicate). The BBC's *Picture Parade* aimed to achieve this in a slightly different manner. For example, the veteran British film director Maurice Elvey presented a regular slot on film history – films from the recent past as well as historical films. This clearly contrasted with the programme's otherwise contemporary focus, and it may well have been a bid to temper (accusations over) its promotional connotations. Often focusing on one of Elvey's own films, sometimes from the silent period, it was commonly organised around a particular theme or genre, ranging from a week on films about legendary highwayman Dick Turpin to one on the various film adaptations of *A Christmas Carol*. Nonetheless, while it occasionally incorporated a directorial point of view, it was usually just a brief illustrated talk with the aid of excerpts and stills, and could hardly be considered overly didactic in tone. Perhaps a more significant difference from *Film Fanfare* was the range of international film culture covered by the series. In the last *Picture Parade* edition presented by Haigh and Bond (1958), Haigh recalled how '[a]ll this time we have enjoyed...bring[ing] to your homes some wonderful excerpts of films from many countries: English and American, naturally, but also French, Italian, Swedish, Russian – and even Chinese'. Although, as Haigh explained here, the primary focus was on British and Hollywood film, *Picture Parade* nevertheless made a concerted attempt to preview films from other national contexts, often in conjunction with features playing at the National Film Theatre in London.

With their more 'artistic' (and, indeed, minority) connotations, there was undoubtedly a bid here to expose the audience to a greater diversity of film ranging beyond the conventional boundaries of 'box-office' fare. Even this cannot simply be perceived as evidence of the BBC's more educational approach to film culture, however, given the shifts in the distribution and exhibition of foreign-language films in the United Kingdom at this time. The 1950s was a time when British exhibitors were increasingly turning to foreign-language films in response to the escalating product shortage from Hollywood (fostered by the decline of the studio system) (see Holmes, 2001b). French (and then Italian) films represented the largest part of this influx, and, coinciding with the decline in family film-going, such films increasingly permeated wider distribution networks and exhibition patterns, enjoying an expanding circulation. While often also retaining their 'artistic' connotations, the increasing popularisation of the Continental film was equally entrenched within discourses foregrounding their 'risqué' nature – particularly in view of their synonymous link with the 'X' certificate.

While also conflicting with the argument that such fare was a key way for the cinema to compete with the tame, domestic medium of television at this time, *Picture Parade's* interest in foreign-language films, and adoption of a 'Continental Cinema' spot, could not exist separately from these discourses. Rather than offering the viewer the odd taste of Chinese or Yugoslavian film culture, it was far more likely to be previewing the more mainstream Continentals – featuring sexy female stars such as Brigitte Bardot, Sophia Loren or Martine Carol. Indeed, in 1957 Haigh noted that Bardot's 'name appeared more than any other' in their Continental spot, and he even indulged in some banter about her popular tags of 'sex-kitten' and 'gorgeous Pekinese'. The point here is that, although the bid to include elements of foreign-language films *did* differentiate *Picture Parade* and *Film Fanfare*, this cannot simply be perceived as being indicative of an anxiety over television's relations with 'popular' film culture, or in some sense linked to an overriding ethos of public service. Once again, a neat opposition between the channels would struggle to emerge.

THE PRESENTER AS AN 'ORDINARY FILMGOER': (RE)CONSTRUCTING TELEVISUAL ADDRESS

The question of how this might relate to the specificities of presenter (and thus audience) address is equally complex. *Picture Parade's* dapper Peter Haigh, with his immaculately trimmed moustache and carefully modulated voice, was a well-known personality on BBC television (and radio) in the 1950s, and in many ways he could be perceived as epitomising the BBC's very middle-class rhetoric at this time. Indeed, given its generalised reputation as offering a more popular and appealing address to television's increasingly mass audience, the use of Canadian presenters on ABC's *Film Fanfare* was, perhaps, an attempt to offer a more casual tone. Yet, in the context of the cinema programme, the accents were clearly also intended to 'stand in' for the United States, and thus loosely signify 'Hollywood'. Certainly, with their desire to promote 'proper' standards for the enunciation of the English language (Briggs, 1965), it is perhaps difficult to imagine the Canadian presenters on the BBC at all at this time. It is worth noting here, however, that the other *Film Fanfare* presenters, Noble, Parsons, Hobley and Fitzgerald, mirrored the tone of the BBC presenters. Hobley, in fact, began his television career with the BBC, and Fitzgerald had presented the BBC's *Current Release* (while Parsons had also occasionally been its interviewer). At the very least, then, this could have made for a degree of continuity across channels as far as the presentation of the cinema programme was concerned.

Even on the basis of such *textual* comparisons, however, it is difficult to reconstruct the original articulation of presenter address – what was intended or conceived, and indeed how it was *received*. Janet Thumim has discussed the 'dilemma' for researchers 'in *seeing*...what was "on television"' at all in the 1950s, particularly when, in comparison with the 1950s audience, they are all relatively 'sophisticated or "skilled" viewers' (2002: 2). My point above does not so much speak to a dilemma emerging from incomparable levels of 'tele-literacy' as pose the question of how present-day researchers can conceptualise the intentions of, and responses to, the medium when it was a *developing* technological, textual and cultural form. This is perhaps particularly so given that (when compared with film, for example) the writing of television's textual past has not been shaped by the same degree of theoretical rigour (although, equally, the paucity of sources makes this difficult). As John Caughie notes, 'There seems to be formal and elaborated theoretical intervention in thinking about television which is written in the process of becoming, in the context of the practical possibilities of what was going on when it was formed' (2000: 15). The point here is that, despite the persistent opposition drawn between the BBC and ITV in this respect, it is far from simple to ascertain now what was perceived as a 'friendly style of presentation' (Black, 1972: 116) on television in 1956. Yet, despite Thumim's comment above about the difficulty of 'seeing' the historical specificity of the programmes we research (locating their intentions, terms of address or audience appeal), this does not mean that we can't make judgements at all. Close analysis of the programme text is still central here, and the existing editions of *Picture Parade* and *Film Fanfare* offer insight into modes of presentational address that are unique to audio-visual footage. I only emphasise two things: first, that this process of interpretation should be open to debate; and, second, that it can also be situated within a wider textual field of evidence – including press reviews, production notes or Viewer Research Reports.[14]

While Viewer Research Reports praised the BBC's cinema programmes for its 'friendly' mode of presentation, just as notable was the Corporation's desire to pursue what it perceived to be an informal mode of address. In the planning of *Current Release*, Cecil McGivern specifically suggested that the programme be presented by a 'representative of the ordinary filmgoer', someone 'whom the public would wish to hear and see'.[15] Certainly, the decision to use a non-professional film critic was also shaped partly by the film industry's 'no criticism' clause, as well as, perhaps, the beginning of television's wider spread to a mass audience at this time. Nevertheless, professional film critics had historically played an important role in radio's coverage of film. Thus, the decision of who should present *Current Release* was perhaps shaped by perceptions of the aesthetic, technological and textual specificity of television, particularly the perceived demands of a developing televisual mode of address. John Corner has referred to this as operating through a 'rhetoric of *understatement*, of the *self-evident* and the *implicitly shared* "Usness"' (1991b: 12, emphasis in original), which drew upon, yet extended, the conventions and possibilities of radio. It is clear from the discussions surrounding *Current Release* that there was some experimentation with how to create the impression of a relaxed informality suited to the specificity of a *visual* medium. Programme scripts indicate how the presenter was to appear 'casually leaning on' – or even 'straddling' – the arm of the chair, for example. Equally, McGivern had correspondence with the producer about how the presenter should be situated, and, indeed, how his presence should be filmed. On one occasion he insisted:

> Your shooting of Fitzgerald was bad. There is no need at all…to aim at visual change and movement in your links. There is all the change of action and movement necessary in your film excerpts. Your narrator must be as still as possible, at ease – and if he is at ease, so will the audience be.[16]

The impression of a casual informality was an approach also intended in *Picture Parade*, and both *Picture Parade* and *Film Fanfare* exhibit very similar strategies in the interaction between presenter and star. While this is part of a much larger question of how film stars adapted to appearing on (live) television (Holmes, 2001a), it is striking that, in both programmes, there was a clear bid to construct a relationship of 'matey' familiarity between presenter and star. Attempting to convey the impression of a friendly 'chat', the bodily proximity between presenter and star was particularly apparent – and was perhaps in part an attempt to draw the star into the rhetoric of a more familiar and proximate televisual mode of address. It is possible that the BBC's Haigh and Bond evinced a slightly more reverent approach to the stars, but it is also worth noting here that (despite the fact that ITV paid far higher fees for star appearances) it was *Picture Parade* that featured interviews with more of the 'big' Hollywood stars. This was a balance perhaps also shaped by *Film Fanfare*'s institutional affiliation with the British film industry and ABPC.

My aim here has been to use a snapshot of the cinema programme in the 1950s as a way of considering the relationship between broader institutional narratives of broadcasting history, and the more localised histories of particular television genres. In focusing on the particular institutional narratives in the British context, *Picture Parade* and *Film Fanfare* offer their own insights into the relations between

BBC and ITV in the 1950s – in ways that both confirm and question the pervasive conceptions of British television history at this time. While far from providing an answer to the critical, methodological and historical relations that might exist between these 'macro' and 'micro' spheres, they at least suggest that these should be conceived as potentially contradictory and open to debate. The programmes also point to the importance of considering these issues within the context of particular *genres*, in which serial drama, quiz shows or news would doubtless offer their own specific inflections.[17] At the same time, existing historical frameworks still represent a pervasive influence on the questions we ask of our research. Despite the aim to question conventional accounts, my comparison here was clearly shaped by prevailing assumptions about how a 'BBC' and 'ITV' programme might be constructed and received in the 1950s – what it might look like, how it might address us and what its institutional intentions might be. Without this framework, there are many other questions that we might ask of these programmes at this time – questions that would enable us to 'see' them in a different way. As more studies of early television genres emerge, discovering what these questions might be is a topic for urgent debate.

6 BBC English Regions Drama

Second City Firsts

Lez Cooke

Television drama historiography has tended to focus on authorship, artefact and genre, establishing a canon of (male) writers and 'classic' dramas, many of which were produced for high-profile anthology series such as *The Wednesday Play* and *Play for Today*, as well as producing sociological and cultural studies of police series, drama-documentary and soap opera. With notable exceptions, less attention has been given to the output of discrete drama departments or to the production of less prestigious anthology series.[1] This chapter takes as its focus a regionally based BBC drama department, BBC English Regions Drama, and an anthology drama series, *Second City Firsts*, produced by English Regions Drama from 1973 to 1978. Using *Second City Firsts* as a case study, the chapter explores the variety of regional drama that was commissioned by BBC English Regions Drama in the 1970s and considers the opportunities that the department, and the *Second City Firsts* series, gave to new television writers.

Research for this chapter has involved uncovering a 'lost history' of half-hour play production within the BBC, an enterprise made more difficult by the fact that many of the half-hour plays produced by English Regions Drama have since been wiped. Of the 73 half-hour plays produced between 1972 and 1978 only 29 survive (see Appendix for a full list of the plays).[2] These half-hour plays were, clearly, not considered to be of any real cultural value, worthy of preserving, and studio recordings in the *Second City Firsts* series were being wiped right up to June 1977. Among the work that no longer exists are plays written by Arthur Hopcraft, Mike Leigh, Mary O'Malley, Alan Plater, Janey Preger, Jack Rosenthal, David Rudkin and Willy Russell.

While I include a brief analysis of some of the surviving plays, all of which I have viewed courtesy of the National Film and Television Archive, the unavailability of many plays makes an assessment of the series as a whole difficult. In the absence of such material, I have drawn on Audience Research Reports and other documentation held at the BBC Written Archives Centre. I also draw on original interviews with some of the writers, script editors, producers and directors involved in the production of these half-hour plays, in addition to original interviews and correspondence with David Rose, Head of Department at BBC English Regions Drama from 1971 to 1981.

Before the 1970s BBC television drama production was largely London-based, with the main studios at Alexandra Palace in the 1930s and 1940s, Lime Grove in the 1950s and White City Television Centre in the 1960s. Some drama was produced at BBC studios in Birmingham (Midland Region), Bristol (South West Region) and Manchester (North Region) – the main production centres in the three 'English Regions' – and also at studios in Glasgow, Cardiff and Belfast, representing the three 'National Regions' of Scotland, Wales and Northern Ireland. The BBC's six regional studios were not equipped to the same standard as the London studios, however, and their function was, on the whole, to supplement the programmes from London, which formed the major part of the schedules.

While there was a Regional Programme in radio, at least until the outbreak of the Second World War, television was initially available only in London and the south-east. When transmission resumed after the war, television was developed as a national service, based in London, with the regional centres producing a relatively small number of television programmes for national distribution. Subsequently, many television dramas that might initially have appeared to be 'regional', such as *Z Cars* (BBC, 1962–1978), were, in fact, produced in the capital. Regional studios did not have the resources, the budget or the personnel to produce a long-running series such as *Z Cars*. Instead, the regional studios produced single plays for national distribution, such as Alan Plater's first television plays, *The Referees* (1961) and *Smashing Day* (1962), which were produced at the BBC's Dickenson Road studios in Manchester.

The opening of the new studios at Television Centre reinforced London's hegemony over television drama production in the 1960s, and when Sydney Newman became Head of Drama in 1963 he decided, according to *Z Cars* producer David Rose, to cut back on regional drama production because he thought the regional studios were not suitably equipped:

> When he arrived he took one look at the regions and said with the coming of colour, editing and this, that and the other, and the cramped size of the studios, he felt it was not the standard that he was looking for that was coming out of the regions, and I think that was fair comment, the backcloths did wobble a bit![3]

By the end of the 1960s, however, steps had been taken to move away from a centralised 'national' broadcasting service at the BBC with the establishment of a number of local radio stations, partly in response to the popularity of pirate radio stations, such as Radio Caroline, Radio London and Radio Essex, which broadcast to local rather than national audiences. In July 1969 a BBC policy document, *Broadcasting in the Seventies*, announced the BBC's intention to expand non-metropolitan broadcasting, and not just radio but also television. According to *Broadcasting in the Seventies* the regional structure of the BBC in the post-war period had been determined by technical, rather than social, considerations:

> The boundaries were drawn up some forty years ago not on any basis of community interest but to match the range of the transmitters. These are regions devised by engineers rather than sociologists. The Midland Region stretches from the Welsh border to the North Sea. The North Region has to cover Liverpool and Newcastle, Manchester and Hull, Lincoln and Carlisle. The South and West Region serves an area stretching from Lands End to Brighton. Over the years we have sought to meet this problem by creating five additional areas within the regions, but we now feel that the time has come to replace this structure. (BBC, 1969: 7)

The three 'English Regions', of North, Midlands and South West, were to be replaced by eight smaller regions and the facilities at the three English regional production centres expanded to enable the regions to supply more programmes to the national television service. To some extent, then, *Broadcasting in the Seventies* was proposing a reorganisation of the BBC along the lines of ITV, with a certain degree of autonomy being granted to the regions and an increase in the amount of regional material on BBC1 and BBC2. Surveying 'A Decade in Prospect' in the 1970 *BBC Handbook*, Director General Charles Curran described some of the initiatives that were being taken with the expansion of regional broadcasting:

> In non-metropolitan radio and television in England there will be some really radical changes. In television we shall have eight new regions which, by 1971, will be producing 400 programmes a year for their own audiences, compared with the 150 a year of the former three English regions… Through the production centres at Birmingham, Manchester and Bristol regional talent and initiative will continue to flow into network radio and television as fully as or more fully than in the past. Birmingham, for instance, will eventually have at its disposal a £6 million television complex at Pebble Mill. In each place there is a senior executive whose terms of reference include responsibility for nourishing creative talent in his part of the country. (Curran, 1970: 23)

Pebble Mill was officially opened on 10 November 1971, having eventually cost £7 million. David Rose was appointed head of a new department, English Regions Drama, with a brief to commission and produce regional television drama for the national network. Having worked at the BBC for a number of years, in the Drama-Documentary Department and as the first producer on *Z Cars*, Rose was well qualified to be Head of English Regions Drama, not least because of his belief in the writer as the most important person in the creation of original drama:

One of the reasons I think we kept the original *Z-Cars* on the road for four years retaining, I hope, some of the qualities of January '62 through to '63, '64, '65 and '66 was because we always venerated the writer. If there was a quality for that series of *Z-Cars* it was to do with our respect for the writer... The first and last thing is the writing as far as I'm concerned. (Millington and Nelson, 1986: 25)

With Barry Hanson as script editor, David Rose set about commissioning drama from writers 'who either live in or who have particular concern for the regions' (BBC, 1972: 73). Hanson had been working at Hull Arts Centre, where he was the first Artistic Director, having previously worked at the Royal Court Theatre, and the connection with regional writers and the repertory theatre movement was crucial to the success of English Regions Drama at Pebble Mill.

The first English Regions Drama productions were transmitted in February 1972 as *Thirty-Minute Theatre* plays. *Thirty-Minute Theatre* had been running on BBC2 since 1965, largely as a training ground for new writers (one of Dennis Potter's first plays was for *Thirty-Minute Theatre*), so it was logical that English Regions Drama should 'nourish creative talent' in the regions by commissioning half-hour plays from regional writers. The 14 *Thirty-Minute Theatre* plays English Regions Drama produced in 1972 were from regionally based (mostly northern) writers, but they were by no means all new writers. Among those contributing plays were Arthur Hopcraft, John Hopkins, Alan Plater, Jack Rosenthal and David Rudkin, all experienced writers who had been writing for television, and other media, since the early to mid-1960s.

These *Thirty-Minute Theatre* plays ranged in kind from Arthur Hopcraft's drama about a 'progressive' Methodist preacher, 'Said the Preacher' (BBC2, 6 March 1972), a studio-based drama directed by Michael Apted featuring Victor Henry as the preacher, to John Hopkins' non-naturalistic filmed drama 'That Quiet Earth' (BBC2, 28 February 1972), written and directed by Hopkins and featuring his wife, Shirley Knight Hopkins. 'That Quiet Earth' was an example of Hopkins' more experimental television work, in the tradition of his groundbreaking *Talking to a Stranger* (BBC2, 1966), and was too obscure for a large number of viewers, many of whom were baffled by it, according to the BBC's Audience Research Report on the play.[4] 'That Quiet Earth' was the only filmed play out of the 14 *Thirty-Minute Theatre* plays produced by English Regions Drama in 1972, only five of which have survived. Of the other surviving plays, E. A. Whitehead's 'Under the Age' (BBC2, 20 March 1972), directed by Alan Clarke, was a play about homosexuality, set in a bar in Liverpool, and featured the Liverpool accents of Paul and Michael Angelis; 'Scarborough' (BBC2, 12 October 1972), by Donald Howarth, was about the relationship between three young people fruit-picking near Scarborough, all the action being set in the barn in which they are sleeping; while 'You're Free' (BBC2, 16 November 1972), by Henry Livings, was a two-hander featuring Rachel Roberts and Colin Blakely as a couple living in a farmhouse in the south of France that they have bought on the proceeds of the husband's pools win. Of these five plays, only 'Under the Age' and 'Scarborough' are clearly set in the regions, although as both these plays were single-set studio plays their regional setting was not readily apparent. The 'regionality' of these plays seems to derive more from their authors being regionally based writers who were not asked to engage specifically with regional subject matter in the plays.

These *Thirty-Minute Theatre* plays were transmitted in two seasons, from February to April 1972 and in October and November 1972. All except 'That Quiet Earth' were recorded in the studio, and this continued to be the pattern with the 30-minute plays produced by English Regions Drama. Of the 73 half-hour plays the department produced from 1972 to 1978, nearly all were studio plays, recorded in the new studios at Pebble Mill; only eight were shot on location, either on film or video. Film tended to be reserved for the longer plays that the department contributed to *Play for Today*. In its first year there was just one of
. these, Peter Terson's 'The Fishing Party' (BBC1, 1 June 1972), but seven more *Plays for Today* were produced by the department in 1973 and 1974, all of them shot on film.

When a third series of half-hour plays was transmitted in February and March 1973 the *Thirty-Minute Theatre* title was dropped. Although the department had close links with the theatre, drawing on writers, directors and actors from regional repertory companies, it had no intention of simply transposing theatre plays to television. By abandoning the *Thirty-Minute Theatre* title the department was seeking to distance itself from any association with 'televised theatre'. As far as David Rose was concerned: 'I didn't like the title *Thirty-Minute Theatre*, I didn't think television was theatre, shouldn't be...so we found another rather clumsy title, *Second City Firsts*.'[5]

The untitled series of six plays transmitted in February/March 1973 was the stepping stone between *Thirty-Minute Theatre* and *Second City Firsts* (the first series of which was screened in October/November 1973). To highlight the fact that the department did not want to be associated with 'televised theatre', and also to emphasise the regional content of the plays, the first drama in the new series was shot entirely on film, on location, in an Asian district of Birmingham. Tara Prem's *A Touch of Eastern Promise* (BBC2, 8 February 1973) tells the story of a young Indian man who fantasises about an Indian film star he learns is coming to Birmingham and who he determines to meet. Filming on location enabled the region to be shown in a way that was not possible in a play recorded entirely in the studio. In studio plays 'regionality' could be expressed through the story, characters and dialogue, and regional accents were sometimes the primary signifiers of regional identity in studio plays, but filming on location afforded the opportunity to show the regional setting in all its verisimilitude, in a way that a studio-based play could not hope to do – although studio plays did sometimes use filmed sequences in order to establish the regional setting before cutting to the studio set for the majority of the play. Few half-hour plays were shot on film, because filmed drama was far more expensive to produce. Filmed drama also required the skills of a film director, film cameraman and film editor – specialised roles drawing on a different repertoire of skills from those of their studio counterparts. A *Touch of Eastern Promise* was directed by Michael Lindsay-Hogg, who had previously directed the Beatles documentary *Let It Be* (1970) and who went on to direct several feature films, plus episodes of *Brideshead Revisited* (Granada, 1981). Not only was A *Touch of Eastern Promise* set in Birmingham, it featured the indigenous Indian community of the city, and the display of regional locations is complemented by the distinctive Birmingham accents of some of the younger Indian characters, while others speak Punjabi. A *Touch of Eastern Promise*, therefore, shows the concern of English Regions Drama not only to go out and film in the region but also to represent the multicultural communities of a provincial city such as Birmingham.

In contrast, the third play in this series of half-hour plays was a studio drama featuring just one actor and minimal studio sets. *You and Me and Him* (BBC2, 22 February 1973) was written by David Mercer and featured Peter Vaughan as Coster, a man with three separate personalities. Imaginatively directed by Barry Hanson, in a departure from his usual job of script editor at Pebble Mill, *You and Me and Him* uses three studio sets to show Coster in his living room, bedroom and office. Through clever use of eyeline matching, and the skilful editing of videotape editor John Lanin, Coster is seen holding conversations with his other selves, in an exploration of divided personality – a familiar theme in David Mercer's work.[6] Clearly, *You and Me and Him* could not have been recorded live, although this would have been possible with other studio dramas in the series, such as David Cregan's *I Want to Marry Your Son* (BBC2, 8 March 1973), which was recorded on one studio set in a conventional, naturalistic studio style. According to Peter Ansorge, who joined English Regions Drama as a script editor in 1975, 'We didn't shoot them live, but you shot great chunks – if not the whole piece, occasionally – in a multi-camera set up, continuously.'[7] While shooting on location, on film, was more time-consuming and more expensive, studio recording was equally demanding, requiring different skills, and in studio production the role of the director was central, as Ansorge explains:

> Studio drama is almost a lost form now. It wasn't theatre, although obviously it's quite close to theatre in some ways, and it wasn't film, but we did think of these little studio dramas as mini-films, if you like. And it was always, in the end, in the hand of the director of the day, because it was all rehearsed and recorded in a single day, and quite often you'd rehearse from ten o'clock until the supper break, you'd have a lunch break, a tea break, and then after the supper break you would go in and you would have two hours to record. [...] In some ways it was much harder than making a first film, where you have a DOP generally telling a first-time director what he shouldn't do. It was quite a demanding skill, that, and so the director in the day of recording and rehearsal

became the pivot of the whole thing, and his or her imagination, and how well he dealt with the multi-camera set-up, the realisation of it, was part of the excitement of the whole process.[8]

Following *A Touch of Eastern Promise* Tara Prem joined English Regions Drama as a script editor, and it was she who came up with the title of *Second City Firsts* for the next series of half-hour plays, transmitted in October and November 1973. Whereas some experienced regional writers had been commissioned to submit plays for *Thirty-Minute Theatre*, the intention with *Second City Firsts* was to premiere work by new writers, hence the 'firsts' in the series title, produced by English Regions Drama in Birmingham, England's 'second city'.

The first play to be shown in the *Second City Firsts* series was 'The Medium' (BBC2, 15 October 1973), written by the Sunderland-based writer Denise Robertson. Its subject was spiritualism: a group of women gather in the house of Beattie (Norah Fulton), whose husband has recently died, to have their fortunes told by a drunken clairvoyant (Winifrede Shelley). Beattie's daughter (Valerie Georgeson) sees that the clairvoyant is a fraud but she pretends otherwise to her mother so as not to destroy her faith in the afterlife. 'The Medium' was recorded entirely in the studio, with no telecine sequences to establish the location, but the Geordie accents immediately announce this as a regional drama set in the north-east, showing that regional identity could be established even when a play was entirely studio-based. Other plays in the first series of *Second City Firsts* included 'If a Man Answers' (BBC2, 29 October 1973), by the Yorkshire actor and writer Brian Glover, and 'King of the Castle' (BBC2, 12 November 1973), the first play for television by the Liverpool playwright Willy Russell. 'King of the Castle' was shot on location in an industrial setting using an Outside Broadcast unit, an alternative means of achieving a sense of place, without the expense of shooting on film. Pebble Mill had recently acquired a new lightweight mobile control room (LMCR) – a two-camera Outside Broadcast unit, using lightweight cameras, which was more flexible than the larger, five-camera, Outside Broadcast unit – and this was the first time that the new lightweight unit was used on a drama production at Birmingham. Unfortunately, recording on videotape made the drama equally vulnerable to being erased as studio plays, and the recording of 'King of the Castle' no longer exists.

The 'new writers' qualification for *Second City Firsts* was not always strictly followed. The first play shown in the second series, 'Humbug, Finger or Thumb?' (BBC2, 18 February 1974), was written by Arthur Hopcraft, who had already written 'Said the Preacher' as a *Thirty-Minute Theatre* play for English Regions Drama and whose *The Mosedale Horseshoe* (Granada, 23 March 1971), filmed on location in the Lake District by Michael Apted, was an important precursor of the filmed dramas produced by BBC English Regions Drama. 'Humbug, Finger or Thumb?' was followed in the *Second City Firsts* series by 'Girl' (BBC2, 25 February 1974), the first of four plays written for English Regions Drama by James Robson and the first of several controversial dramas that the department was to produce. The controversy surrounding 'Girl' concerned the portrayal of a lesbian relationship between Jackie (Alison Steadman), a young army recruit, and Chrissie (Myra Frances), a corporal with whom Jackie has an affair. Jackie is leaving the army because she is pregnant, and Chrissie comes to see her before she goes. She tells Chrissie that her pregnancy is the result of being raped and that she still loves her. The drama takes place in one room, but includes a flashback to show Chrissie and Jackie in bed together. At one point Chrissie puts a Dusty Springfield single, 'This Girl's in Love', on the record player, referring to the song as being 'top of the gay girls' hit parade', and they dance together, singing along to the song. While the record plays the volume of the music increases, introducing a moment of heightened melodrama into the drama during which their illicit relationship is celebrated. 'Girl', incidentally, contains what is probably British television's first lesbian kiss, and the sensitivity of the project caused the Controller of BBC2 to preview the programme and to rewrite the introductory announcement to it.[9]

The second series of *Second City Firsts* included two plays shot on location. 'The Actual Woman' (BBC2, 11 March 1974), written by Jack Shepherd, was filmed on location outside Birmingham by Philip Saville, using the LMCR, while 'Match of the Day' (BBC2, 18 March 1974), written by Neville Smith and directed by Stephen Frears, was shot on film. A comparison between these two location-based dramas, shot on different formats, might have been illuminating, but, once again, the recording of 'The Actual Woman' no longer exists. A very complimentary review of the drama, however, shows that the recording was still available a year and a half after its first transmission for a repeat screening in October 1975:

> 'The Actual Woman' is the second play in the last series of *Second City Firsts* which the BBC considered to be worth repeating (BBC2, 11 October, 10.15 pm) before they embark upon their new series. And, certainly, producer Barry Hanson has every reason to be pleased with this vivid tour de force.
>
> It is, to begin with, remarkably literate. Author Jack Shepherd has a fierce flow of dialogue that bites and glows, together with a perception of human beings living precariously on the edge of their emotions, and Philip Saville is a director who has a particular gift for the presentation of words, balancing them against the visual aspects of a production in a way that gets the best out of both. (Holt, 1975: 13)[10]

Although no recording is available to enable an analysis of the visual style of 'The Actual Woman', a viewing of 'Match of the Day' shows that the drama was clearly liberated from the constraints of the studio by being shot on film, making extensive use of flashbacks and voice-overs in addition to a variety of interior and exterior locations. The title has a double meaning, referring to the wedding that forms the basis of the story and the obsession with football (in particular, Everton FC) of its central character, Chance (Neville Smith). Chance narrates the events, seen in flashback, leading up to the wedding of his sister, as well as those that occur on the day of the wedding, including his attempts to chat up a woman at the reception while he is also trying to get the football scores. The entertainment value of the drama is considerably enhanced by some lively dialogue and Liverpudlian humour. It is clear from the accents alone that 'Match of the Day' is a regional drama, but its regional identity also emerges from the fact that Neville Smith is writing about people with whom he can identify and situations with which he is clearly familiar.[11] As with Denise Robertson's 'The Medium', the authenticity of 'Match of the Day' arises from the writer's regional affinity, fulfilling the objective of David Rose to place the writer at the centre of drama production at Pebble Mill.

While many of the writers commissioned by English Regions Drama had regional theatre connections, one of the plays in the third series of *Second City Firsts* directly acknowledged the special relationship the department had with regional theatres. 'Fight for Shelton Bar' (BBC2, 18 November 1974) was a 30-minute version of a longer play from the Victoria Theatre Company in Stoke-on-Trent. Directed by the company's artistic director, Peter Cheeseman, the play was staged for television in the documentary-drama style pioneered by Cheeseman at Stoke and described the struggle to prevent the local steelworks in Shelton from being closed down. Although the television adaptation was produced entirely in the Pebble Mill studios it used captions and photographs to give a documentary reality to the drama, and had actors speaking to camera in an attempt to replicate the direct audience address of the theatre production. Produced in 1974, the same year that the play *Fight for Shelton Bar* was performed at the Victoria Theatre, the television version formed part of a successful campaign to keep the Shelton steelworks open.

The *Second City Firsts* series enabled a number of now very well-known writers to have their first television scripts produced. Alan Bleasdale made his television debut in 1975 with 'Early to Bed' (BBC2, 20 March 1975), shown in the fourth series of *Second City Firsts*. The drama tells the story of Vinny (David Warwick), an 18-year-old student, who is having a sexual relationship with Helen (Alison Steadman), the young married woman living in the terraced house next door. Like 'Match of the Day', 'Early to Bed' was shot on film, which again enabled the drama to achieve a greater sense of place and regional identity than some of the studio dramas were able to achieve. It begins, for example, with a shot of a pithead, establishing the location as that of a Lancashire mining community, and the scenes filmed in the small town help to illustrate the limited opportunities there for Vinny, establishing his need to get away. 'Early to Bed' was an apprentice work for Bleasdale, and he acknowledged the contribution of the film's director, Les Blair, who 'made a script of some promise, but no great quality, into something worth watching' (Millington and Nelson, 1986: 27).

Also in the fourth series was 'The Permissive Society' (BBC2, 10 April 1975), the first of two *Second City Firsts* by Mike Leigh, both studio productions and the only studio dramas, apart from *Abigail's Party* (BBC1, 1978), that Leigh has ever produced. The scenario is typical of Leigh's work: a slice of working-class life, set mainly in a living room, featuring a rather mismatched young couple and the boy's older sister, who goes out on a date only to return at the end of the play having been stood up. Nothing much happens, and, like most of Leigh's work, 'The Permissive Society' (the title is clearly ironic) is a character study. The claustrophobic studio set suits the drama well, however, reinforcing the sense of the characters being trapped in lives with limited horizons. Once again, 'The Permissive Society' illustrates that it is not essential to film on location in order to convey a sense of characters being trapped in their environment.

As with the plays for *Thirty-Minute Theatre* and *Play for Today*, the primary objective of *Second City Firsts* was to commission regional writers rather than regional drama. The distinction is important, because it meant that not all the plays produced by English Regions Drama were obviously 'regional' in subject matter. For example, Ian McEwan's 'Jack Flea's Birthday Celebration' (BBC2, 10 April 1976), shown in the sixth series of *Second City Firsts*, was a studio drama about a young man who is writing a novel called *Jack Flea's Birthday Celebration*, the content of which, it transpires, is remarkably similar to the subject of the play. Thematically the drama is typical of McEwan's first collection of short stories, *First Love, Last Rites* (1975). In fact, McEwan saw the play 'as really belonging in that volume' (McEwan, 1981: 10–11). 'Jack Flea's Birthday Celebration' is not particularly 'regional' in subject matter but the fact that the play was produced in Birmingham did have a distinct advantage, according to McEwan:

> At the end of a day's rehearsal the four actors – who all came from far away – could not go home. They had to hang about together in restaurants or in the hotel bar. No one could quite escape his or her part. By the end of ten days a very odd and gratifying level of controlled hysteria had been reached and this suited the claustrophobic nature of the play perfectly, as did the detached quality of Mike Newell's camera script. (McEwan, 1981: 11–12)

The play's director, Mike Newell, is now better known for *Four Weddings and a Funeral* (1993), among other feature films that he has since directed, and he is one of several *Second City Firsts* directors who went on to have successful careers in the film industry. Les Blair, Alan Clarke, Stephen Frears, Roland Joffe, Mike Leigh, Michael Lindsay-Hogg and Philip Saville all directed half-hour plays for English Regions Drama at Birmingham in the 1970s. While English Regions Drama may have privileged the writer, directors made an important contribution, as indeed did set designers, given that most of the productions were studio plays.

By no means all the *Second City Firsts* were successful. 'The Frank Crank Story' (BBC2, 17 April 1975), screened a week after Mike Leigh's 'The Permissive Society', was one of the less successful productions. A debut play by a machine minder and jazz fan, 'The Frank Crank Story' needed a lot more work at the script editing stage, and it is difficult to see why it has been preserved when other plays by Mike Leigh, Alan Plater, David Rudkin and Willy Russell have been wiped. Yet the importance of the *Second City Firsts* series was that it gave writers an opportunity to experiment and to have original work produced, rather than having to conform to the more formulaic strictures of the continuous drama serial, which is what most new writers have to do today. It also gave an opportunity to an unprecedented number of new writers: 42 writers contributed to the nine series of *Second City Firsts* over a period of six years, while another 17 writers contributed to the two series of *Thirty-Minute Theatre* plays and the untitled series of six half-hour plays from 1973. While not all these writers were making their television debut, most of those who wrote for *Second City Firsts* were. Some of them went on to write other work for television, and a couple (Bleasdale and Leigh) have since contributed to the 'canon' of British television drama with work such as *Boys from the Blackstuff* (also produced by English Regions Drama) and *Abigail's Party*. The chief significance of *Second City Firsts*, however, is that it provided a forum in which regional writers could try their hand at television drama without having to write a full-length contribution to *Play for Today*.

From the plays that survive, it is clear there was a considerable diversity in the work produced in the nine series of *Second City Firsts*. They include naturalistic studio plays as well as social realist dramas, intimate personal dramas as well as campaigning agitprop dramas such as 'Fight for Shelton Bar', plays about the West Indian community in Birmingham (Barry Reckord's 'Club Havana') and about lesbians in the army, plays about football, journalism, dogs, clairvoyants, strikes and politics. The fact that the plays were only 30 minutes long and mostly recorded in the studio may have limited what they were able to achieve, but the writers were given the freedom to do what they wanted within that limited canvas.

In many cases the limitations of the confined studio set placed more emphasis on the writing and the performances, but in the hands of a creative director such as Philip Saville a studio drama such as 'Rotten' (BBC2, 13 May 1978), the last of the *Second City Firsts* to be transmitted, could be transformed into something extraordinary – in this case a non-naturalistic drama using electronic effects, split-screen, montages and superimposition to tell the story of a boy who lives a fantasy life inspired by the Beatles, when he is a child, and then, as a teenager in the mid- to late 1970s, by punk (the title refers to Johnny Rotten of the Sex Pistols). Written by Alan Brown, 'Rotten' was both a contemporary 'state of the nation' drama and a testament to the creative ingenuity that English Regions Drama and the *Second City Firsts* series inspired. Like most of the drama produced at Pebble Mill under David Rose, the *Second City Firsts* series extended the range of dramatic representations in the 1970s, providing a televisual forum for regional writers and encouraging the kind of diversity, originality and eclecticism in television drama that is sadly lacking in British television today.

APPENDIX: BBC ENGLISH REGIONS DRAMA: A CHRONOLOGY OF HALF-HOUR PLAYS (BBC2, 1972–1978)

1st transmission date		Availability
	Thirty-Minute Theatre	
21.2.72	'An Arrow for Little Audrey' (Brian Finch)	n/a
28.2.72	'That Quiet Earth' (John Hopkins)*	NFTVA
6.3.72	'Said the Preacher' (Arthur Hopcraft)	NFTVA
13.3.72	'That Time of Life' (David Cregan)	n/a
20.3.72	'Under the Age' (E.A. Whitehead)	NFTVA
27.3.72	'Bypass' (David Rudkin)	n/a
3.4.72	'And for My Next Trick' (Jack Rosenthal)	n/a
10.4.72	'The Sit In' (Keith Dewhurst)	n/a
12.10.72	'Scarborough' (Donald Howarth)	NFTVA
19.10.72	'Tonight We Meet Arthur Pendlebury' (Alan Plater)	n/a
26.10.72	'Ronnie's So Long at the Fair' (Jay Humber)	n/a
2.11.72	'Ten Torrey Canyons' (Brian Clark)	n/a
9.11.72	'I Wouldn't Tell on You, Miss' (Susan Pleat)	n/a
16.11.72	'You're Free' (Henry Livings)	NFTVA
	Untitled Series	
8.2.73	*A Touch of Eastern Promise* (Tara Prem)*	NFTVA
15.2.73	*And All Who Sail in Her* (Andy Ashton)	n/a
22.2.73	*You and Me and Him* (David Mercer)	NFTVA
1.3.73	*The Great Acrobile* (Roy Minton)	n/a
8.3.73	*I Want to Marry Your Son* (David Cregan)	NFTVA
15.3.73	*Atrocity* (David Rudkin)[12]	NFTVA
	Second City Firsts	
Series 1		
15.10.73	'The Medium' (Denise Robertson)	NFTVA
22.10.73	'Mrs Pool's Preserves' (Michael Sadler)	n/a
29.10.73	'If a Man Answers' (Brian Glover)	n/a
5.11.73	'The Movers' (Ian Taylor)	n/a
12.11.73	'King of the Castle' (Willy Russell)**	n/a
19.11.73	'Patrons' (Eric Berger)	n/a
26.11.73	'That Time of Life' (David Cregan)[13]	n/a
Series 2		
18.2.74	'Humbug, Finger or Thumb?' (Arthur Hopcraft)	n/a
25.2.74	'Girl' (James Robson)	NFTVA

1st transmission date		Availability
4.3.74	'Bold Face – Condensed' (Peter Rawsley)	NFTVA
11.3.74	'The Actual Woman' (Jack Shepherd)**	n/a
18.3.74	'Match of the Day' (Neville Smith)*	NFTVA
25.3.74	'Lunch Duty' (Rony Robinson)	n/a
Series 3		
28.10.74	'Pig Bin' (Brian Glover)	n/a
4.11.74	'Sunday Tea' (Edwin Pearce)	n/a
11.11.74	'Silence' (John Fletcher)	n/a
18.11.74	'Fight for Shelton Bar' (adapted by Peter Cheeseman)	NFTVA
25.11.74	'Squire' (Tom Pickard)*	NFTVA
2.12.74	'Too Hot to Handle' (Jim Hawkins)	n/a
16.12.74	'The Festive Poacher' (Ian Taylor)	n/a
Series 4		
20.3.75	'Early to Bed' (Alan Bleasdale)*	NFTVA
27.3.75	'Swallows' (John McGahern)	n/a
3.4.75	'Waiting at the Field Gate' (James Robson)	n/a
10.4.75	'The Permissive Society' (Mike Leigh)	NFTVA
17.4.75	'The Frank Crank Story' (Alan Taylor)	NFTVA
24.4.75	'Released' (Stephen Wakelam)	n/a
Series 5		
25.10.75	'Club Havana' (Barry Reckord)[14,15]	NFTVA
1.11.75	'The Writing on the Wall' (devised by Mike Bradwell and Hull Truck)	n/a
8.11.75	'How It Is' (Anita Bronson)	n/a
15.11.75	'On the Good Ship Yakky Ikky Doola' (Bob Mason)	n/a
22.11.75	'Thwum' (Mike Stott)	n/a
29.11.75	'The Healing' (Laura Lemson)*	NFTVA
Series 6		
13.3.76	'Trotsky is Dead' (Tony Bicat)	NFTVA
20.3.76	'The Visitor' (Denise Robertson)	n/a
3.4.76	'Do You Dig It?' (John Harding and John Burrows)	n/a
10.4.76	'Jack Flea's Birthday Celebration' (Ian McEwan)	NFTVA
17.4.76	'Black Bird Shout' (Paul Hyland)	n/a
24.4.76	'Travelling Free' (Sean McCarthy)	NFTVA
Series 7		
14.11.76	'Summer Season' (Brian Glover)	n/a

1st transmission date		Availability
21.11.76	'Knock for Knock' (devised by Mike Leigh)	n/a
28.11.76	'Glitter' (Tony Bicat)	NFTVA
5.12.76	'Dreamboat' (Ian Taylor)	n/a
12.12.76	'Percy and Kenneth' (Mary J. O'Malley)	n/a
Series 8		
3.5.77	'Twelve off the Belt' (Ron Hutchinson)	NFTVA
10.5.77	'Postcards from Southsea' (J.C.W. Brooke)	n/a
17.5.77	'Daft Mam Blues' (David Halliwell)	n/a
24.5.77	'In the Deadspell' (James Robson)	n/a
31.5.77	'Waifs and Strays' (Chris Bailey)	NFTVA
6.6.77	'Fattening Frogs for Snakes' (Janey Preger)	n/a
Series 9		
8.4.78	'The Back Page' (Andrew Nickolds and Stan Hey)	NFTVA
15.4.78	'Shall I See You Now?' (Mary O'Malley)	NFTVA
22.4.78	'The Lady Irene' (Tom Hadaway)	NFTVA
6.5.78	'Mucking Out' (Robert Holman)	NFTVA
13.5.78	'Rotten' (Alan Brown)	NFTVA

Writer's name(s) in brackets.
* Shot entirely on film.
** Shot on location using an Outside Broadcast unit.
NFTVA: viewing copy in National Film and Television Archive.
n/a: no recording available.

ACKNOWLEDGEMENT

This chapter was part of doctoral research on regional television drama for a three-year AHRC-funded project, 'Cultures of British Television Drama 1960–1982'.

PART THREE
Production and Institutions

INTRODUCTION

This section takes the production of television as its focus, each chapter differently connecting historical case studies to issues of institutional development, programming history, and the construction of the historical television audience. The first three chapters here respond to Jean Seaton's call to catch the 'nuances and character' (2004: 152) of institutions through detailed historiography, though they approach this task in different ways and in relation to different institutions, moments and issues. Emma Sandon's account of the early history of BBC Television employs an innovative research methodology, gathering and analysing the oral histories of key personnel who worked at the BBC's Alexandra Palace studios between 1936 and 1952. This is a timely study, given that oral production histories have been marked as an 'urgent priority' (Cooke, 2003: 4) in the field of television historiography. Sandon's essay is a detailed and nuanced account of the ways in which a 'life history' approach to oral history gathering illuminates the operation of nostalgia and negotiated memory in these institutional histories, and offers us an exemplary model for this kind of research (see also Skutch, 1998, Finch, Cox and Giles, 2003, and Born, 2004).

The following chapter, by Darrell Newton, directly addresses Mary Beth Haralovich and Lauren Rabinowitz's claim that 'the object of study of most television histories has been a nominally white TV' (1999: 9). Newton's analysis of policy documents and programme files in the BBC's written archives draws a vivid picture of the ways in which the television service sought both to address and to culturally produce the West Indian settler in the context of mass immigration in the 1950s. This study thus exemplifies the ways in which the institutional archive might be reinterpreted with a focus on particular identities – racial identities in this instance, but, alternatively, the negotiation and production of gendered, religious or sexual identities. Newton's handling of institutional audience research data (both qualitative and quantitative) also represents a valuable method for reaching and reading the historical audience.

The third of these institutional histories is Jamie Medhurst's chapter on the Welsh independent television company Teledu Cymru. Whilst others have discussed the historiography of early television *programming* as the reconstruction of 'ghost texts' that exist 'as shadows, dispersed and refracted amongst buried files, bad memories, a flotsam of fragments' (Jacobs, 2000: 14), Medhurst shows us here that similarly fragmented institutional histories may be reconstructed via a variety of sources not held in a single institutional archive (including board of directors' minutes, personal diaries, private correspondence, newspaper accounts and interviews with surviving personnel). Medhurst's study proposes a form of institutional 'archaeology', drawing on a mosaic of sources, a particularly pertinent methodology when researching the history of companies that are no longer in business. His account also redresses a historiographic bias towards the centrality of the BBC in institutional histories of British television.

Finally, Erin Bell and Ann Gray offer us a history of what John Corner terms 'television as making' (2003a: 275), addressing Máire Messenger Davies' concerns about the dearth of production histories, or 'research about people who make television programmes and how these people work' (Davies, 2006: 21). Bell and Gray draw on their wider study of the history programme, using qualitative interviews with key historian-participants in this genre to unpick its recurring discourses of production. They produce a fascinating analysis of the development of presentational styles in the field of history television, evaluating the 'doing' of history on television, and delineating the ways in which those producing this genre understand and engage with its textual history. This section of the collection thus draws connections between institutional histories and production research, and offers innovative approaches to the institutional archive that enable key gaps in the history of the medium, its programmes and its viewing practices to be filled.

7 Nostalgia as resistance

The case of the Alexandra Palace Television Society and the BBC

Emma Sandon

This chapter looks at the dynamics of oral methodologies in television historiography, using as an example the Alexandra Palace Television Society (APTS) oral history collection. I drew on this archive of audio recordings by members of the APTS who worked in the BBC Television Service between 1936 and 1952, to re-evaluate the period[1] in the light of previous accounts (see Briggs, 1965, 1979).[2]

THE SOCIETY

The APTS began in 1992, when Michael Henderson brought together people who had worked at Alexandra Palace,[3] and by 1994 there were 237 members.[4] Henderson was of the opinion that histories of the first two decades of television, at a time when television was 'live' and recordings of programmes were few, were inaccurate because of the lack of first-hand accounts. He wrote that 'the main purpose of APTS [is] getting what the Historians call our "Living History" on public record'.[5]

The formation of the APTS coincided with a transformation of television broadcasting following the Broadcasting Act of 1990. Henderson envisaged a semi-official history being published as a result of his initiative. When the BBC showed little enthusiasm for being involved, Dr John Stevenson, from Oxford University, was invited to the first reunion, and he encouraged members to record their memories. Over the next two years 52 hours of audio taped memories were recorded in 27 recordings, involving 83 members of the society, whilst a further 14 members sent in written submissions.[6] Oxford eventually failed to follow up with any commission for the writing of a history from this material, and the project was taken up by the University of Sussex, which appointed me in 1995 as a doctoral researcher to interpret the audio collection.

By the time I attended the reunion in 1995, two anniversaries were approaching: the 60th anniversary of the opening of television and the 50th of its post-war reopening. Some APTS members were critical of the programmes being made for these anniversaries. They felt that they were not of the same quality or as well researched as those made when they had worked for the BBC, and they tended to disagree with their interpretations of the period.[7]

THE AUDIO COLLECTION

There were 16 group and 11 individual contributions in the original collection. The recording quality was variable; whilst the majority were clear and informative some were badly recorded, and one or two were difficult to understand. Some tapes were very general and others quite focused. Group recordings encouraged members to recall, but at times it was impossible to identify speakers, while others were too old or ill to remember much. Individual recordings ranged from the detailed recollection to the quirky contribution. Overall, the collection succeeded in creating a general picture of the service and the day-to-day atmosphere of life working at Alexandra Palace. The mainly uncritical stance towards the BBC gives a nostalgic flavour to the recordings, however. Whilst they convey the excitement of working for an experimental service, they also reinforce the existing portrayals of a period of engineering ingenuity and technical innovation, and tend to perpetuate the idea of the service producing a quaint, outdated or rather stuffy programme mix.[8] Accounts of technical achievements and developments are dominant in the tapes but the actual productions are not so well covered, and producers are not well represented. There was only one drama producer in the society, and the areas of outside broadcasting, talks, music, variety and light entertainment were thinly or partially covered.[9] While the collection could be drawn on for some factual and empirical evidence, it seemed that another approach to interpreting the archive might be more productive.

ORAL HISTORY METHODOLOGIES AND BROADCASTING HISTORY

Historians concerned with the early period of broadcasting have used oral sources empirically, though not as a main source. Asa Briggs based his voluminous official history of broadcasting in the United Kingdom on written sources, and, although oral history constituted one element of his approach, he thought oral records were unreliable (1960: xi; 1979: v). He used unrecorded interviews with those in management within the BBC, as well as with those who had left the organisation, but it did not seem to occur to him to draw on other people who had worked at Alexandra Palace (1980: 7, 11). Edward Buscombe, in his 1980 critique of Briggs' policy and management-weighted history, argued that the 'true' history of broadcasting remained to be written, in which the programmes and programme makers would be privileged (1980: 75). Yet the idea that employees will necessarily come up with a truer picture of the BBC 'from below' underestimated the power of such a public institution. This was a point that Tom Burns made when, for his sociological study of the BBC, he interviewed people working on the actual programmes and on the studio floor. Burns remarked on the ability of interviewees to evade voicing an opinion about the BBC and its role in broadcasting when talking to him about their work (1977: 132). Other contributors to broadcasting history in the early years, including Paddy Scannell and David Cardiff, have succeeded in using oral sources to solicit alternative opinions from producers known for their radical and political views, or who became active in the trades unions (1991: xv).[10] Similarly, Elaine Bell used oral sources as empirical evidence to embellish, complicate or contradict official written sources (1986).

In recent years oral history methodologies have been influenced by ideas that draw on psychoanalytical and narrative theories, and that recognise the constructive and social nature of memory. Researchers are now encouraged to pay increased attention to the whole dynamic of oral history work, beginning with their initial motives and selection of subjects, through to the process of interviewing, transcribing and selecting, and finally publishing from material recorded. It is not just the relationship of the interviewer to the respondent that is important but the fact that memory is subject to the shaping and nuances that change any account. In fact, one of the aspects of memory that has been acknowledged recently is the fact that the process of remembering is a constant negotiation of the past with the present – indeed, more often than not, it is about dealing with the present (Wood, 1992: 148). One of the most interesting developments in this new work in oral history that points to the complex nature of oral recordings and subjective approaches to history (see Perks and Thomson, 1998) has been the engagement with how memory is part of the process by which people create their sense of collective and individual identities, be they class, gender, ethnic or national identities.[11] When people construct narratives to make sense of their memories, they are often concerned to project an image that fits with their own identification with social and political ideas and groups. The way people make meaning or sense of the world can be different from the explicit content of the interview. Taking into account how past events are related, in the light of these overarching insights into memory and identity, it can better be recognised that oral histories must take account of issues of nostalgia, pride and self-justification, sorrow and regret, even trauma and pain, and of silences, both collective and individual. In other words, all oral accounts will be highly mediated.

APPROACHES TO INTERPRETING THE APTS ARCHIVE

Integrating some of these insights into my work on the APTS project, my first approach was to augment the original APTS tapes with recorded interviews of my own, and I used a questionnaire approach to whittle down the number of interviews to manageable proportions. In all, 125 members responded to my questionnaire, 24 of whom had been involved in the original APTS recordings, 11 had been interviewed by the Broadcasting Entertainment and Cinematographic Theatre Union (BECTU) oral history project[12] and 45 had also been involved in other publications and programmes. I focused my attention on music and variety programmes, and specifically on the development of light entertainment as a form, as that was where I could perceive a gap in existing histories, and it was clear that there were members who had worked in these areas. I also decided to look at areas of contradiction in the recordings, such as the examples of conflict and divisions of labour in terms of class and gender referred to briefly in a couple of the tapes, and which served to counter the nostalgic picture of camaraderie and teamwork amongst staff (Nicholson-Lord, 1992).

I decided on a life history approach for my interviews.[13] This contrasted with the original recordings and was designed to bring up different aspects of the history of the television service, as well as expanding on aspects already referred to. I ran one-to-one, in-depth interviews with 11 people,[14] often returning for a subsequent session. I wanted to know much more about the interviewees' class, education, expectations, experience and motivations, as I thought these might shed light on the roles they played within the service and the influences they may have had on – and their opinions of – the programming. With some I raised questions about contradictions or issues raised on the original recordings. In order to counter the picture of early television as being just 'radio with pictures', I was keen to know what media and entertainment experiences they were bringing to the service, such as radio, cinema and theatre. I was also interested in what they did during the Second World War, and how it affected them and their memories of British cultural, political and social life at the time. Finally, I attempted to solicit their broader reflections on television programming then and now, the BBC, and public service broadcasting.

MEMORY, REMINISCING AND NOSTALGIA

The second approach I used was to examine both the original collection, and the additional interviews I ran, within the context of recent theories of memory, reminiscence and identity. The annual reunions of the APTS, held at Alexandra Palace, have played an important role in facilitating remembering. They were very lively; discussion and remembering took place amongst groups and between individuals throughout the day. These were people of advanced age – in their seventies, eighties and nineties – many of whom had travelled a long way. The collective reminiscing led to the recording activities. The dynamics of the group meetings – who met with whom, who hosted the recording events, the inclusions and exclusions – proved to be quite revealing in themselves. For example, class divisions were quite marked: engineers and producers did not mix, and those who had been in management positions did not socialise with those who had worked in clerical and technical grades. Not everyone on the APTS list went to the reunions or was invited to recording groups. Members hosting recordings tended to invite their immediate colleagues. Oxbridge men who worked in Outside Broadcasts recorded together, and pre-war pioneers met to produce another tape. Many of the group recordings were convened by male engineering staff. In one case in which a woman was part of a group recording of technicians, she was not able to intervene in the ensuing discussion. Women engineering and technical staff contributed their own tape, however, which turned out to be one of the most revealing in the archive collection. Female personal assistants and secretaries to producers recorded a useful if rather polite contribution, whilst nine male designers produced a very in-depth and lively discussion of their expertise. Three actors recalled their first television performances in a recording organised by Mary Malcolm, an announcer, who was also responsible for another session focusing on presentation, including in-vision announcers, a presentation assistant, a make-up assistant and an actor. The other mixed-group tape, which drew together an actor, two producers and a librarian, was hosted by the Head of Make-Up. Other contributions consisted of individual interviews or monologues.

A great deal of what has been recorded by the APTS is anecdotal, material that has often in the past been avoided by historians; for example, Eric Hobsbawm argues that 'historians cannot remain content with images and anecdotes, however significant' (1995: 289). Indeed, as Alistair Thomson points out, in his analysis of the official history written by Charles Bean about the Australian experience of the First World War, in this case the historian used the anecdotes and stories of the soldiers to corroborate his narratives of courage, motivation and Australian identity (1994: 46–47). Luisa Passerini noticed in her study of working-class men and women in Turin under the Fascist regime, however, that what seemed at first to be either irrelevant or inconsistent answers were of two sorts, silences and jokes, which, when interpreted as a form of anecdote, conveyed an irreverent attitude towards the regime (1979). This notion of irreverence rang true for the APTS collection and was helpful in understanding the proliferation of anecdotal stories. It became clear that many of the stories illustrated how the staff of the television service had managed to produce programmes in spite of insufficient resources from BBC Broadcasting House. Anecdotes were also used to symbolise the spirit and feelings of the time. One story, mentioned on a number of occasions, was the '*Clive of India* story':

> I will tell you the story of George More O'Ferrall; that will do it for now, because it shows the spirit that went on – it's just a marvellous example of television at work in those very early days... George had dreamed up the idea and got all the sources but, when it came to it, was not sufficiently disciplined or controlled as a practical producer, practical director, to make it work, but he had given us all the tools, and we then did it. And that was Alexandra Palace – that was

television in those days. It didn't matter which crew you were on or who you were, everybody was the same.[15]

For Bill Ward, this story illustrated not just collective effort but the fact that producers/directors were not the only heroes. Alessandro Portelli found that euphemisms, jokes and a change of subject were often used to cover over conflicts and embarrassments, and this certainly was the case amongst APTS members whenever there was any mention of class or gender divisions amongst the workforce (1998: 67). Far from being irrelevant, anecdotes were important for my understanding of attitudes and allegiances within the APTS.

The emphasis on enthusiasm and teamwork, and working to a common cause during 'the good old times', was repeated again and again. Commentators, such as John Caughie writing about early television drama, have expressed exasperation at these pioneer narratives with their 'showbiz' elements when, whatever happened, the show still had to go on (1991: 30). Alexandra Palace did, indeed, present almost impossible technical and physical problems, which were overcome by people thrown together for a common enterprise. The intensity of live production made the working atmosphere exhilarating, if exhausting.

> LS: As you know, the studio in Alexandra Palace was not very large, and the conditions under which we worked were very extraordinary, because you had the orchestra up against the wall at one extreme end and at the other end of the studio there would be the singers, actors and so on, with all technical gubbins in the middle taking up all the space. And the only way we could have any kind of interaction was for Bumps conducting at that end and me taking a pass beat on this end, looking over my shoulders to see if we were still in the same opera, as it were; and the chorus, there was no room at all for them, so they had to be put on a little balcony, if you please, on the edge. So, I not only had to skip over the cable for cameras trying not to get in their path...on the sidelines...but also had to dash out to the outskirts of the studio onto the balcony to conduct the chorus whenever it came in.
>
> Q: And this was – in which studio was this?
>
> LS: This was the big studio in Alexandra Palace.
>
> Q: So, in your article you write about an assistant conductor even working from the fireplace; was that you?
>
> LS: Yes.[16]

Mary Malcolm, a presenter, ascribed this collaboration to the amateurishness of the operation, which made it so enjoyable. It was almost part of the war effort, with a 'camaraderie almost of the battlefield...we all shared enthusiasm and a pioneering feeling'.[17] Gilchrist Calder, an actor, said it was the happiest time of his life, when you knew everybody, when people helped each other and there was teamwork, whereas today production is very anonymous.[18] Many people emphasised that it was not just a matter of getting a show off the ground, it was about the quality and kinds of programming and performances they were achieving. Calder said that the fact that everything was so difficult meant people performed well even if, technically, standards are better today. In this vein, Stuart Harry Latham was stage manager before the war, and later became a producer: 'By 1939 I had taken part in 42 live transmissions. I was fascinated by it, it was very exciting. Original directors and technicians were brave.'[19] People were learning techniques and adapting the medium as they went along, developing the aesthetics and technologies of television.

> One great thing about being a pioneer, ...you don't make any money, you don't make any money. The people who come after you make the money, but no one can tell you what to do; you've got no one sitting on your head saying 'Do it this way, do it that way', because nobody knows. You have to find out yourself, but the joy of finding out and winning and making progress and letting everybody else know what you've done, the satisfaction in that is far, far greater than any money can buy.[20]

Nostalgia was expressed about the collective spirit, which contrasted so strikingly for them with working in today's television industry. In the opinion of many of the members, the commercialisation of the television industry since the mid- to late 1980s has brought with it a lack of innovation and experimentation, combined with conservative scheduling and commissioning policies. For those who had continued to work for the BBC, and those who, after they left the BBC, worked as jobbing producers and directors or as freelance engineers and technicians, their experience of working for television had become uninspiring, programme making had become formulaic, and it no longer involved a collective team endeavour to achieve something extraordinary and new.

LOYALTIES, RESISTANCE, SILENCES AND ABSENCES

Accounts in the recordings were not directly critical of the BBC, and I found that there was a marked reluctance to discuss openly such topics as the working conditions or political conflicts. Tom Burns commented on these issues of loyalty and identity when he interviewed staff in the BBC between 1963 and 1973, which he attributes to there being a public service ethos (1977: 66). He saw this as distinct from television 'professionalism', which developed later. In the case of the APTS, however, not many members seemed loyal to the BBC as such; many moved to commercial television for more money, and more creative freedom – or so they hoped. In 1954 the BBC threatened that if employees left they wouldn't be able to return, though many of them in fact did. People were asked if they had been made an offer by commercial television, and, if they had, they were either given notice of dismissal or offered more money to stay.[21] Briggs notes that staff who were forced to leave the BBC, who did not like its ethos or who criticised the organisation became 'rebels' (1980: 11). This shift from being loyal to a collective identity to being a 'rebel' was contingent on the level of recognition a member received retrospectively from a group or organisation. That process of recognition was still being negotiated by the APTS (even though individuals had received rewards such as CBEs, MBEs, OBEs or knighthoods), making the reticence of members understandable.

Remembering experiences in particular ways has also had the effect of sometimes silencing alternative ways of articulating the experiences. Studio manager Basil Adams had his history ready for me when I arrived for the interview – a repetition of stories in which he himself, or his subjective experience, was excluded. He was from a generation who believed that facts are facts and that history is made up of empirical evidence, and cannot be described as an interpretative method of analysing the past. In other words, the idea that subjective accounts can be historical is a perspective that came in after the APTS members' time. It is also a view that problematises the idea of objectivity, a condition the BBC has prided itself on achieving, and one many of its members did not question. Bill Ward, on the other hand, placed himself centrally in the narrative and spoke more openly. He told me about key figures he felt I should speak to and urged me to mention those whose names he felt had not been sufficiently acknowledged by the BBC:

> I told you I would digress, but some names are important because they are no longer around, and one name I must, must mention – they probably have come up before, but two men played an incredible role, an incredible role in the early days, pioneering days, in the early days of television; one was pre-war and one was post-war. The pre-war name was D. H. Munro – now, he should be given a posthumous medal, because he was incredible, his energy was unbelievable… And the other name was Cecil McGivern, who also went away unrewarded, and was in bad favour by the hierarchy of the BBC, but he played an incredible role; he was much loved by all producers and directors.[22]

He also wanted to mention Duncan Ross:

> BW: [A]nd a name you may not come across, he's dead now, but for God's sake write him up somewhere, somewhere, talking about scriptwriters: Duncan Ross – heard of him?
>
> Q: Yes, I have heard of the name.
>
> BW: Duncan Ross was a documentary writer, but a dedicated one – God, he was a dedicated one – and Duncan Ross and Ian Atkins did a series called *The Courts of Justice*; superb series. Duncan died in a bedsit in Wood Green sometime after the war, in total poverty, almost unknown, yet Duncan gave some marvellous scripts to television. He did a programme on the Great North Road, the A1, which was the Great North Road and was used by lorry drivers and so on, and

he did a documentary on the Great North Road and went and lived as a hobo for a month, going up and down the Great Road, cadging lifts, sleeping rough, just to get his background research material to write the series. He was a totally dedicated, wonderful writer.[23]

Loyalty to the British state was commonly expressed, and many, particularly the men who were on active service in the Second World War, took great pride in their war records. They often described activities in battle terms:

OBs [outside broadcasts] and light entertainment were – we likened ourselves to fighter pilots, as opposed to the bomber pilots, that were drama. You flew a little, in television terms, by the seat of your pants, which the fighter pilots did, whereas the stolid, pipe-smoking drama producers, with lots of rehearsals and great precision, were the bomber pilots.[24]

The British war ethos led interviewees to turn off the recorder whilst relating what were considered official secrets. Many men returning from the war resented those who had had an easier time in a home posting, and a number of people talked about how difficult it was to get work after the war. This was at all levels of the workforce. Robin Luxford, in order to move into a job in sound in television, joined the BBC as an office boy and then applied internally for work.[25] A resentment towards the women who had been recruited into technical positions during the absence of men at war was expressed indirectly by some male engineers.

A professional pride was displayed by many members, and certain difficulties would not be admitted. Some were hostile towards unions and later generations for demanding better conditions. Others were proud and disdainful of my suggestion that they might have learnt skills from other people. Bill Ward was extremely irritated by my questioning about how he had gained his skills, insisting that everything was new and he had worked it out himself, while Basil Adams' pride was stung by my suggestion that he might have wanted training: 'I think I should have been insulted.'[26]

The gender differences in respondents were very apparent. The men in particular refused to admit to any personal or emotional issues and wanted only to talk about the happy times and memorable moments. They became quiet or resistant when I attempted to explore areas that would have required personal reflection. A number were suspicious of my attempts to involve them in analysing their past, such as Philip Bate, music producer: 'I don't think I analysed very much how I felt and so on, I was just in many ways getting on with the job and doing the thing that I enjoyed doing.'[27] A number mentioned having 'nervous breakdowns' either during the war or in the early 1950s, but none were prepared to enlarge on the impact of war on their personal lives, or on the strains of the working conditions at the time. Basil Adams attributed his breakdown to great pressure to achieve high standards in the face of competition from commercial television. Briggs' account confirms this (1979: 279).

The women were more willing to admit to difficulties, and talked happily about not knowing what to do, getting things wrong and the conditions of work.

> BH: Telecine! Nobody taught me anything, so when I first picked it up it went backwards, and frontways and sideways, and inside out and you just had to learn by yourself your own mistakes.
>
> GD: I nearly put the film on upside down.
>
> BH: That's right. Nobody told you anything – it's extraordinary.
>
> GD: No, they didn't; they didn't notice what I'd done (*laughs*).
>
> BH: No, they just said: 'Get on with it, find out.'[28]

Sylvia Peters, an announcer, said there were 'terrible conditions: the lighting was so hot it gave you headaches, and the drafts… [A]nd we had to learn everything – long scripts, no autocue, and we were on the air all evening and doing seven to nine announcements a night. Hard on the brain.'[29] Elizabeth MacGregor talked of the effects on her health of stress at work, yet the job 'had to be done', and she talked with pride about her skill as a grams operator. Notwithstanding these admissions, a stoical attitude was still predominant amongst the women.

There was a generational need to be seen to have 'coped', as well as a legacy of military attitudes from the Second World War and the British public school mentality – something that many of the men had experienced. Less directly, personal references to certain difficult experiences were clearly more permissible if one talked about absent colleagues:

> BW: I came under DH [Munro], DH before the war – I was just one of the lads on the floor, that looked and saw him at work, but he, he was before the war… But he just was a bundle of energy, he lived and breathed television. In fact, the reason he left television after the war, I understand, was because his doctor advised him that if he continued he would die of a heart attack, and he said: 'You must get away from this, this monster which is eating you up and causing you so much stress you will die.' And so he left, and I believe joined the Coal Board – I'm not sure, something like that.[30]

Apart from ill health, drinking was referred to as an occupational hazard in the service, and there were stories about particular people. Yet the APTS members are from a generation that does not like to perceive itself as 'washing its dirty linen in public', and, understandably, all these references were barred from publication.

COLLECTIVE AND INDIVIDUAL IDENTITIES

A collective BBC identity was not just about being part of the BBC or the Alexandra Palace Television Society; it had been imposed to some extent.

Working for television carried codes of 'professional practice', which did not encourage people to criticise their colleagues publicly. The interviews reveal many examples of the conflict this imposed on individuals. Lionel Salter, an accompanist, had grievances against the BBC, which he did not want recorded, but he did relate the unsatisfactory way in which he was moved from his position as Head of Music and Opera. Philip Bate, a producer, referred to 'a personal intrigue', which forced him to retire early, but he wouldn't elaborate. Elizabeth MacGregor was reluctant to admit that there was any friction between people over what was produced for television, but she did talk about the problem of women being regarded as unable to do particular jobs. Other collective identities existed within the service. Barrie Edgar loved his work as producer on Outside Broadcasts, and was uncritical of the BBC in an interview that gave some good examples of how 'the old boy network' functions. Ian Orr-Ewing, another producer, talked about recruiting people 'you played cricket with' and who came from Oxford. Another member mentioned freemasonry as a bonding force between some people.

Trade union loyalties meant that many of the male engineers were defensive about gender roles at work, whilst female members of the technical staff made it clear that bullying by the male employees existed. There was a strong collective identity amongst those involved in the BECTU oral history project, alongside their APTS identity. Nevertheless, this union identity, which was articulated in class terms by referring to the men on the studio floor as distinct from those in charge, was clearly in conflict with gender roles at work. One of the men attempted to blame management for incidents of gender discrimination over who was allowed to work on sound and camera, whilst two of the women insisted that the men themselves were responsible. Further exploration revealed that the union had protected men's positions by downgrading women's technical roles and prohibiting them from work on the studio floor (even though some were union members).

A collective identity as APTS members was not shared by all. The fact that some producers clearly did not wish to socialise with the engineering and technical staff was reflected at reunions and in the oral recordings, where the production and technical staff did not intermingle in the group interviews. For example, Orr-Ewing talked about the 'we and they' situation between producers and engineers,[31] whilst Gilchrist Calder and Christine Hillcoat recalled how Harold Cox despised James Bold because of the clothes he wore![32]

NATIONAL IDENTITY

Members identified themselves as British and on the whole were united over the British cultural tradition they were promoting, in comparison to European standards. The British were leaders in performance, according to Elizabeth MacGregor:

It was interesting in these early days at the Palace too, because we had – after the war – we had all the ballet companies from abroad coming and performing, and it was a very good advertisement for our Royal Ballet; they always showed up so well when they were there, they were so disciplined and so smart and well groomed and well mannered. I used to feel very proud of them.[33]

Furthermore, nobody criticised royalty, and many talked respectfully about their involvement with the 1953 Coronation programmes or other royal television occasions.

Although not loyal to the BBC, they were proud that they had proved the people at Broadcasting House wrong: that television had succeeded and that commercial television could not have taken off without them. In this context, the nostalgia of the APTS recordings is open to more nuanced readings. Whilst many of the original people mourned the perceived loss of programme quality and range at the BBC, and some shared a distaste for the increasing commercialisation that started in earnest under John Birt, their nostalgia was not necessarily to do with the values of Sir John Reith or the BBC. This was reflected in the name of the society. Many had no regrets about moving to commercial television but, while resisting a BBC identity, they still sought its recognition. They were proud of the achievement of setting up the television service and their work in developing television. They largely saw the effort as collective, rather than an aggregate of particular individuals. This collective identity was one that was created at Alexandra Palace in contrast to Broadcasting House, which looked down on television as a medium that produced only entertainment. The considerable snobbery about television at the time was confirmed by many of the APTS members: 'As I say, radio looked down upon television as an upstart, and as something only fit for the servants' quarters anyway. I don't think they wanted to know anything about us and we went our own sweet way regardless.'[34]

Commercial television was clearly instrumental in creating the image of the BBC in the monopoly period. It was seen as out of touch with popular tastes, serious and pompous; this image was unchallenged by the BBC itself, which was concerned to disassociate itself from its past Reithian years.[35] Yet the early television service was not really as Reithian as has often been described. Reith had had nothing to do with television, but he did show his distaste for a service run by 'the Fools on the Hill'.[36] The attitude that television was just producing entertainment was prevalent amongst people in radio, and was as much to do with rivalry as with concerns about the social purpose of broadcasting. One of the most important revelations of the APTS collection, therefore, was that members did indeed pioneer television entertainment in its early years. Popular entertainment was developed by the BBC Television Service, not commercial television. Commercial television benefited, particularly in the area of entertainment programming when people left the BBC to join it.[37]

CONCLUSION

What initially appeared to be an institutional collection of oral recordings by former employees of the BBC Television Service turned out to be more revealing than simply providing a record of the early years. The collection was intended to put the flesh on the bones of the written archives, and whilst it did that in certain areas, such as giving technical and engineering details, it initially appeared not to provide much to overturn the existing histories that did not take the programme output seriously. The process of recording and reminiscing is not just about providing a record of how it was, however, but also addresses the needs of the present. New oral history methodologies allowed me to explore different factors in the process and selection of memories that the members recorded, leading me to focus on a neglected but important sector of the television output of those years, as well as following up on the contradictions and conflicts that arose in the existing accounts. The significance of the collection was that the recordings did, in fact, shed new light on the past, and provide an alternative history to that of the BBC's 'official histories' – albeit not a 'history from below', in Buscombe's sense. I began to understand that the nostalgia that dominated the recordings was not expressing a loyalty to a past BBC, nor for the BBC as an institution, but could be read as signalling a collective memory of the resistance of APTS members to the BBC (or, further, a BBC identity) at the time of their struggle to make the fledgling television service a success. This resistance was, however, tempered by the desire on the part of members to receive some form of recognition from the institution of the BBC in the present; an acknowledgement of their role within the context of the public histories being created to mark the anniversaries of the beginnings of the television service. If I had not read beyond some of the overt meanings of the archive I would have misunderstood the extent of the power an institution such as the BBC is able to wield in order to produce loyalties or conformity amongst its staff. That is not to say, however, that institutional and generational issues of pride, conformity and confidentiality did not inhibit the respondents; there were stories hinted at, tantalising morsels of information dropped off the record, and professional silences maintained, all highlighting the difficulties that researchers encounter in writing public histories. Nonetheless, while some research questions were frustrated by these processes of loyalty and resistance, other narratives came to the fore, and a new picture of the early BBC Television Service did indeed emerge from my research. Television at Alexandra Palace served to provide and develop television entertainment in a post-war, war-weary Britain, problematising accounts that see commercial television as the only force for introducing popular culture and entertainment to television. If this focus on entertainment is in danger of reversing the picture of early television to the extent of negating the importance of serious programming, such as talks, outside broadcasts and drama, the point has been to add a new dimension to our understanding of the period and to existing writing, as well as alerting researchers to the richness of the available sources.

ACKNOWLEDGEMENT

I would like to thank the Alexandra Palace Television Society for allowing me to access their audio collection, and those members who agreed to be interviewed. I am also grateful to Dr Rodney Walshaw for his expert help in editing this piece.

8 Shifting sentiments

BBC Television, West Indian immigrants and cultural production

Darrell Newton

As part of the public service agenda under Sir John Reith, the BBC became a major tool for the cultural production of millions. Through programmes offered under the first Director of Television, Gerald Cock, the service produced televisual constructs of British 'culture' for generations. Audiences had a choice of teleplays, both BBC and Gaumont British News, and musical programmes, each demonstrating the ability of television to provide windows upon the world. When considering the presence of black people within British television history (in the case of this study, African Americans and Afro-Caribbeans), BBC's first public broadcasting day of 2 November 1936 featured musical guests Buck and Bubbles, an African American dancing and singing duo. Within a year singer and actress Elisabeth Welch was featured in musical programmes, beginning in October 1937, from Alexandra Palace. Welch, who had become a favourite of audiences on BBC Radio years before, continued to provide musical entertainment to television audiences, as did other black performers such as Winifred Atwell, Paul Robeson and Adelaide Hall.

After the suspension of television during the Second World War, broadcasts from Alexandra Palace resumed in 1946, yet management reminded the Beveridge Committee that broadcasting should be used 'constructively in the general social interest, and the "educational impulse" maintained' (Paulu, 1961: 22). Meanwhile, a different kind of black presence on BBC Television disrupted the racial alterity and the exoticised construct of blacks previously seen on television. West Indian immigrants arriving in 1948 aboard the *Empire Windrush* became a landmark event, particularly when shown on *Television Newsreel* (BBC, 1948–54), a programme that used the highly familiar format of 'cinema' newsreels. Along with these settlers came a history of colonialism, employment concerns and seething racialism. Soon programmes on race and immigration were planned by the BBC. The advent of these programmes was timely, in that many Britons were concerned about the

113

impact these settlers would have upon notions of national identity. As a coloniser and as an imperial power, Britain's discursive power was reinforced through BBC production practices. In doing so, the service reinforced a social history that drew upon colonial notions of West Indians while examining historical evidence through the lens of post-war nationalism. Aspects of West Indian culture were constructed with patronage; one that reinforced cultural imperialism as voice-overs for British Pathé newsreels reminded audiences that these immigrants should be welcomed as 'citizens of the Empire sailing to the Mother country with good intent'.[1] Despite this affirmation of liberalism, the service also began to discuss what was called 'the Jamaican Problem' in some of their programming – a condition allegedly brought about by an increase of immigrants from the Caribbean (BBC/Pathé broadcast shooting script, 1955).[2]

Within this institutional case study I examine the manner in which BBC Television cautiously undertook the responsibility of assisting white Britons in considering, if not accepting, West Indian immigrants and their assimilation via selected programmes. Beginning in the 1940s, I provide a historiographical meta-analysis of the BBC's cultural production of West Indian settlers and their transition into British culture. Through contextual and textual analyses, I explore current affairs programmes that attempted to interpret the immigrant experience for the benefit of two distinct audiences: white Britons being educated on the social impact of these peoples, and the immigrants themselves, who were advised on acceptable behaviour. Archived memoranda between BBC Television management during the 1950s and 1960s were essential to this research, along with Audience Research Reports conducted during these same decades. These documents, along with shooting scripts, were examined at the BBC's Written Archives Centre, and were invaluable as historiographic narratives that demonstrated the cultural saliency of the service and its efforts to address immigration during the 1950s. This chapter is part of a larger piece of qualitative research that also includes a more extensive analysis of television and radio programming, along with personal interviews of black Britons working within British media, including the BBC.[3] Inherent to my research have been regulatory and social issues, the cultural phenomenon of race, and aspects of BBC Television's broadcast policies as related to West Indian imagery. Within the study, I focus upon the BBC as a non-commercial network considered free of the pressures thought to be inherent to commercial advertising and sponsorship, freeing the network to engage in cultural practices of its choosing.[4]

According to documents examined at the Written Archives Centre, broadcast policies were sometimes driven by Audience Research Reports conducted during the years in question, underlining the importance of these reports as historiographic resources. While they never completely and irrefutably reflect actual attitudes held by the viewing public in the years collated, they do provide an indicator of the social and cultural environment of the day. These records also provide a chronology of efforts undertaken by management, including handwritten responses to policy and anecdotal afterthoughts as related to West Indian actors, and community activists. While this method of research ultimately requires semiotic analysis of representations cast by BBC producers and writers, written documents provide an insight into the underlining of 'difference' and subjectivity that resulted when programming analysed the impact of West Indian immigration. Due in part to colonialism, subsequent patronage abounded. While it would be difficult to reconstruct this programming critically using mere transcripts and synopses, this chapter examines some of this material and highly important decisions undertaken by management about such programming. This source material helps to demonstrate the social issues enveloping post-war Britain and the conditions under which the service attempted to establish the assimilation of West Indians as a social impetus.

What is understated within this documentation, however, is how these Afro-Caribbeans were marginalised by social authors, seldom having the opportunity to engage in *how* they would be represented within these programmes. How could their voices be heard and their inherent desires for social enhancement known? What effect does this absence of voices have upon a historical study of BBC Television, representations of race and the canonical formation of programming texts? It wasn't until the 1960s that BBC Television, under the direction of the BBC's then Director General Hugh Greene, called upon West Indian community leaders to discuss ways that the service could better serve their needs as new citizens. These discussions created possibilities within a social and institutional environment that had been foreshadowed by social tensions, some of which were examined by programming in the 1950s, yet seldom from the perspective of West Indians themselves. An assessment of these representations of Afro-Caribbeans as immigrants and their impact upon British television audiences is thus shown here to be a historical concern within studies of British broadcasting.

LIGHT ENTERTAINMENT AND THE WEST INDIAN

During the earlier days of television, many of the programmes transmitted were versions of popular radio programmes and defined as 'musical or comedy shows, filled with a variety of singers and dance routines'.[5] Some of the earliest representations of blacks came in the guise of BBC radio performers such as Elisabeth Welch, who had already been exposed to audiences in the 1930s. BBC Television first allowed Welch to 'appear' to home audiences on Thursday 28 October 1937, in the programme *Song and Dance: A Little Show*, which featured English song and dance favourites Frances Day, Edward Cooper and the BBC Television Orchestra. Prior to this broadcast audiences merely heard Welch's voice, and were often unaware that she was black (Pines, 1992: 22). When performing at Alexandra Palace for BBC Television, Welch explained that make-up was unnecessary in that 'everybody was white, white, white – you only had eyes and black lips' (Pines, 1992: 22–23). Welch's reference to the BBC's monochromatic cameras and lack of make-up infers an absence of racial coding, in that everyone, including her, appeared 'white'.

Ten years later West Indian actor Edric Connor first appeared on the service in a BBC variety show entitled *Music Makers* (BBC, 22 June 1948), the same date as the arrival of the *Empire Windrush* at Tilbury Docks. Later, West Indian performers were featured on the variety programme *Bal Creole* (BBC, 1950), which included Trinidadian performer Boscoe Holder and his wife Sheila Clarke (Bourne, 1998). His group, the West African Rhythm Brothers, was later addressed in a 1951 memorandum from the BBC Controller of Television, Cecil McGivern, to producer Bill Ward. The memo suggested that the group be included on an upcoming broadcast of the show *Caribbean Cabaret* and that the performance be 'as loud and savage as possible' for viewers.[6] The merger of abject fascination with the exotic 'Other', which was thus highlighted as the cultural production of West Indians in light entertainment, relied heavily upon the fascination of 'going native' – at least, for the length of a musical number. Though the BBC attempted to address issues of race in later documentaries and teleplays, these cultural productions became more controversial when contrasted with West Indian immigrants arriving on the *Empire Windrush* – an event televised to only a modest portion of the population, given that fewer than 130,000 licences were held in 1948, and yet one that could not be ignored, particularly in light of newspaper coverage of their arrival and cinematic newsreels.[7]

SCIENTIFIC CONSTRUCTS OF RACE AND BBC TELEVISION

In an attempt to address concerns about racial differences, the BBC formulated programmes that analysed misconceptions and provided 'scientific facts' about race. In a memo sent on 5 January 1952 a series of planned 'Race Programmes' on the BBC was discussed by Television Talks Producer George H. Noordhof:

> Grace [Wyndham Goldie] is putting together a series of programmes on the racial question and she wishes to start with a programme dealing entirely with the scientific aspect of the problem. In this programme for which I should be responsible, the scientific points made would be brought into direct relation with the type of argument which would be followed in...[MP] Christopher Mayhew's thesis during the remainder of the series.[8]

In turn, Goldie, serving as Assistant Head of Talks, received a memo later that year from James Bredin addressing the planned series. The programme, which would become part of the *Africa Series: Scientific Programme* planned for television, was given the working title *The Scientists Look at Race*. Topics included notions of how racial categories were historically perceived or how cultural differences and 'ideas about Jews, Negroes, Latins, Ayrians, the Island race (British) and European (as opposed to non-European)' might be understood.[9] The programme would then begin with an introduction from anthropologist Dr Jack Trevor of Cambridge University, who would discuss 'the way in which the ordinary man sees race: i.e. in terms of posture, gesture, talk, clothes and walk'.[10] Programming notes indicated that the scientists would then 'put on paper' specific points they wanted to make, as agreed at a previous meeting. In an insidious reference, the memo then reads that a 'further meeting of all parties will then be held with the intention of persuading the scientists to fit what they want to say to the conclusions which we want them to reach'.[11]

The programme was ultimately entitled *Race and Colour: A Scientific Introduction to the Problem of Racial Relations* (BBC, 9 November 1952). According to a draft script of the programme, those who participated in the all-white panel discussion included Christopher Mayhew, MP; interviewer Ritchie Calder; Dr Trevor; biologist Dr Julian Huxley; director of the Blood Group Reference Laboratory, Dr Arthur E. Mourant; and Maurice Freedman, Lecturer in Anthropology, London School of Economics and Political Science. Also participating was discussant David Attenborough.[12] Trevor addressed misnomers about 'races', such as the incorrect notion of what were called 'the German race and the Slav races', and discussed 'skulls and other bones', particularly the 'Negriform' and 'Caucasian'. When Dr Trevor was asked about the sociological impact of racial prejudice, he stated that racial prejudice did not exist. He felt:

> There are all sorts of group prejudices and some of these are dressed up in the garb of feelings against other races, but different racial groups do not dislike one another just because they are of different appearance. If this was so, then we should expect to find the same prejudice shown to Negroes by whites the world over.[13]

A few moments later, Calder asked Trevor if he would allow his daughter to marry a black man. He made it clear that he would have to 'answer "no" to that question, and it should not be too difficult to see why'. He said that in England they, as whites, 'were somewhat more liberal in their attitudes toward coloured people than in other countries around the world'. He warned, however, that it was still difficult for a coloured man and his wife, 'white or coloured', to be completely accepted in society. He ended his discussion by saying that, if he had answered 'yes' to that question, it 'would have meant that the coloured problem had been solved'.

Despite these controversial issues and subsequent discussions, audiences were not impressed. The BBC's Viewer Research Report of 10 November 1952, based on 218 questionnaires completed after the programme, stated overwhelmingly that viewers were disappointed by the programme's focus. The show ran at a peak viewing time of 7:45–8:25 p.m., and had an audience rating below the current average (62) for other television discussion programmes and 'chat shows'.[14] When compared to the Viewer Research Weekly Summary, the show had an audience of 35 per cent of the adult TV public, below an average of 46 per cent for recent scientific talks and demonstrations. More importantly, it was discovered that the programme fell far below the 68 per cent to 81 per cent of viewers garnered for 12 programmes that ran under the series title 'International Commentary', broadcast from autumn 1950 to spring 1951.[15]

According to the Viewer Research Report for *Race and Colour: A Scientific Introduction to the Problem of Race Relations*, many viewers regarded the issue of race and 'colour' as 'tedious or unpleasant and therefore unsuited to television'. While some viewers were pleased that a programme enlightened them on a subject of national importance, the scientific discussions were far too technical. One viewer regarded the programme as an 'advanced lecture on anthropology', and there was difficulty in assimilating technical jargon such as 'phrase codes' and 'blood categories'. The most common criticism of the show was that the guest experts had not discussed 'the real issues of the racial problem' created by immigration, or offered any viable solutions. Audience members wanted to hear what measures could be enacted to keep problems to a minimum. Soon after management had examined these survey results the BBC began to consider documentaries that specifically examined the social impact of West Indian immigration, with an emphasis upon how these hopeful citizens could adapt to English customs.

SOCIAL REALITIES AND THE 'COLOUR BAR'

In 1955, in an effort to examine issues raised but not completely addressed by programmes such as *Race and Colour*, producer Anthony de Lotheniere began researching a news programme that would become one in a series of *Special Enquiry* shows. The programme would examine the impact of newly arrived West Indians and other non-white immigrants upon Birmingham residents. De Lotheniere had planned to interview West Indian bus drivers who had recently begun working for the transport companies – particularly important in contextualising the immigrant experience from those who experienced this transition. Background notes compiled by De Lotheniere's assistant, Peter Stone, indicated that a great deal of resistance to the interviews existed among whites working at the Hockley bus garage.[16] According to a rough outline of the programme, entitled *Special Enquiry No. 3: The Colour Bar*, white drivers felt that an unfair amount of praise would be given to these men on the programme. Within days the *Birmingham Gazette* (5 January 1955, 1) had a headline reading 'Bus strike threat stops TV film: undue publicity for coloured men: so BBC won't take cameras to Hockley'. Despite their best intentions, the BBC initially cancelled the show after weeks of research and filming. The reaction of the BBC to the white Hockley drivers in Birmingham immediately altered the organisation's ability to frame 'true' stories of the West Indian experience in the United Kingdom autonomously. In this instance, cultural authority was shunted by a management desire to take a safer approach to the issue of racial integration.

Later that year de Lotheniere began to research the idea of returning to Birmingham to continue the project.[17] Letters were written to Dr Kenneth Little, an anthropologist at Edinburgh University, to determine why coloured people came to Britain, relying again upon 'scientific' knowledge to examine race, as earlier Talks programming had done. Birmingham was still of interest to de Lotheniere because of 'the topical interest aroused by the large-scale arrival of immigrants from the West Indies'.[18] The producer also followed up with an apologetic letter to the head of the local busmen's union, Harry Green, indicating how sorry he and his staff had been to cause 'ill feeling[s] down at the garages'. He followed with a reassuring message.

> We went down to Hockley yesterday – and we were invited into the canteen for a cup of tea – on the strict understanding that we did not talk a word about the buses or coloured men. It was a very good arrangement and we talked hard about the Eighth Army and coal mining! Our camera, by the way, was left locked up in the car outside![19]

In 1955 BBC Television transmitted the *Special Enquiry* programme, retitled *Has Britain a Colour Bar?*. A principle focus of the show was how West Indians were settling in since their arrival in Birmingham. The programme provides little or no actual interviews with West Indians, Pakistani immigrants or their perceptions of life in the city, however. A rough draft treatment of the programme, written on 28 January 1955 by de Lotheniere, suggested that host Robert Reid would open the programme by introducing the subject of a 'colour bar'. He would then outline a brief history of this 'new large scale immigration from the West Indies' via the following points from the outline script

(1) British Colonial policy has fostered belief in Britain as the 'Mother Country'.

(2) During war we were happy to have 'colonials' fighting in the Services and working in British factories. *FILM TO ILLUSTRATE THIS* (from 'Hello West Indies').

(3) After war a few stayed in Britain. Others on return to their own countries found poor economic conditions and they later came back to this country. *FILM*: Immigrants landing from Empire Windrush in 1949 with sound piece by Jamaican. Since then – with jobs going in this country – many thousands more have come over.

(4) Many immigrants are assisted to get here by societies making loans at 10 per cent interest. HEADLINES OF CURRENT SITUATION.

Are they being absorbed? Is a Colour Bar emerging – or not? Housing? Redundancy? What about controlling immigration? If they're British can we control them?[20]

A scene-by-scene analysis of a rough treatment for the programme reveals a mixture of highly cautious optimism with a general sense of disquiet towards West Indian workers.[21] One segment features two young West Indian men coming into a pub, dressed in overcoats.[22] The scene (staged for dramatic effect, as the show's treatment indicates) shows white male patrons of varied ages talking and drinking. One of the black men pounds his fist on the bar to get the bartender's attention. The voice of the narrator, which sounds white, middle-aged and British, says, 'Manners are different, too. In Jamaica, this is the normal way to attract the attention of the man behind the bar.' The camera then shows patrons grow immediately silent and gaze at the duo. The narrator's voice then states, 'In English pubs, they don't approve of it. Innocent actions and gestures are misunderstood and suspicion hardens on both sides.' De Lotheniere and a BBC camera crew began to craft a narrative of proper behaviour for immigrants in a British social setting.

Of the 51 scenes in the treatment for the programme, 30 highlight unemployment, racism, fears of miscegenation, housing and labour disputes. Dramatised and actual interviews with landladies and 'average' (white) citizens give dystopic responses to questions such as 'Is there an active colour prejudice in Birmingham?', further codifying concerns over the black (and Asian) presence in the city. In other scenes meant to highlight lifestyle choices, West Indians are shown shooting dice, hanging around on street corners and sitting in pubs with white women as white men scowl. The choice of only one West Indian interviewee (who was slated to address racism) reinforces the strategy of white British discursive authority to frame these issues strategically, in this case for docudramatic impact. While an effort is made by producers to demonstrate a positive outcome for these settlers, the suggestion of cultural differences is made apparent within the operations of the texts. Despite the changing social discourses and shift of constitutive power, the cultural authority of the BBC is thus reinforced, as is its autonomy as an 'observer'.

Years later a follow-up instalment of *A Question of Colour* was transmitted on Friday 14 November 1958. David Martin of the BBC's Midland Film Unit produced the programme, which returned to Birmingham to find out how the 'coloured members of the population were faring'. Before filming began on Martin's project, Norman Swallow, Assistant Head of Films and Television, sent a memo providing ideas for the documentary that were positive and reaffirming to anti-xenophobic discourse. Swallow noted that the second story in Birmingham was seen to be 'a cheerful one, at least on the surface. A great deal more cheerful than it was in 1954.'[23] He reminded Martin that a '*Special Enquiry* segment during the period 1955–57 averaged 71 and the previous programme about coloured people in Birmingham (Week 5, 1955) gained an Index of 77', which he found encouraging.[24] In his memo, called '*A Question of Colour* Notes', he suggests that audiences be reminded that racism previously encountered by the BBC crew would be exposed to audiences in the follow-up programme.[25] Individuals who expressed racist views would also be re-examined. In a reference to a landlady, Swallow made this suggestion:

> Put the splendid landlady later on. Cut her down as discussed. [Then] end, after the sequences, with street scenes of Birmingham. Over these [the presenter] says that 'this city and its people are perhaps an example to the rest of Britain. Proving that a colour bar is neither necessary nor excusable…Britain, in 1958, is still a place that can promise a worthy future for everybody…whatever his colour…(cut to shot of coloured child…whatever his age (Or something of the sort!).[26]

Though relying on a docudramatic narrative, Swallow's directives were pro-integration, as the BBC demonstrated a desire to heal social rifts and expose racist practices. As a means of accentuating positive aspects of the immigrant experience in Birmingham, it was suggested that the show's title 'avoid the words "prejudice" and "bar"'.

According to an audience research project for the second *Question of Colour* and an observation by Swallow, the show seemed a 'very good idea to most viewers in this sample of the audience'.[27] The criticisms voiced by several viewers sampled included, first, the fact that, as the programme dealt with one town, it did not give a fair picture of the national situation, and, second, the programme offered no new or surprising information. Otherwise, the Research Department found that audiences considered it to be 'interesting and a useful programme'. Most viewers in the sample felt that subjects 'had been well chosen' as representatives of immigrants and that they 'behaved naturally in front of the cameras, and answered the questions put to them frankly and sincerely'.[28]

As the Corporation began to incorporate more issues concerning the 'racial question' into its news and documentary programming, there was an attempt to calculate the amount of 'Negroes' and other coloured people who had appeared on the BBC throughout the 1950s. There had been criticisms at a meeting of the Northern Ireland Advisory Council, led by Controller Robert McCall, that the service had used coloured people only for popular programmes that addressed music, controversial race issues and 'special series'. In an effort to address this concern, an urgent memo by McCall was sent to Swallow on obtaining information 'regarding Certain Programmes'. The memo inquired about programmes coloured people had appeared on and how many there had been. McCall stated:

> I suggested…that in fact coloured people were frequently employed in programmes of high quality. Apart from the obvious examples of Paul Robeson and Mattiwilda Dobbs, there were many other artists who had been projected in our programmes in the last 12 months. What I really want from each Departmental Head is half a dozen examples of programmes in which coloured people – Indian, African, West Indian, etc. – have been heard as serious artists or have taken part in serious programmes such as discussions or talks.[29]

In a follow-up memo that addressed 'Coloured speakers in religious television programmes during 1958', Oliver Hunkin (Assistant Head of Religious Broadcasting, Television) wrote to Swallow to note that guests included various overseas students, the Bishop of Uganda, religious official Angela Christian of Ghana discussing colour prejudice, and the Reverend Vedaneyagon Gnanamuthu on the Church in India.[30] Also highlighted was the *Spotlight* programme (1957) that included West Indian guests. Another film, from the United Nations (12 May 1952), dealt specifically with the Declaration of Human Rights. The editors of Women's Programmes explained in the memo that the department did a '13-minute programme recently on *Mixed Marriages* and often have coloured people in their programmes – e.g. a Nigerian midwife'. *Second Enquiry's A Question of Colour* was also included as the Midlands' contribution to 'coloured' programming.

Despite these efforts, a number of West Indians organisations wrote letters to BBC management criticising programming choices. A major complaint was that race programmes simply didn't go far enough in stressing the similarities of the cultures, as opposed to problems. This concern was re-emphasised by the BBC's Director General, Hugh Greene, who, at a meeting with Regional Controllers in March 1965, expressed concerns that 'special programmes for coloured immigrants' shouldn't emphasise the 'apartness' of the coloured community.[31] It was also during 1965, however, that the *Colour in Britain* radio series on the BBC's Third Programme was receiving critical acclaim for providing a balanced look at race relations within the country. In addition, 'special' broadcasts for the immigrant communities of the north-west (such as *English by Radio*, which was programmed for Indian and Pakistani immigrants) were planned. These programmes underlined a belief by Greene that management should re-examine educational programmes about racial relations and, more importantly, cultural assimilation. In agreement was famed West Indian cricketer Sir Learie Constantine, who also served as a member of the BBC General Advisory Council, yet other members were convinced that most immigrants worked in the United Kingdom for a number of years but then returned to their home countries with the income they had earned. From the meeting notes with Hugh Greene, Robert Stead, Controller of the North Region, stated that it was 'dubious as to whether immigrants would even bother to listen to such programmes judging from the evidence already in hand to the lack of initiative many immigrants were showing toward helping themselves acclimate to British life'.[32]

THE COLOURED CONFERENCES

In July 1965 the Press Officer of BBC Television sent a message to several news organisations announcing a series of conferences in which BBC management would meet with selected 'coloured' guests to discuss immigration issues. A press announcement from the BBC Evening Press Officer, Dulcie J. Marshall, was distributed to the Press Association, Exchange Telegraph, Reuters (UK Desk) and the United Press International's Television Department. Each responded by sending representatives to cover the meeting and subsequent discussions. The first conference, held on 6 July, was specifically tailored to discuss 'the problems of Indian and Pakistani immigrants'.[33] The second conference was held on 13 July, in the Council Chamber at Broadcasting House, with representatives of the West Indian community as 'the guests of the BBC'.[34] The meeting was led by Greene, who welcomed representatives from more than 20 organisations that were concerned about the impact of immigrants in London, the Midlands and the North. The focus of the meeting seemed highly encouraging, in that the Director General felt that the BBC, as a public service broadcasting authority, had a duty to assist immigrants in whatever way it could. As indicated in the minutes of the meeting, Greene stated that the service recognised that the problems of West Indians were unique, and the main purpose of the conference was to 'provide an opportunity for the BBC to learn from those present what the West Indian problems were and how the BBC could help'. The organisations taking part had been identified by the BBC in a list of 'Societies and Organisations' that identified 'coloured' groups in the mid-1950s as important sources for televised interviews and talks by BBC management. These groups included the popular West Indian Students Union, the Stepney League of Coloured People, the Anglo-Caribbean Club and the League of Coloured Peoples.[35]

The Director General also reminded the attendees that there were two sides to the BBC's problem. One was to decide how the BBC should make West Indians feel at home in the United Kingdom, and the other was to educate public opinion, both in general and in the particular communities in which West Indians lived. With regard to the second part of the problem, it was unfortunate that there was no system of local broadcasting, because this could prove an excellent way of reaching the communities, and discussing their day-to-day problems. Therefore, the BBC had to depend on existing regional and national radio and television series with support from the External Services. Management stated, however, that the BBC would avoid 'excessive condemnation of what West Indians did in the United Kingdom, and would not be condescending', while the 'guiding aim would be to put the other side of the picture when dealing with subjects concerning West Indian immigrants'[36]. While Greene stated that the primary concern of BBC management was to improve relationships between British people and West Indians, participants were reminded that there were differences that the 'mass of people were not capable of accepting'.[37]

Within the proceedings, attendees also had the opportunities to express concerns over the BBC's plans for future race-related programming. Among the many suggestions made by the attendees, one related to 'more documentaries to give the other side of the West Indian situation', and suggested that 'programmes giving the historical background of the link between Britain and the West Indies would be useful'. Educational programming by television and radio was urged to focus upon educating the *British* public in accepting West Indians as *citizens*, not just *educating* West Indians to be citizens. Cited by R.E.K. Philips was a BBC programme about life in Jamaica, *A Little Bit of Madness* (1965, in conjunction with the Jamaican Broadcasting Company), which showed a very small aspect of life in the islands, yet helped to 'spread the idea that every black man in the street was uncivilized' and practised 'lower ethical standards'. BBC news reports that stressed 'areas of conflict' were criticised by Mrs Jeffery of the Kensington bureau, as were stories that highlighted racism against West Indians.[38] Jeffery felt that these reports often excited 'the lunatic fringe', and stated that the focus of these reports should be to 'damp down such issues' instead of 'bringing attention to them'.[39] When the press gave undue attention to these events, it was felt that the BBC should help to counterbalance such reports by stressing 'cooperation between groups' facing common problems, such as 'run-down areas in British cities'.

A highly important issue raised by Leeds University lecturer E.D. Butterworth was the continued onus on the BBC to educate the populace about subsequent race misunderstandings. He stated that, on the question of prejudice, it was wrong to assume that people would automatically reach the right conclusions if they were presented with the facts about the constructs of race. He reminded Greene and other attendees that there was a 'need both for education of the leaders of the community, the intellectuals', and the general public as to the reasons for the 'British attitude to race'. As evidence of this, Butterworth discussed a recent study, published by UNESCO (the United Nations Educational, Scientific, and Cultural Organization), about the 'unimportance of biological differences'. He explained that the 'BBC should be concerned not just with affecting public opinion at the present, but with affecting potential public opinion in the future'.

There were also numerous suggestions from every attendee as to how the BBC could develop its role in educating audiences of all ages, with more programming that demonstrated positive aspects of integration and follow-up sessions. The meeting concluded that the West Indian issues and opinions should be referred to within specified programming; the suggestion made by many attendees, however, was that the service should 'not be thinking in terms of special programmes addressed to West Indians, whether immigrants or people born and long settled in the United Kingdom', but programmes that took into account the fact that white and coloured people were living in a mixed community, and would be listening and watching these programmes together.[40] When asked, the West Indian participants felt that the conference was helpful, but that the events had not led to any specific commitments from the Corporation. Nevertheless, the representatives were highly concerned that, once again, 'BBC programmes in general should lean toward integration rather than emphasising racial differences'

– something the service had done throughout its history in its constructions of West Indian culture and ethnicity.

CONCLUSION

In this chapter I acknowledge BBC Television's approach to the highly sensitive issues of race, immigration and xenophobia. Through an examination of programming in the 1950s I have been able to consider briefly how the public service onus of the BBC provided an opportunity for producers and management to disrupt discourses of prejudice via their institutional practices, and I have researched the supporting documents that provide a history of these efforts. During the late 1940s images of the *Empire Windrush* transmitted by the BBC codified the West Indian as a post-war phenomenon, despite the presence of blacks in Britain since the fifteenth century. The service attempted nonetheless to provide a balanced representation of immigrant experience, while demonstrating a liberal social position within confines of racial relations. The Talks Department of BBC Television was engaged in a mission to analyse the question of racial origins for the benefit of its audiences, while scientific interpretations of race merely reinscribed aspects of difference. The BBC consulted organisations and individuals of colour in an attempt to tailor the proper kind of programming to help their cause. Though often misaligned, there was an effort to accept the responsibility of promoting racial assimilation, a task still considered highly difficult to this very day. What we deduce about the programmes offered by the service during the 1950s is made evident by documentation and programme files. Within news specials, the West Indians were framed in a sympathetic fashion that attempted to humanise the assimilation experience.

Within these programmes subjectivity was reinforced, however, as the service attempted to provide a social blueprint for racial relations between white British and black West Indian immigrants. While this research examines only part of the efforts of television management during the 1950s and up to 1965, a series of the special programmes that were aired could not explain racial inequality as purely a social structure without considering the origins, patterning and transformation of racial difference. This subjection was primarily ideological, as the racial identities of Britain's post-war audiences were reinscribed without the benefit of conscious inculcation. Therefore, racial formation and post-colonial difference continued to be social constructs, which subsequently became a way of comprehending and explaining these new citizens. During the period examined within this study, however, no written archival data reflected a desire by BBC management to provide programming that adequately explored the origins of xenophobia and white racism. Through the cultural authority of BBC television, West Indian immigration and the ensuing problems were visually encoded as 'actual', creating representations of immigrants not through transculturalism but by the authority of the BBC. The programmes that engaged with racial difference and assimilation provide an important, albeit limited, historical framework shaped by the public service obligation of the BBC. All the same, in the absence of input from West Indian immigrants on the required scale to provide more insight into what their needs were as audiences, many questions and potential answers were, and remain, muted. These immigrants, as settlers, needed further opportunities as agents of change to tell their own stories and develop multiple narratives of the Afro-Caribbean experience – particularly through the ostensibly liberal social framework of BBC Television.

9 Piecing together 'Mammon's Television'

A case study in historical television research

Jamie Medhurst

This chapter seeks to reconstruct a history of Welsh television that has been largely absent from broadcasting histories in the United Kingdom. Its focus is the short-lived – but crucially important in terms of Welsh cultural history – ITV company Wales (West and North) Television, or Teledu Cymru.[1] The chapter is based on the historical and archival research undertaken for the author's doctoral thesis (Medhurst, 2004a).

The 'piecing together' of the chapter title is a reflection on the process by which much historical television research is undertaken. As will be seen, in researching the origins, operation and eventual demise of Teledu Cymru, the task was akin to an archaeological dig. A picture of the company was 'pieced together' using a range of primary and secondary sources, including board of directors' minutes, personal diaries, private correspondence, newspapers and interviews with surviving company personnel. In this respect, Gill Branston's notion of television archaeology is apposite, and the archaeological metaphor can be adapted for consideration in television history. Branston argues that '[i]magery of archaeological excavation can be eloquent in evoking the fragility and difficulty, as well as the pleasure, of making argument and proof in historical enquiry' (1998: 51–52). In a similar vein, John Caughie, in comparing the primary visual material available to cinema and television historians, argues that, given the fact that so much early television material does not exist in recorded form, 'this makes the recovery of the early history of television form and style an archaeological, rather than a strictly historical, procedure' (1991: 25). Jason Jacobs also refers to the historical study of television as 'the study of loss' (2006b: 114), and Janet Thumim argues that work on television history inevitably focuses on what she calls 'the imaginative recall of a lost object' (2002: 1). These statements can be applied to the study of Teledu Cymru. Very little programme material remains from Teledu Cymru – a short film insert is all that has survived. Many programmes were broadcast 'live' and were therefore not recorded, and, although the company that took over from Teledu Cymru, Television Wales and the West (TWW), inherited the film material, this was disposed of when Harlech Television took over the Wales and West ITV franchise in 1967.

The reference to 'Mammon's Television' also merits explanation. In January 1962 a Welsh-language pamphlet entitled *Teledu Mamon* ('Mammon's Television') was published by Radical Publications of Carmarthen. Written by Aneirin Talfan Davies, Deputy Head of Programmes at the BBC in Cardiff, under the pseudonym of 'Sodlau Prysur', it was an attack not only on commercial television but on those key figures in Welsh public life who were associated with the Teledu Cymru venture (notably the Plaid Cymru (Welsh Nationalist Party) president, Gwynfor Evans, and Dr Haydn Williams, chairman of the board of the television company). It was an important and crucial intervention, and one that has hitherto received very little attention in Welsh historical writing. Opinion on the pamphlet in the historical work by Bernard Sendall (1982), John Davies (1994) and Evans (1997a, 1997b) places it as a relatively minor, momentary eruption of discontent within the Welsh political and cultural elites. This passes over much of real interest in the pamphlet, however, appearing, as it did, in the middle of a major governmental review of British broadcasting, the Pilkington Committee, and nine months before Teledu Cymru was due to go on the air for the first time. I hope to remedy this in this chapter.

TELEVISION AND WELSH HISTORY

Despite the supposed centrality of the broadcasting media in the creation and maintenance of a national consciousness and identity in Wales,[2] the media are noticeable by their absence from Welsh historical writing. During the 30-year period from 1974 to 2004 not a single article on broadcasting was published in the main Welsh historical journal, the *Welsh History Review*. During the same period the social history journal *Llafur* published two articles on broadcasting history, the first as part of a special media history section in 1997 (Evans, 1997a) and the second in 2002 (Medhurst, 2002a). A survey of some of the main historical journals during these years – *Twentieth Century British History*, *Contemporary British History*, *History*, *The Historical Journal* and *Past and Present* – also yields nothing in terms of the history of broadcasting in Wales. In 1986 Geraint H. Jenkins edited the first of what was to become a landmark series in Welsh-language historiography, *Cof Cenedl* ('The Nation's Memory'), 'in part [his] riposte to the insidious effects of the "British history" mentality'. The aim of the series, according to Jenkins, was 'to cultivate a deeper and more intelligent sense of the nation's history among the Welsh-speaking public' (Jenkins, 2002b: 113). Essays on the broadcast media have been conspicuous by their absence, however, with only one such contribution featuring in the 21-volume series at the time of writing (Medhurst, 2003).

There is no *one* explanation for the absence of academic writing on broadcasting history in Wales. One explanation is offered by the media historian Hans Dahl, who argues that the contemporaneity of the broadcast media – dealing with 'the here and now' – results in a resistance to historical exploration (Dahl, 1994: 552). Another possible explanation is the historical centrality of the printed word to the support and maintenance of Welsh language and culture (Jones and Rees, 1988). As such, television could be considered the poor relation and not worthy of study in a scholarly or academic context. Another possible reason is the fact that television has been viewed by a number of key Welsh writers as posing a threat to the indigenous culture of Wales and has been sidelined accordingly in terms of its worthiness of study. Gwynfor Evans, in his 1964 book on the beliefs of a Welsh nationalist, *Rhagom i Ryddid* ('Onwards to Freedom'), stated clearly that television has had a more deleterious effect on the Welsh language than anything else, but at the same time he argued that the technology could be harnessed for the good of the language (Evans, 1964: 115). The poet D.H. Culpitt, writing in 1961, may have had his tongue planted firmly in his cheek, but his verse resonates with the feelings of many towards television at the time. The poem loses something in translation, but roughly translated it reads:

The Devil's forks can now be seen
On the corner of the chimneys of Hendre Fawr;
To the place of good words
Came rock 'n 'roll and cha-cha-cha...
Take Your Pick and Treble Chance
Came to the home of the neighbour of the manse...
And we hear talk of Perry Como
Amongst adverts for Tide and Omo.
To the hearth where once the song reigned
The devices of hell now reign,
And in the cottages of Wales
The one-eyed devil is now in place.
Judgement day is here! Friends come
To the retreats! O people flee!

(Culpitt, 1961)

Some 20 years later the playwright Emyr Humphreys argued that 'the television set has insinuated itself like a sinister visitor from an alien universe and sits in the corner of every household exerting its hypnotic rays and quietly changing the natures of the inmates even as they go about their daily business' (M.W. Thomas, 2002: 173). At the same time, however, Humphreys admitted that this statement was based on a 'general sense of unease' as opposed to hard evidence (173).[3] In summary, given the perceived centrality of the broadcast media to life in Wales, the general histories of Wales do not reflect this role. It is also true to say that, in the growing number of publications on broadcasting history, it is more often than not the case that Wales features as a 'side issue'.

In terms of historical work on the Welsh media, the pool is relatively small. Aled Jones' work on the press in Wales has been an invaluable contribution to Welsh historical scholarship (Jones, 1993), whilst John Davies' detailed and painstaking volume on the history of the BBC in Wales has been one of the major contributions to Welsh media historiography in recent years (Davies, 1994). More recent work includes a volume that provides a historical and contemporary account of the media in Wales (Barlow, Mitchell and O'Malley, 2005). The strength of the volume lies in its marriage of a narrative historical account with a theoretical approach to the media in Wales. Nonetheless, despite this growing body of work, very little exists on the history of commercial television in Wales. It is as though the BBC has 'stolen the limelight', which, it could be argued, reflects a general BBC-centric view of broadcasting in the United Kingdom as a whole. This is changing slowly, however, with increasing historical scholarship focusing on ITV in Britain (for example, Johnson and Turnock, 2005). The most detailed work on Welsh broadcasting to emerge in recent times has been that by Davies, *Broadcasting and the BBC in Wales*, in 1994. Davies clearly locates himself in the tradition that sees broadcasting (and television in particular) as being central to the creation of a national consciousness and identity. In this respect, he supports Aneirin Talfan Davies' argument that broadcasting in Wales needs to be seen as a 'battle for the nation's rights' (Talfan Davies, 1972), and Michelle Ryan's assertion that '[t]elevision in Wales has been defined as one of the key areas in the struggle for a national identity' (Ryan, 1986: 185).

TELEDU CYMRU

The purpose of my research was to provide, in light of the existing historiography, a fuller and more detailed account of the history of Teledu Cymru than had been written to date. It aimed to set the history of the company within a wider historical context and provide a critical account of the origins, nature and collapse of Teledu Cymru based on a broader range of primary, secondary and interview sources than had hitherto been the case. It also aimed to assess the strength of the explanation for the origins, conduct and demise of Teledu Cymru that exists in the historiography, and to evaluate the extent to which the dominant nationalist paradigm needed to be re-evaluated in light of the evidence studied. Before moving on to consider the 'piecing together' that took place in my own research, it is worth pausing to provide a brief history of the company itself.

The roots of the company can be traced back to the post-war period and, in particular, the 1950s, when calls for a Welsh television service increased as the perception grew that the mass media were a pervasive influence in society (this is discussed later in the chapter). These calls culminated in a 'National Television Conference', held in Cardiff in September 1959, at which over 80 organisations and local authorities supported the notion of a Welsh service, offered either by the BBC or the Independent Television Authority (ITA). The turning point, from the perspective of Teledu Cymru, came in August 1960, when the ITA announced that it was seeking a programme contractor for the west Wales region. Four consortia submitted applications, and the following year the contract was awarded to the Wales Television Association. The company had emerged from the two 'National Television Conferences', held in Cardiff in September 1959 and July 1961. The company began to broadcast to south-west Wales via the Preseli transmitter on 14 September 1962. Eventually, the Arfon transmitter in north-west Wales opened (in November 1962), followed by the Moel-y-Parc transmitter in the north-east of the country in February 1963. At the end of May 1963, however, the company ceased all locally originated programming and acted as a relay station only. The chief reasons for this were the poor take-up of the service by potential viewers and a dire financial situation; these are discussed later in the chapter. In January 1964 Teledu Cymru was taken over by the ITV company that had been operating in south Wales and the west of England, TWW.

The evidence relating to Teledu Cymru has shown that a number of factors worked to create a situation that was far from ideal in the operation of a commercial television company. The relationship between Nathan Hughes, the General Manager, and his staff and the board of directors was clearly difficult. This is apparent from reading the minutes of the board together with personal correspondence between board members. The main reasons for this were personality clashes and the often impetuous zeal of Hughes. The directors as a body were not faultless, however, in several ways. Their hands-on approach was seen as obstructive to the effective running of the company by a general manager who saw it as his role to manage on a day-to-day basis. The erratic attendance record of the directors at board meetings lays them open to accusations of not devoting their energies to the overall direction of the company. It could also be argued that the poor attendance suggests a low level of commitment on the part of some directors (see Appendix II for a list of directors). The board, which, arguably, should have been united, was marked by internal division. In addition, the nature of the leadership provided by Haydn Williams was a source of conflict within the board.

The problems of management in the company at board level and below were illustrated in the handling of financial issues. The financial situation of the company was weak from the start, due in part to disappointing advertising pre-bookings and the advertising recession that hit the commercial television sector in general in the early 1960s. The situation was not helped by an apparent lack of overall control or management of the finances and a lack of financial strategy. Whilst evidence has been difficult to come by, what material exists (for example, in the minutes of the board of directors) suggests that such control was inadequate. At the same time, external factors hampered the financial state of the company. Transmitters were late in coming into operation and the set count remained lower than expected. For example, in the west and north-west areas covered by the

Preseli and Arfon transmitters, only 83,000 of the anticipated 115,000 households changed sets to receive Teledu Cymru. The reluctance to adapt television sets and receivers resulted in a low income and, therefore, increasing losses on the part of the company.

Teledu Cymru reached the target for original programming set by the Postmaster General in January 1963 (ten hours of Welsh-language and English-language Welsh-interest programming produced by the company), and was a pioneer in its Welsh-language provision (particularly in the area of Welsh-language news and current affairs and sport). Maintaining this provision proved difficult, however, because of the deteriorating financial situation and the cuts that had to be made. The decision to provide quality programming to a small area in 'good evening hours' was a risky venture, and therefore the financial constraints under which programmes were made and scheduled affected quality and viewer take-up.

The lack of cooperation from the television relay companies was, in effect, the final nail in the coffin for Teledu Cymru. As commercial ventures themselves, the relay companies were focused on financial gain rather than cultural 'good'. In increasingly anglicised parts of Wales (such as the south-east and north-east) they clearly did not see any obligation to carry the programmes of the new company, given that TWW or Westward programmes were proving to be attractive to their customers. With insufficient resources, Teledu Cymru could not offer competitive programming that would have aroused enthusiasm in the relay companies. At the same time, the companies faced the problem that viewers were not enthusiastic about viewing Teledu Cymru. This is evidenced in a letter sent to the company's Chairman by Television Audience Measurement (TAM) Ltd in April 1963. The TAM survey for the north-east area discovered that 53 per cent of homes never watched Teledu Cymru programmes, and the letter refers to the 'depressingly bad news' for the ITV company. Teledu Cymru also faced the difficulty of having to break into a market already served by TWW and the BBC due to overlap areas: viewers in the Teledu Cymru area could already receive BBC programmes, and those in the south-west of the country could also see programmes from the south Wales and west of England ITV contractor, TWW. In addition, the signal from the ITA transmitter at Winter Hill, which had been transmitting Granada Television programmes to the north-west of England since 1956, reached homes as far away as Anglesey, in north-west Wales.

PREVIOUS WORK ON TELEDU CYMRU AND MY OWN RESEARCH

Those who have written on the history of broadcasting in Wales have tended to see the rise and fall of Teledu Cymru as being essentially a failed nationalist enterprise, and stress the role of nationalist (political and cultural) pressure groups in the formation and demise of the company. Alan Butt Philip (1975: 248–250), David Bevan (1984: 87) and Ifan Evans (1997b) all stress the nationalist pressure group influence on the project. Davies points to the failings of this form of nationalism to encompass south Wales (Davies, 1994: 230), whilst Dai Smith underlines the failings of the rural language-based model that excludes the industrial south-east (Smith, 1999: 44, 46). Bernard Sendall also accounts for the failure of Teledu Cymru in terms of the 'impetuous excess of zeal...common to men who are convinced of the rightness of their cause' (Sendall, 1983: 76).

These writers, therefore, articulate the foundation and failure of the company in terms of the nationalist politics of the period, but all, apart from Evans, fail to provide empirical support for their arguments. Furthermore, some of these writers relate the company's failure to a set of external difficulties over which Teledu Cymru had little or no control. These include transmitter difficulties (Davies, 1994: 228; Sendall, 1983: 80) and financial problems stemming from the sparsely populated area that the company served (Davies, 1992: 627; Butt Philip, 1975: 249–250). Although these conclusions are adequate, in the sense that they go some way to explain the reason for Teledu Cymru's demise, they are still based on insufficient coverage of all the available evidence.

My aim was to revisit the histories of Teledu Cymru and study the company in light of what had already been written about it. It became apparent that previous histories had not utilised the full range of sources available and had therefore failed to set the company in the wider UK broadcasting context. The three key factors that emerged from my own research were the importance of the prehistory of the company in explaining its eventual demise; the *Teledu Mamon* pamphlet, which merited only a cursory mention in previous histories; and the setting of the Teledu Cymru venture in the wider UK broadcasting context, particularly in the debates involving the Pilkington Committee, the Post Office and the ITA. Each of these will be discussed.

PREHISTORY

Previous studies did not attend to the prehistory of Teledu Cymru. This prehistory is rooted in the pressure group politics of the period after 1949 (at the time of the Beveridge Committee on broadcasting), particularly cultural pressure groups. The Teledu Cymru initiative stemmed from the widespread view that the media influenced cultural life, and as such needed to be harnessed to a nationalist agenda. The lack of consensus over what the agenda should be – public service, commercial, Welsh, English – led. to a situation by 1959 (the time of the first 'National Television Conference') in which there were no unified proposals coming from Wales. The advent of commercial television in Wales in 1956, together with the fact that the BBC's television coverage of Wales was only partial, provided a platform for political intervention. From 1956 onwards the level of activity amongst political and cultural pressure groups increased and the role of the ITA and the government became increasingly prominent.

At this point, the complexity of Welsh politics meshed with the changing nature of television in Wales and engaged with Westminster politics. Added to this was a BBC under increasing pressure from ITV and a growth in the institutional rivalry between the two broadcasters. The environment from which the Teledu Cymru initiative emerged was, therefore, one that fused Welsh politics with Westminster politics. Previous accounts have failed to pay regard to this complex interweaving of factors in their considerations of the origins of Teledu Cymru. This prehistory, therefore, provided an unstable context for the operation and progress of the company, and can be seen as an influential factor when assessing the reasons for its demise.

TELEDU MAMON

Previous accounts of Teledu Cymru also failed to note the importance of the 1962 pamphlet *Teledu Mamon*. *Teledu Mamon* appeared at a key point in the debate over the relationship between television, the Welsh language and culture in Wales, and the *timing* of the publication – during the government-established Pilkington Committee's review of broadcasting (1960–1962) and in the early phases of the Wales Television Association – is an issue that has been overlooked by previous histories. It is very important, as the pamphlet appeared at a time when there were widespread doubts among those interested in the subject about the project's viability, and the pamphlet is best understood in this climate of doubt about the project and of quite fierce divisions within Welsh elites over issues of principle and viability regarding the television company. Many, for example, questioned whether a Welsh television station funded by advertising revenue would ever be able to do justice to the Welsh language and culture given the inherent commercial pressures.

This forms the backdrop against which *Teledu Mamon* appeared. I have argued elsewhere that *Teledu Mamon* crystallises a complex set of interweaving debates that are prevalent in Welsh discourse at the time of its publication (Medhurst, 2004b). These issues revolve around religion, language, culture, commercialism, politics and the unity of Wales, and it is these that have been disregarded up until now. The nationalist perspective adopted by previous histories, therefore, is only partially useful in understanding the history of Teledu Cymru. Nationalist politics undoubtedly played a crucial role in the venture, but technical issues, Westminster politics and institutional rivalry all played major roles as well.

TELEDU CYMRU AND UK BROADCASTING

Although the Pilkington Committee formed a significant backdrop against which television developments between 1959 and 1963 were played out, it has not been considered in this way in the historical writing on commercial television in Wales. Sendall refers to the work of the committee (albeit in one sentence) and suggests that the Post Office was reluctant to make any decision that might prejudge the committee's report (Sendall, 1983: 72). Davies discusses Pilkington in the context of the BBC and places more emphasis on the recommendations than on the process itself in the context of ITV (Davies, 1994: 230–233).

As a result of Pilkington, for broadcasting the period was one of flux and relative instability; the fact that the government-appointed committee was deliberating meant that the Postmaster General was unable to make major policy decisions prior to June 1962 due to not wishing to pre-empt the results of the committee. At the same time, as Jeffrey Milland has argued, Pilkington was predisposed towards the public service model of broadcasting as embodied in the BBC (Milland, 2004). It castigated what it saw as the 'trivial' nature of commercial television and recommended the award of the third national channel to the BBC. This, then, could be seen as standing counter to the government's pro-commercial television stance. In the midst of this emerged Teledu Cymru – the timing could not have been worse, for the government, the BBC and the ITA were naturally working on a schedule dictated by the fact that the committee was in progress. It is this aspect of the political scene that has not been taken into consideration in historical accounts of Teledu Cymru.

CHALLENGES

The historian Asa Briggs, writing in 1980, outlined some of the major problems facing historians wishing to write on the history of broadcasting (Briggs, 1980). Amongst the problems was that of access to visual materials. In terms of written material, the vast quantities of paper produced in conjunction with a single programme can sometimes present the researcher with an immediate case of information overload. Accessing this kind of written documentation is, of course, much easier/comprehensively available in the case of the BBC than for any other British broadcasting company, as the Written Archives Centre in Caversham provides a well-catalogued central resource for the broadcasting historian. Yet accessing visual material can be difficult, if not impossible, in some instances. It was not until the development of recording that pictures emanating from this most ephemeral of all media could be captured and stored. Even then, the requirement to archive material broadcast was not made a statutory requirement (for the ITV companies, at least) until the 1981 Broadcasting Act. In some instances also, film (and later videotape) material was discarded or wiped either to make space or so that videotapes could be reused. Thus, a combination of technical capability and pragmatic management decisions has left the televisual heritage of the United Kingdom in a patchy condition, to say the least.

A key factor explaining the lack of televisual evidential material is the fact that the technology to record and preserve the programmes was in its infancy during the late 1950s and early 1960s. In a recent survey of programmes thought to have gone missing (presumed wiped) from British television archives, Dick Fiddy notes that 'the early technical difficulties associated with the recording of live television programmes and the later injudicious wiping and junking policies of the major British broadcasters has meant that hundreds of thousands of hours of precious television material is missing from the official UK television archives' (Fiddy, 2001: 3). Only 1 minute and 25 seconds of material exists from the days of Teledu Cymru, and what exists of TWW material is fragmented and consists mainly of film inserts that were used in live programmes.[4] There are a handful of complete programmes in the ITV Wales Archive from the days of TWW (1958–1968) but very little printed documentation remains, and ITV Wales have only the 'Programme as Broadcast' (PasB) material.[5] Likewise, Granada Television has only one almost complete programme of *Dewch i Mewn*, which ran from 1956 to 1962, although there exists in the Granada programme archive a considerable amount of paperwork related to the series. The programme is important in that it was the first Welsh-language programme to be broadcast on ITV and was transmitted three times a week between 4.20 p.m. and 5.00 p.m. As it was transmitted from the ITA's Winter Hill transmitter, it reached many of the Welsh-speaking parts of north Wales, even reaching as far west as Anglesey. The paperwork includes draft scripts, financial sheets noting payments to contributors, and studio plans. Having studied these, like Jason Jacobs in his work on pre-1955 television drama (Jacobs, 2000), I was able to construct an idea of the content and structure of the programme.

In the absence of programme material, I had to use programme journals to recreate a sense of the programming type: a full set of the *Teledu Cymru* programme listings journal is held at the National Library of Wales. The journal is a valuable historical source. Due to the absence of programme material and written programme documentation, it provides the only record of the company's output and the place of that output in the overall ITV schedule. The paper also reflects the duality of the company. For example, the cover of the first edition (16–22 September 1962) shows a picture of a scantily clad woman, Lisa Peake, star of the Sunday night drama 'The Sin Shifter' (part of the ABC *Armchair Theatre* series). Max Bygraves appears on the front cover of the 7–13 October edition, promoting his appearance on the *Sunday Night at the London Palladium* programme. The first 'Welsh' cover appeared in the 14–20 October edition and it promoted a Teledu Cymru feature programme on 'the problem of alcoholism in modern society'. So, despite the clear cultural mission of the company, the magazine reflects the fact that attracting a large audience to popular and populist programmes was still a commercial necessity.

As has been noted, one of the weaknesses in past work relating to Teledu Cymru has been the range of evidence upon which past histories have drawn. I engaged with a wide variety of sources of information that provided evidential material upon which I was able to base judgements. These included the ITA archives (now held at the British Film Institute) and the National Archives in London, the BBC's WAC in Caversham, the National Library of Wales in Aberystwyth, the Granada Television Archive, the ITV Wales Film Archive, board and committee minutes, personal correspondence, newspaper and journal articles, and interviews with former production and management staff, together with secondary source material such as articles, theses and books. In interrogating these sources, I worked systematically through the evidence, measuring its significance, studying (in the case of official minutes, for example) the nature of the discourse and looking for recurring themes in contemporary newspaper material. I set out to use the sources to create a comprehensive and coherent narrative of events on which to base my analysis.

In interrogating the sources, I was aware of their inherent biases. Board minutes are written for a specific purpose, and I was told by one interviewee not to believe what I read in them.[6] Personal diaries are another valuable, though equally biased, source of information. I was fortunate enough to be granted access to the diaries of T.I. Ellis, a prominent member of the Welsh establishment, secretary of Undeb Cymru Fydd and a member of the board of directors of Teledu Cymru. These proved to be an invaluable source, as they often gave a personal insight into the wider picture. Whereas a minute might give an impression of satisfaction, a diary entry can often throw a very different light on matters. On more than one occasion Ellis would note that a meeting of the directors had not gone smoothly or that things were a mess; this was not reflected in the official minutes. Diaries can therefore provide context and depth to a sanitised board minute. They can even tell a completely different story. Ellis was a member of the company's Programme Committee, and to read the minutes of that committee for 10 May 1962 (four months before the company went on-air) one would assume that all was well. An entry in Ellis's diary for that day, however, reads: 'A lot of talking – I do wonder at times whether or not we are making any progress.'[7] Likewise, on 30 July 1963 (at the height of the company's financial difficulties) the diary entry reads: 'I have been faithful to the cause throughout the months and I am beginning to tire of the whole situation by now.'[8] There is no hint whatsoever in the board minutes of Ellis's true feelings.

Interviews with producers and executives from the early days of ITV in Wales proved to be valuable, but they also highlight important historiographical issues. Care is needed when interviewing, but the information obtained can provide the rare insights sometimes needed.[9] The whole story of the Teledu Cymru failure (and the reasons for that failure) remains a sensitive issue to this day. In April 2003 I delivered a lecture to the Aberystwyth Old Students' Association annual reunion based on my research. Sitting in the audience was an ex-Aberystwyth student who also happened to be a former senior producer at the BBC *and* at Teledu Cymru. He came up to me at the end and, having congratulated me on the lecture and saying how much he had enjoyed it, turned away and added, 'Of course, you can't tell the true story because you weren't there, and I was...' Similarly, as time passes, the memory plays tricks. In August 2004 I interviewed Nathan Hughes, General Manager of Teledu Cymru. Hughes now lives in Texas but was visiting the National Eisteddfod of Wales then. His account of his time at the company was fascinating, but when pressed on certain matters (e.g. things that had been said at programme committees) he either denied all knowledge or provided a different version of events from that recorded in the public domain.

CONCLUSION

My research – based as it was on a wider range of sources than had hitherto been consulted – demonstrated the need to view the history of Teledu Cymru from a wider perspective than previous histories had done. E.H. Carr has argued that history is 'a continuous process of interaction between the historian and his facts, an unending dialogue between the present and the past' (Carr, 1990: 30). Like Sean Street, I see myself as having been in constant dialogue with the past (Street, 2006: 31–32). At the same time, I was aware of Janet Thumim's description of the historical endeavour: 'The historian's task is to dis-cover, to unearth, sufficient material to allow the object of study to begin to speak for itself so that the historian may begin to form an idea not too determined by his or her own preconceptions' (Thumim, 1998: 91–92).

The historian must critically evaluate all types of evidence available on a particular topic and order them into some sort of semblance without colouring the outcome with preconceived ideas. I began the research with a relatively clear idea of what I would *like* to have discovered – that a united Wales fell in line with the call from a leading group of prominent Welsh entrepreneurs and supported the Teledu Cymru venture. I also expected (or wanted) to lay the blame for the demise of the company at the feet of the ITA for its lack of support of the venture. During the course of the research, however, I had to re-evaluate these ideas and preconceived notions in the face of what I discovered and unearthed from the evidence. As Richard Evans has stated, 'The first pre-requisite of the serious historical researcher must be the ability to jettison dearly-held interpretations in the face of the recalcitrance of the evidence' (R.J. Evans, 1997: 120).

Thumim has argued that the historical endeavour 'is a task fraught with difficulties, perhaps an impossible task, but nevertheless one worth attempting' (Thumim, 1998: 92). Having spent seven years researching the history of an overlooked, yet landmark, episode in broadcasting history, I, for one, would certainly agree.

APPENDIX I: KEY DATES

24 June 1949	First meeting of Broadcasting Committee (Beveridge).
18 January 1951	Beveridge Report published.
15 May 1952	Government White Paper on broadcasting establishes the ground for the introduction of a commercially funded television service.
15 August 1952	BBC Television begins in Wales with the opening of the Wenvoe transmitter in Glamorgan.
13 November 1953	Second government White Paper proposes establishment of commercial television service.
30 July 1954	Television Act (introducing commercial television to the United Kingdom) receives Royal Assent.
22 September 1955	Independent Television begins in London.
26 October 1956	TWW awarded the contract for the ITA south Wales and west of England region.
September 1957	Granada television launches its Welsh-language programme *Dewch i Mewn*.
14 January 1958	TWW begins transmissions from the St Hilary transmitter in Glamorgan.
19 November 1958	University of Wales Television Committee meets for the first time.
18 September 1959	First 'National Television Conference' held in Cardiff.
13 November 1959	First meeting of the 'National Television Conference' Continuation Committee.
13 July 1960	Government announces its intention of establishing a Committee of Enquiry into broadcasting in the United Kingdom (Pilkington Committee).
4 August 1960	Sir Robert Fraser, visiting the National Eisteddfod in Cardiff, announces that the ITA will be establishing an ITV company in the west Wales area.
12 September 1960	Meeting of potential sponsors (which eventually transformed into the Wales Television Association) to discuss putting forward a bid for the west Wales ITV contract.
7 April 1961	ITA invites applications for the west and north Wales contract area.
15 May 1961	Wales Television Association submits an application to the ITA.
30 May 1961	Interviews for the west Wales licence held in Cardiff; four groups interviewed: Television Wales Norwest, Wales Television Association, Cambrian (North and West Wales) Television, Cambrian Television.

6 June 1961	Licence awarded to the Wales Television Association.
20 June 1961	Wales Television Association learns that Postmaster General has given permission for a transmitter to be built in north-east Wales at Moel-y-Parc.
7 July 1961	Second 'National Television Conference' held in Cardiff.
1 August 1961	Postmaster General writes to the BBC to inform them that Channel 13 would be allocated to the ITA in north-east Wales, thereby hampering the BBC's six-transmitter plan for Wales.
1 September 1961	Teledu Cymru registered as a private company.
January 1962	*Teledu Mamon* published by Radical Publications of Carmarthen.
5 June 1962	Pilkington Report published.
14 September 1962	Teledu Cymru broadcasts for the first time, from the Preseli transmitter.
11 November 1962	Teledu Cymru broadcasts for the first time from the Arfon transmitter.
28 January 1963	Teledu Cymru broadcasts for the first time from the Moel-y-Parc transmitter.
17 May 1963	Teledu Cymru board of directors meet in Shrewsbury and decide to end all originated programming as a result of the financial crisis. As a result, Haydn Williams resigns as Chairman of the board.
27 January 1964	Teledu Cymru is officially taken over by TWW.

APPENDIX II: TELEDU CYMRU BOARD OF DIRECTORS

Hon. Islwyn Davies
S. Kenneth Davies
T.I. Ellis
Gwynfor Evans
Lady Olwen Carey Evans
Moses Griffith
Alderman Llewelyn Heycock
Tom Jones
Sir David Hughes Parry
Dr Thomas Parry
Sir T.H. Parry-Williams
Emrys Roberts
Eric Thomas
Colonel Cennydd Traherne (Vice-Chairman)

Sir Miles Thomas
William Thomas
David Tudor
David Vaughan
Dr B. Haydn Williams (Chairman)
P.O. Williams
Colonel J.F. Williams-Wynne

10 History on television

Charisma, narrative and knowledge[1]

Erin Bell and Ann Gray

The recent explosion of history programming across a number of television networks and channels prompts us to ask how we get the history television that we do. To answer this we address the contexts of production and attempt to relate these to different kinds of history programming on television. Production studies are rather thin on the ground in television scholarship, but our research first looks at the role that academic historians play in programme ideas and execution. Arguably, they can be seen as the originators of work that develops historical knowledge, some of which is considered suitable for development into television programming. Very little is known about the processes whereby an expert body of knowledge is mediated, shaped and transformed through television for mass audiences. In the case of history and representations of the past, this raises pressing and pertinent questions as narratives about national and other pasts are constructed, distributed and marketed through television. It further raises the question of how TV history programmes fit into the broader history of television, especially when, as we shall consider, several early TV historians actively campaigned for independent television as part of their role as public intellectuals.

Our research will, we hope, provide a history of history programming on television, using an innovative method that uses interviews to unpick discourses of production within a particular genre. The first phase of our interdisciplinary research project involves a pilot study, which seeks the opinions and experiences of academic historians involved in TV history programmes. Between October 2004 and October 2005 we carried out open-ended interviews with a sample group of nine historians, of around two hours' duration each. We further plan to interview more historians, and have also begun interviewing TV producers. By using this qualitative and exploratory method, we are seeking to elucidate the ways in which scholars working on different aspects of TV history account for and interpret their various experiences. Stuart Davies and Crispin Paine have done similar research with museum professionals; in both projects, attitudes and ideas about popular representations of the past have been garnered through interviews from 'insiders'. As Davies and Paine comment, 'Professions are knowledge-based occupations and so it is legitimate to examine what knowledge they have, how they use it and what are their professional preoccupations' (Davies and Paine, 2004: 55).

Nevertheless, there are, obviously, further methodological issues relating to how the 'producers' of television, both TV executives and other professionals such as historians, remember – or misremember – the history of the programmes they worked on. Their accounts are significant, though, and highlight both the benefits and pitfalls of using this research method for those interested in the ways in which the history of television itself is written and researched. For example, although the historians interviewed are experts in their specific fields, this did not, in most cases, include the history of television, and so analysis of their understanding and description of the wider processes in which they have been engaged must bear this in mind. By considering what these 'outsiders' perceive to be going on, however, we receive additional insights into TV history and history on TV; some, for example, were active in other areas of what might be described as 'public history', such as museology, and brought this to their understanding of the making of history programming.

All the historians interviewed have been involved in TV history at a variety of levels. Usually they have advised researchers over the telephone, and have also appeared as 'talking heads' in the same or another programme. They have all been involved in at least two programmes. Seven are male, which, coincidentally, is a reflection of the gender imbalance amongst university historians in the United Kingdom, where we estimate only around a quarter are women.[2] Our respondents were aged between 30 and 60, and most worked at northern English universities, two of which were 'new' universities. We have been careful to safeguard the anonymity and confidentiality of our interviewees, and to ensure this we have removed references to programmes that might allow them to be identified. Although this may limit the extent to which we can make explicit statements about programmes, and the ways in which different TV channels and production companies approach making history programmes and work with professional historians, we believe that we have still succeeded in identifying themes in history TV programming, whereas a narrow focus on historians' accounts of specific programmes might have proved misleading. For the purposes of this chapter we have focused on two recurring themes from the interview material, which shed some light on the operations of television history. These are the interviewees' own representation on camera as historians and their views on the style and modes of address of TV historian presenters. This material is analysed with reference to notions of charismatic television personalities and dominant narrative structures, and suggests that these modes of address and televisual forms offer the viewer particular relationships to knowledge and ways of knowing.

Much of the debate about television history since the 1970s (Kuehl, 1976/2005; Watt, 1976; MacArthur, 1980) has remained couched in terms of the medium's inability to do 'proper' history. A more recent edited collection that does attempt to present work that goes beyond debates over 'good' and 'bad' TV histories is *The Historian, Television and Television History* (Roberts and Taylor, 2001), which Graham Roberts describes as part of a 'multi-disciplinary historical study of television' (Roberts, 2001: 2). Several of the chapters are still concerned, however, with what makes 'proper' history on TV. These include James Chapman's consideration of 'what makes *The World at War* "good television" and "good history"' (Chapman, 2001: 127) and Ian Bremner's insider account of *A History of Britain* (Bremner, 2001). Our interdisciplinary research, however, aims to go beyond this, considering, as several of our interviewees did, the role of television in producing and disseminating knowledge about the past.

Some historians and media professionals view television's primary role as that of entertainment, and consequently the pressures to produce watchable television, often within limited budgets, that will attract a reasonably sized audience mitigate against the kind of history programming of which many historians would approve. For example, one of our interviewees, having highlighted factual errors in several programmes and voiced his disillusionment with programme makers, said:

> I wish that I could speak to a public audience and make them understand these things, but…where production companies are chasing money…they're not going to be willing to take the risk in doing things in a more sophisticated and complicated way. Instead we're going to get Simon Schama, standing up reciting his A level notes. (Interview B)

This interviewee described what he saw as the thwarted attempts of university historians to educate an audience through TV history. In contrast to these attempts, media professionals appear to favour strong presenter-historians, whom he sees as conduits for over-simplified narrative accounts of the past.

As this suggests, the professional norms of television producers have led to certain types of history programming being made that rely upon key elements including on-camera presenters, linear narrative and accessible visual material. Again, this suggests that the medium itself imposes limitations on how and what kinds of history reach the screen. An increasing number of historians do recognise the value of this form of public communication in disseminating historical knowledge, however, and are embracing the medium in its own terms. Predictably, one such champion is Simon Schama, historian and presenter of *A History of Britain*, the 15-episode series broadcast in three parts from 2000 to 2002 by the BBC, who draws attention to TV history as a potentially more imaginative medium than printed history, and infers, by drawing on the popular nineteenth-century Whig historian Thomas Macauley,[3] that it is of equal value:

> If it has the courage of its own convictions, and reinvents its own way of visiting the past, not just struggling to translate the issues of printed history…, then it has a fighting chance…of making a history which is not only 'received by the reason but burned into the imagination'. (Schama, 2004: 33)

The historian Justin Champion also speaks of the potential that television holds for history: 'It can take you to the familiar spot of land, into the castles and cathedrals, through the country houses and fields, into the bedrooms and private places... Portraits, tapestries, skulls, coins, statues, all speak of the dead who once were' (Champion, 2003: 153). Another TV presenter historian, Tristram Hunt, criticises those of his fellow historians who are 'often willing to celebrate the lost customs of oral history and traditions of storytelling [but] are unwilling to accept a modern variant... [O]ur society is telling stories about ourselves to ourselves – a concept which is perhaps more easily understandable to sociologists and anthropologists than historians' (Hunt, 2004: 90). One of our older interviewees reflected upon the potential of contemporary television to fulfil his desire earlier in his career to be involved in history outside the academy, saying that he

> [a]lways had a sense as a young academic that I would like to make a general impact...but I always thought of that in terms of books, a pretty old fashioned traditional outlook... [T]he media itself has changed so that you're able to reach a much broader audience, even if it's only a small TV audience. (Interview A)

Taking our cue from this recently re-energised debate, arguably inspired by the expansion of history programming, our research is an attempt to go beyond notions of 'good' or 'bad' television history. We hope that this research may, to paraphrase John Corner, make 'valuable progress towards a more comprehensive sense of what television's role in the circulation of contemporary knowledge, "bad" or "good", really is' (Corner, 1999: 115).

PRESENTING HISTORY

Simon Schama, in a recent article, refers to A.J.P. Taylor as the 'grand-daddy of all television historians' (Schama, 2004: 24). Indeed, Taylor has become the archetypal presenter-historian. In the inaugural BBC History Lecture,[4] Schama links Taylor's style to history as a kind of civic oration, akin to the Greek performative art of storytelling. Jeremy Isaacs, producer of Thames Television's *World at War* and former Controller of Channel Four, describes how Taylor 'stood alone in the studio and talked to camera. Without a prop or a note, without a hesitation or a syllable out of place, Taylor gave a dazzling demonstration of his lecture technique...just the historian, epigrammatic, provoking, compelling' (Isaacs, 2004: 37). Indeed, at the time Taylor was noted as 'the only lecturer to face the cameras for half an hour without visual aids.' (Taylor, 1967 [1963]: 1) One of our respondents echoed these views: 'A.J.P. Taylor...was standing up there, and telling you his view, he wasn't encouraging you to debate it, just he was requiring a bit more brainpower to follow what he was saying, because there were no...maps and cameras floating around in the background' (Interview B). Ian Kershaw goes further by confirming Taylor's legacy to contemporary television history: 'The Schamas, Starkeys and Fergusons follow in Taylor's footsteps and have inherited the mantle of those who believed long ago that the historian's job was to use their skills and knowledge to bring big and important historical themes to the attention of a mass audience' (Kershaw, 2004: 120).

What has been systematically eradicated from these memories of Taylor's programmes is the content. Through his pedagogic style he challenged his audience and encouraged them to think by basing his narratives on questions such as 'How do wars begin?' (*How Wars Begin*: BBC, 1977). In addition, his lecturing style was, surprisingly, perhaps, given the era and his status, not at all patronising. Compare this to episode 8 of A *History of Britain*, 'The British wars', in which 'Schama tells of the brutal war that tore the country in half',[5] acting as a conduit for historical truth. Although Jerry Kuehl has reminded historians that TV audiences do not consist of undergraduates (Kuehl, 1976/2005: 180–181), some of Taylor's lectures were initially given before the university, before being 'a little shortened in the third programme of the BBC… The text represents what I said a little more coherently; but still as lectures' (Taylor 1969 [1957]: 9). Indeed, the BBC producer John Irwin had originally suggested that Taylor present some of his Oxford University lectures to a wider television audience.

Furthermore, and unlike most historian-presenters in the late 1990s and early twenty-first century, Taylor was openly critical of the BBC and championed the cause for independent television, becoming vice-president of the Popular Television Association in the mid-1950s, a body campaigning for the introduction of commercial television.[6] Having recorded several series for both ITV and BBC from 1957 onwards, this criticism led in part to a nine-year hiatus, ending in the mid-1970s, when producer Edward Mirzoeff invited Taylor to return to the BBC. Upon his return Taylor's work included *How Wars Begin* (1977), and its companion, and Taylor's final, series was *How Wars End* (Channel 4, 1985). Thus, the memory of the style has overshadowed the content of Taylor's series, and his actions outside the TV studio, for both media professionals and historians. In the cases of both Taylor and Kenneth Clark, the history of TV historians has been largely obscured; unsurprisingly, when TV executives provide accounts of the earliest era of TV history, they underplay such issues, and in doing so they limit the possibility for comparison with more recent presenter-historians such as Schama, who have also become involved with broader issues, such as school history lessons (BBC News, 2002).

A much more paternalistic style was adopted by Kenneth Clark, who Ian Kershaw leaves out of his list of 'mantle bearers'. Clark was an important and significant presenter-historian, whose series *Civilisation* was also a groundbreaking programme. Subtitled A *Personal View by Lord Clark*, the series was transmitted between February and May 1969 on BBC2. Clark was invited by David Attenborough, then Controller of the fledgling channel, to front this innovative 13-part series,[7] the first of its kind in colour. Clark had been a successful director of the National Gallery during the war, had written scholarly books on art and, importantly, was interested in television. Indeed, a decade after Taylor, Clark supported independent television and was the first Chair of the Independent Television Authority, and he had also made programmes for ITV. Although Clark is clearly addressing the audience through his pieces to camera, his tone is one of patronising elitism, epitomised in his introduction to the first programme, in which he asks 'But what is civilisation?'. He answers his own question with 'I can't define it in abstract terms (*pause*) yet. But I think I can recognise it when I see it.' *Civilisation* ran over budget, causing Attenborough to schedule it twice in the week, halving the per hour costs. It was, with the minority of colour television set owners, a huge success. People held *Civilisation* parties, inviting less fortunate friends to view the programme. Attenborough was keen to sell it to US television but the networks were not interested at the time. Clark, no doubt using his contacts in the art world, arranged screenings in the National Gallery of Art in Washington, DC, and attracted large audiences.

Many series bear the adjective 'landmark' but, arguably, *Civilisation* is one that earns this description. Executives at the BBC immediately grasped the potential for this new genre of 12- or 13-part authored documentary, for which they coined the term 'sledge-hammers' (Attenborough, 2002: 214). Aubrey Singer, the then Head of the Science Department, commissioned *The Ascent of Man* with Dr Jacob Bronowski, filmed in 1971 and 1972 and broadcast by the BBC in 1973, and others followed: Alastair Cooke on the American Bicentennial; J.K. Galbraith on economics. Attenborough himself resigned from his post as Controller of BBC1 and BBC2 in 1973 in order to make the natural history series *Life on Earth* (BBC, 1978). Clearly, then, the author-presenter is a figure central to this genre of programming, and one that has, arguably, been resurrected in recent years in history television. Significantly, *A History of Britain* was originally intended to consist of 'worthy interviews intercut with location filming', but BBC1 Controller Michael Jackson's move to Chief Executive of Channel Four meant that 'modern protocol demanded' a presenter, and in 1997 Schama was offered the role (Bremner, 2001: 64, 70). Furthermore, Janice Hadlow, at a recent conference,[8] spoke of the desirable characteristics of presenters – or, as she put it, 'essayists of the TV world' – as being the ability to entertain and engage, to demonstrate a certain element of showmanship and, above all, 'charisma for the camera'. This represents a move away from the explicitly paternalistic Clark and the 'charismatic academic' Taylor, towards more charismatic presenter-historians who do not lecture the audience even though they do address the viewers, and of whom some are arguably paternalistic, albeit by more subtle means.

Drawing on Richard Sennett's (1992) discussion of modern charisma, Espen Ytreberg suggests that 'the broadcasting "personality" exudes a personal charm that functions to soothe and reassure the audience' (Ytreberg, 2002: 765). Ytreberg is talking mainly about hosts of talk shows, but he notes that this kind of self-presentation is central to contemporary broadcasting across entertainment and popular fiction, as well as in the genres of popular journalism. 'The audience is invited to believe in what the charismatic says because the charismatic communicates his or her personal belief in it so intensely' (Ytreberg, 2002: 765). The 'new generation' of historians and their styles of presentation can be collectively described in this way. Indeed, Michael Wood was described by the *Sunday Express* as 'the Indiana Jones of factual television',[9] whilst Schama is 'the keeper of British history' and 'the man who made history sexy' (Billen, 2003).

The issue of presentation is also key to the analysis of authority in TV history, and to some extent the interviewees identified this. The historians commented on their physical representation on camera, one saying that 'television is actually a very intimate medium, because people see you often quite close up, and you're dropping into their front room…you need…to be dressed casually I think, because otherwise it comes over as very formal…' (Interview C). Another described 'such a close-in shot on my head, that I couldn't actually physically move around outside of the box the lens had created', which, he felt, 'loses about half of what I do when I lecture, because I'm not mobile, and I don't feel that I can put as much energy and dynamic into it' (Interview B).

It is difficult for a professional historian to maintain physical authority on the screen unless he or she is allowed to do so by the producers; visual representation is crucial in this respect. Jeanie Attie's review of Ken Burns' *The Civil War* (PBS, 1990) similarly refers to the limitations placed upon the historian Barbara Fields, who appears as a talking head, with footage of her 'carefully spliced, at times cutting her off in mid-thought', meaning that she appears 'neither physically comfortable nor intellectually buttressed by the wisdom contained in books' – unlike another (male, non-historian) commentator (Attie, 1992: 98). It should come as no surprise, then, that presenter-historian-led productions, which rely on the charisma of the individual Schama or Starkey, create that same charisma by allowing the presenter to roam freely in front of the camera, rather than the far more common situation in which restrictions are imposed on historians.

Charismatic presenters do not arrive ready formed but their television persona often develops and builds over time. Schama's early five-part series *Landscape and Memory* (BBC, 1995) provides us with evidence of the historian-presenter who has yet to develop the confident style of the charismatic television personality. Clearly, this is due in part to the programme's limited budget and consequent low production values. *Landscape and Memory* modestly combined film with the presenter speaking only from a studio set. His style and mode of presentation is formal and static. He wears a suit, although not a tie, and relies totally on his close-up speeches to camera to engage and persuade the audience.

Schama was persuaded to take on *A History of Britain* (2000–2002) by Janice Hadlow, and in that series his presenter style has been developed. He is less formal, the higher budget affords much location filming, and he is constantly striding into shot, speaking from historic sites, thereby enhancing his authority and presenter power. Quite clearly, he has undergone something of a 'makeover', in that he is now beardless, has been through a series of distinctively styled spectacles to contact lenses and seems to have benefited from some dentistry. The series was heavily hyped within the BBC's 'History 2000' project and marketed with a special issue of the *Radio Times* devoted to *A History of Britain*. It was presented as 'landmark' television but sold around the 'personality' historian. The May 2001 cover of the BBC's *History Magazine*, launched in 2000 as another part of the 'History 2000' project, carried a photograph of Schama with the caption 'The History Man'. With this cover appearance, Schama becomes not only a fully fledged charismatic presenter but, what is more important, a brand. Ian Bremner has stated that the series was 'supposed to be a worthy successor to those classic series, *Civilisation* and *The Ascent of Man*' (Bremner, 2001: 64). Bremner further remarks that, in contrast to *A History of Britain*, such series 'underwhelm' the modern viewer (Bremner, 2001: 64), but in the wake of the success of Schama's series they have been repackaged as DVDs and relaunched by the BBC.

Whilst Ytreberg's arguments about the dominance of charisma in broadcasting are useful, they are insufficient for a detailed analysis of the author-presenters of history programming. Although they demonstrate on-screen presence and use their personal style to persuade and captivate, there is a further aspect to their appeal: the nature of their address. They are presented as knowledgeable, they are experts and, above all, they are intellectuals. They speak with eloquent fluency, with enthusiasm and with the certainty that their access to a fund of knowledge affords. Their performances are powerful, in visual and literary terms alike. Add to this beautifully shot and composed images, and we have beguiling television. This power to beguile is afforded to the charismatic author-presenters and is a key component of their authority and legitimacy.

It could be argued that the notion of 'charisma' is more comfortably applied to the white male presenter, and this is certainly true of the new generation of historians. Interestingly, few of the male historians interviewed identified this as a 'problem area' in TV history, which may suggest the essentialising of white male experience here, as in other aspects of life (Gray, 1997b: 98). A female respondent referred to the comment of one TV executive in the early 1990s, however, when responding to the idea of having a female presenter-historian: 'No one wants to be lectured at by a woman' (Interview J). Indeed, the same interviewee asserted that 'there is still a deeply seated, innate sexism within the television industry, and within the commentators on the television industry, and that must have a knock on... [T]here are a couple of women in *Coast* (BBC, 2005), for instance, who are female historians, so I hope it will change' (Interview J).

The use of male voices in most series perpetuates 'a culturally constructed assumption that it is men who speak of the actual world and that they can do so in an authoritative manner' (Nichols, 2001: 55). Bettany Hughes, who authored and presented *The Spartans*, a Lion Television series, first screened in 2002 on Channel Four, is one of the few female historian-presenters, but her persona is depicted and marketed in terms of youth, glamour, travel and tourism. Presumably, she is not considered to be sufficiently authoritative to carry 'grand narrative' landmark history programming, such as *A History of Britain*, which Schama orders his audience to view as 'an adventure in self-recognition'.[10] Whilst gender clearly is an issue here, Bettany Hughes, like her male genre counterpart Michael Wood, does not have a university affiliation, and therefore the legitimacy afforded to certain types of TV history programming by academia. She has recently been unfavourably contrasted with Simon Schama and incorrectly described as having 'no academic claims' to legitimise her TV work, which undoubtedly stems from her representation on TV as a glamorous traveller. Indeed, the archaeologist Angela Piccini has criticised Hughes' *Seven Ages of Britain* (Channel 4, 2003) for 'feminising' the past: 'It is veiled and mysterious, but might be available to us with the right chat-up line' (Piccini, 2004). Such comments echo those of the historian Peter Novick a decade earlier, when he conflated 'the language of bad history' with 'the language of women' and was denounced by feminist scholars (cited in Smith, 1996: 567). In a similar way to Hughes, Wood's persona is presented as that of the explorer and adventurer, encapsulated in the description on the DVD of his series *In Search of Myths and Heroes* (Maya Vision International, BBC, 2005) as 'an epic travelogue, a historical adventure and an exploration of some of humanity's most enduring myths'. In both cases the subject matter, period and geographical locations covered by their programmes can be seen as peripheral to current debates, which seek to link TV history to contemporary British identity.

The marketing of author-presenters is, plainly, critical to the construction of their public persona, and the different ways in which they are publicised underlines their claims to authority and the direct relevance of their narratives to contemporary Britain. The authority created for historians such as Simon Schama via the media is refuted by many of their peers, however. For example, Schama's lack of expertise in the areas covered by *A History of Britain* was criticised by our interviewees, as were any programmes fronted by a historian who did not have the relevant specialism. One described such a presenter as not having sufficient 'stature to carry it off…he is not known for his expertise' (Interview F).

TELLING HISTORY

Clearly, the author-presenters of TV history are central to the success of history programming not only in terms of ratings but also in their support for the programmes' claims to legitimacy and credibility. The presenters themselves, however, inhabit particular kinds of historical narrative. Issues relating to this were identified by some of our interviewees. In general, the presenter-historian's TV persona was seen as distracting, and, in the case of Simon Schama and David Starkey, was linked to narrative history. As an interviewee commented: 'I find it pompous, and slightly authoritarian, and it's not a style of history that I feel comfortable with…' (Interview D). He continued by referring to the link between form and content in presenter-led programmes: 'What is suggested by those programmes is that there's only one way of telling a story... So the format determines it but the content goes along with that, because usually the kinds of historians that appear...are highly opinionated...[a]nd that, you'd imagine, would write old-style narrative history anyway' (Interview D). Interestingly, this is a similar point to that made by John Corner when he suggests that presenter commentary is, 'literally, story*telling*' (Corner, 2003b: 99). This describes the single presenter leading the audience through his personal account of the past, as emphasised by, for example, Clark and Schama, but which, because of the weight of the programme and the lack of alternative viewpoints, appears to speak the 'truth'. One respondent made the related comment about her opinion of the gendered nature of knowledge, commenting that

> women are more ready to go 'This is what I think, and I'm going to tell you that this is what I think, because this is the evidence and therefore this is the conclusion I have drawn', and I do think, and it's horrific to make such a generalisation, but I do think that men are happier to go 'This is how it is', and it's not, it's what they think (Interview J).

If this is the case, and as most presenter-historians are men, much presenter-led TV history may follow this form. Initially it seemed feasible that the interviewees would support only programmes aiming at 'truth', given their criticism of basic factual errors. Dirk Eitzen suggests that his fellow historians evaluate documentaries 'according to how well they do what academic historians are supposed to do' (Eitzen, 1995), and that typical areas of criticism are factual inaccuracies and the type of questions posed and answered.

Nonetheless, many of the interviewees were aware, although they did not refer to them specifically, of ideas relating to the analysis of documentary, such as those offered by Bill Nichols. In his *Representing Reality* Nichols describes how the documentary's use of narrative and structure, using introductory dilemmas, building tension and then ending with closure, infers a privileged access to reality and moral authority, which he called the 'discourse of sobriety' (Nichols, 1991: 107–108). Although this would suggest that historians support the idea of the documentary as offering privileged access to reality, the parallel reliance in this particular form of historical programming upon narrative and moral authority, both carried by the author-presenter, was criticised. One interviewee commented on what he perceived as a return, in the decade following 1995 of TV history programming, to 'extraordinarily conventional storylines, whether it's particular monarchs, or histories of big global themes or histories of nations' (Interview G). The presenter-led linear narrative form also suggests that, for example, both documentaries and history can be finite narratives. Furthermore, this can stimulate discussion that is only about the subject and not its mode of representation. As Nichols has asserted, however, 'What films have to say...can never be separated from how they say it' (Nichols, 1991: xiii). The same interviewee similarly highlighted the need to consider 'strategies of proof and exemplification, and what is used to stand for what' (Interview G), and other interviewees were critical of these kinds of presenter-led, linear history programmes, for the same reason.

In contrast to this perceived growth in more conservative TV history, many interviewees called for the use of conflicting historical accounts, even within presenter-led series. One suggested that '[m]aybe there's a way you can have an argument that runs through, but have a diversity of voices that contribute to that, and might raise doubts' (Interview D). Indeed, the production team with which this interviewee had worked were determined that the narrated, oral-history-based programme they were producing in the early 2000s, which allowed such a variety of voices, should be 'not like David Starkey' (Interview D). Corner too, like the historian interviewed, has noted the potential for the use of 'little stories' of individuals to create tension between the narrative of the documentary and 'the imaginative possibilities to emerge from the case-studies selected to illustrate it' (Corner, 2003b: 99).

Unsurprisingly, then, most interviewees rejected series such as *A History of Britain*, and one historian saw TV history as missing an opportunity to give 'marginalised groups' a voice, when instead 'what you're actually doing is bringing in the good and the great, like Simon Schama, with lots of resources to tell a particular narrative history, that is actually his watered-down version of what the academics have come up with, but [the] potential is there for something rather more radical' (Interview C). Schama's frequent justification of presenter-led history is rebutted here and viewed as a symptom of lost opportunities in TV history programming.

WATCHING HISTORY

Clearly, the audience for television histories is a central aspect of understanding how notions of the past enter into the public domain, and the historians interviewed were also extremely interested in this. Such a response from professional educators is not surprising. They are keen for people to be more engaged by television history programming, as a route into a broader interest in, and critical appreciation of, the past. Studies of television audiences have tended to focus on popular genres, and we have found useful a body of work that is investigating how people gain knowledge about the past from a range of sources.

Those responsible for heritage attractions and museums are interested in how visitors 'may be rendered "mindful" so that they will be actively processing information and questioning what is going on' when visiting sites (Prentice, Guerin and McGugan, 1998: 5). Richard Prentice, Sinéad Guerin and Stuart McGugan draw on Gianna Moscardo's work, influenced by educational psychology, which proposes that in any given situation – for example, viewing television or visiting museums – people are either mindful or mindless.[11] Mindfulness involves the recognition that 'there is not a single optimal perspective, but many possible perspectives on the same situation', which means that information can be processed and, importantly, questioned (Moscardo, 1996: 381). It also empowers individuals, in that they display 'greater recall of, and learning from, interpretation' (Moscardo, 1996: 384). This does, of course, depend on other factors relating to the individuals involved. As one interviewee commented on his own experiences,

> Museum visitors…come with their own agenda, and they have their own reasons for visiting the museum…and they can be very resistant indeed to any 'message' or 'narrative' or line that the museum wants to project… [Further, the] programme maker is in a similar position to…the person who pulls together an exhibition…: they have a line that they want to project…but…then you also have to think…about the audience. (Interview C)

Mindlessness, in contrast, is a 'single-minded reliance on information without an active awareness of alternative perspectives' (Moscardo, 1996: 380). Familiar and repetitive situations, such as traditional museum displays, or perhaps certain kinds of TV history, may encourage this. Indeed, one interviewee commented that a large number of people had said "'I saw you on that programme, that was great, that subject's really interesting", but they can't actually remember what the argument was anyway' (Interview B). This could apply to familiar generic programme formats, or to frequently revisited topics. Thus, viewers, like museum visitors, may respond more positively to 'mindful' TV. This has the incidental effect of raising self-esteem (Moscardo, 1996: 382), one of the 'feel-good' factors associated with much TV programming. As Corner has asserted, 'The giving of pleasure is the primary imperative of most television production' (Corner, 1999: 93). Moreover, TV has 'extended the pleasures which gaining knowledge involves' (Corner, 1999: 96); Bill Nichols refers to this as 'epistephilia', pleasure in knowing (cited in Corner, 1999: 96).

TV has also popularised knowledge for mass audiences. Many specialist knowledges, as Anthony Giddens has identified, have been rearticulated as mass-mediated knowledge, and have been far more widely distributed (cited in Corner, 1999: 116). As Corner notes, however, some criticisms of TV history have complained about the ways that TV blurs 'different orders of knowledge', with 'little regard for the procedures of knowledge production and the protocols of evidence and argument' (Corner, 1999: 97). Furthermore, available knowledge may be restricted in a variety of ways: this *may* be a function of bureaucratic control, or a consequence of the commodification of TV (Corner, 1999: 109), but the outcome is often a reliance on tried and tested topics and modes of delivery.

DOING HISTORY

We conclude now by looking at two kinds of television history narrative, both within the 'tried and tested' author-presenter genre, and ask what versions of historiography they represent. In addition, we consider what kinds of viewing positions – 'mindful' or 'mindless' – are offered to the audience by the narrative structure and presenter style. This is not to say that we seek to define 'good' and 'bad' TV history, but that we consider which types of narrative and presenter style have more potential to allow space for 'mindful' engagement.

A History of Britain presents a fund of 'stories' about the past. Schama argues that history is *about* telling stories and that he wanted to get across his passion for history through this series. Thus he puts together and often juxtaposes stories about people and events, which present an overall narrative about 'who we are' and 'how we got here'. This linear narrative style is more likely to close the minds of viewers to any possible alternative view. It also refutes the notion that history is a process, in particular one of interpretation, provisionality and differing perspectives. Here we are given one perspective, albeit a self-confessed personal view, which through a range of visual and aural elements makes truth claims that are powerfully carried through the texts. How viewers engage with history programming is a key point here, and merits further research, but by looking at what spaces the texts offer for viewers to construct meaning we can see the potential, or lack of it, for their engagement.

By contrast, Michael Wood's *In Search of Myths and Heroes* adopts a different narrative structure, that of discovery and quest. In terms of television genres this programme draws on picturesque and spectacular images from 'far off lands' reminiscent of holiday and travel programmes. In adopting the narrative of the quest, however, he – and, by extension, the viewer – goes off in search of 'the truth', or the 'real' substance of mythology. This is an interesting example of author-presenter history programming, in that it actually problematises history, suggesting that, at the very least, history is open to interpretation and is subject to a process of examination of evidence and the assessment of different accounts. Furthermore, Wood, in addition to consulting experts and original texts, also asks people residing in the countries he visits about their everyday knowledge of myths and stories. In the programme, therefore, we have a multiplicity of voices and a variety of points of view, which invite the viewer to speculate and play with the ideas put forward. This may perhaps explain the positive opinion of Wood's work held by more than one interviewee (Interviews B and J). Instead of history as grand narrative, work such as Wood's may be seen as history as detective story, which shows in part, albeit in a variety of 'exotic' locations, the processes of historical research and the various possible interpretations of the same sources.

The authored narrative, then, is a particularly closed way of telling history. Schama, like Clark before him, is at great pains to insist that this is a subjective view and that it is **A** *History of Britain* and not **The** *History of Britain*. When asked by Mark Lawson[12] how he would respond to criticisms of his single white male authoritative voice throughout the series, echoed by one of the respondents, his answer was revealing. First of all he referred to history programmes in the United

States, examples of which included many voices, which represented different positions and points of view. He described this kind of programming as offering a 'salad of opinions'. This, he said, left the viewer thinking that they knew exactly what happened. Schama argued that the most compelling history is shamelessly engaged and not objective, and said that he would far rather present his own view and invite people to question and challenge it. Plainly, his view contradicts the way in which audiences are understood to engage with television, and does not recognise the 'mindful' and 'mindless' distinction suggested by Moscardo's work, which relies upon a multiplicity of viewpoints being available to the viewer. He also overlooks the way in which this programme, and others like it, are presented. The aim of the series, its style, aesthetics and high production values, as well as the accompanying book and DVD, are all packaged as if they are presenting the definitive history of Britain. In addition, Schama's presence as a white, albeit Jewish, male striding around the locations, explaining events, situations and identifying causes and consequences, is a familiar style of television that, whilst it pre-dates him, certainly carries an unquestionable authority and legitimacy. As one feminist scholar has written of museums, visitors often 'do not "read" what they see as the selection and interpretation of one person' in part because they have 'no access to alternative material, meanings, and arrangements' (Porter, 1988: 104). In these circumstances, what resources are given to the viewer to facilitate a critical and questioning response to the authoritative and articulate Schama?

In conclusion, we can contrast the two presenter styles in epistemological terms as 'he who knows' (Schama) with 'he who wants to know' (Wood). In the former, knowledge is the property of the expert and can, moreover, be imparted to the layperson (the viewer). This resonates with notions of bardic television developed by John Fiske and John Hartley (1978), who suggest that television offers a space for the modern-day equivalents of soothsayers and priests – and, we might add, the civic orator and public historian identified by Schama. The latter 'wants to know' and seeks to discover the 'truth' behind legends. Whilst this may well be a mere narrative device, used to achieve some narrative closure, knowledge is nevertheless being constructed by putting together a series of clues, the provenance of which includes non-experts offering experiential accounts that are valued as knowledge. The underlying contradiction here is that, whilst Schama's series has entered the annals of classic 'landmark' history television, it is Wood's series that is arguably more intellectually stimulating and offers more 'mindful' pleasure through knowing by understanding, perhaps reflecting the medium's pre-existing and enduring ideas of what makes 'good history'.

ACKNOWLEDGEMENT

This research is supported by the Arts and Humanities Research Council.

PART FOUR
Audiences

INTRODUCTION

Available historical accounts of the development of television in Britain have generally neglected the experience and contexts of television *viewing*. Studies of viewers and the domestic conditions under which television was acquired and watched have been largely absent from the picture. (O'Sullivan, 1991: 159; emphasis in original)

Each of the accounts in the final section of this book is concerned with the historical audience of television. As with several of the studies that appear in this collection, Tim O'Sullivan's chapter, 'Researching the viewing culture: television and the home, 1946–1960', proposes a methodology for studying television history that embraces multiple sources and their contradictions in order to gain a sense of past television viewing practices. O'Sullivan galvanises his earlier oral history work on the acquisition of television (1991) by drawing on contemporary and retrospective viewer accounts of TV acquisition, as well as available audience research. Further, he persuasively argues that it is critical for historians to know more about the basic, geographical growth of technical transmission facilities and the broadcasting infrastructure that allowed the cultural development of a national, fully networked, regional television service in order to understand fully television's increasingly ubiquitous role in the viewer's everyday life, during the period in question.

Also arguing for the historiographic value of pre-existing audience research to the television historian, Henrik Örnebring's vivid analysis of material from the Mass-Observation Archive counters one of the most commonplace 'myths' of British television viewing. Demystifying the image of reverent viewers, huddled round their own (or their neighbours') television set for the first time for the Coronation of Queen Elizabeth II, Örnebring draws on the rich accounts of this 'media event' that were collected for the Mass-Observation Archive in a number of innovative ways. Close analysis of this material leads Örnebring to argue that television viewing in this period was far more complex than a simple case of 'awe and wonder' at the 'white heat' of a new technology offering unprecedented access to the institution of the monarchy, and that television was, in fact, negotiated into domestic and non-domestic space in a multitude of different ways. The images located by Örnebring of familiarity, irreverence and, sometimes, downright indifference in viewers' relationship to the medium offer a radically new perspective on this moment in British broadcasting history.

As suggested in the introduction of this collection, Rachel Moseley's account of television drama for teenagers in the United Kingdom between 1968 and 1982 exemplifies the tripartite historiographic approach, which might be seen as the future of historical television scholarship, bringing together concerns with television programming, television production and institutions, and an interest in the television audience. Sketching a history of key programmes in this cycle, including *Going Out* (Southern TV, 1981) and *Maggie* (BBC, 1981–1982), Moseley constructs a fascinating picture of the ways in which television companies (and their regulators) sought to construct teenagers discursively, attempting to inform, educate, regulate and contain them through a variety of programming strategies. Furthermore, this historical study supplements archival research and textual analysis with original interviews with key personnel working in this field (specifically, influential producer Phil Redmond), and makes a strong argument for revisiting this neglected area of British television history, thus ultimately reinserting these programmes into the historical canon on the grounds of their critical significance. If, as O'Sullivan suggests, television viewing is a much-neglected area of historical research, the essays collected here seek to fill some of the gaps in our knowledge and understanding of historical television viewing, though from markedly different perspectives.

11 Researching the viewing culture

Television and the home, 1946–1960

Tim O'Sullivan

> Study of television has often been preoccupied with the contemporary moment, it has been the study of a perpetual present. (Corner, 1999: 121)

It is a welcome sign indeed that the serious study of television in general, and research into the history of television in Britain in particular, have now achieved a kind of critical mass or maturity signalled by the appearance of that self-reflexive, critical enterprise: historiography. In recent years there have been some interesting skirmishes around the possibilities contained in the putative label 'Television Studies' as delineating a distinctive and defined field, or even an emergent discipline.[1] In the light of these, it is both instructive and important that we should consider television historiography.

Attention to the current state of the historiography[2] of British TV should allow for systematic reflection on how (under what conditions and with what particular tendencies, points of view *and* blind spots) *the story* of television, its development – and, inescapably, its consequences – have been told. In probing both 'what' and 'how' we know about television history, it should also address, critically, the principal resources[3] that have fuelled these accounts, and how these received wisdoms have been synthesised (or not) into wider versions of the social and cultural history of the last 60 years or so.

Television has begun to be recognised as one of the most decisive cultural technologies of modern times, if not *the* most – both the *product* and as a significant, visible, *agent* of modernity. A conduit for, and a cause of, recurrent moral panics, it is the classic modern scapegoat, par excellence, reflected in its visibility within the private sphere of the household, articulated with its now ubiquitous presence on (and as) the world stage, and in the mediation and shaping of the values, directions and meanings of the contemporary public sphere. In adapting and capitalising on the inherited diversity of journalistic, documentary and entertainment traditions and forms, combined with its ability to provide spectacular 'intimacy at a distance', television occupies a special and contested place in what John B. Thompson (1995: 129) has called 'the rise of mediated publicness'.

This chapter starts by making some brief observations about current TV transformations and their relationship to the history of television. It then summarises issues raised in some of my early work on the oral history of TV in Britain from 1945 to 1960, which aimed to rethink and document the growth and the *domestication* of the viewing culture in that period, and how the aims and scope of this work have subsequently developed. In short, I suggest a methodology that embraces multiple sources and their contradictions, drawing, for instance, on contemporary and retrospective viewer accounts of TV acquisition, available audience research, oral history and, in light of this, attention to the developing broadcasting infrastructure and its cultural mediation. The chapter concludes by means of a (revisionist?) sketch of some issues and questions, which confront and concern the current state of the historiography of television in the United Kingdom.

BEYOND THE 'GOGGLE-BOX': TELEVISION HERE AND NOW

One of the many complicating factors facing contemporary historians of television is the way in which the television of the present is a constantly changing and volatile kind of chimera, through which we try to make connections and comparisons with the past.[4] As Philip M. Taylor, for instance, has noted in this context, the television apparatus itself is rapidly mutating, beyond the received idea of TV, constantly contradicting television 'as we know it':

> The 'goggle box' which usually sits in the corner of an average household's living room is about to change considerably. The TV set is about to get wider, flatter and interactive. Having already migrated into bedrooms and kitchens, it may even possibly change its location from the floor to the wall. The digital revolution signals the end of an era for analogue technology, including television as we have known it… […] Under such circumstances, it will surely not be long before historians begin to talk of a 'golden age of television' – by which they will mean the analogue era in which choice of programming was simple because it was limited and in which programmers could be reasonably sure that their output was being watched by a sizeable chunk of the population at the same time, providing a point of common reference and subsequent social interaction. (2001: 171–174)

We have surely already reached and gone beyond this point, in an era when advertising slogans for new, digitally connected televisions foreground the 'Flat is cool' aesthetic and promise that you can 'Create *your own* channel', 'Bring

Hollywood into *your* home', and even (my favourite) 'Rearrange television around *your* life' (see O'Sullivan, 2005). These are some of the advertising slogans of the volatile moment, part of the 'perpetual present'. With their seductive mix of visuals and music, the adverts foreground the idealised, unfettered power of modern digital television viewers, now 'magically' free to watch just whatever they want, just whenever they want to.

Recent surveys suggest that televisions in the United Kingdom are switched on for an average of five or more hours per day, and that TV viewing provides a background for almost every activity in the home. In view of this it should not come as a surprise that '[m]ore than one in two Britons – more than half the population – believe they would *"feel lonely without a television"*'.[5] As Stuart Hood neatly observed over 25 years ago, television has become 'as natural as gas, water and electricity' (1980: 1). Deeply and almost 'invisibly' etched and stitched into the textures and routines of familiar, everyday domestic life and the home, television has become part and parcel of the taken-for-grantedness of what Paddy Scannell (1996) calls the 'dailiness' of everyday existence and identity.[6] Undoubtedly, there is now a lot more television around. John Ellis (2000a), for instance, has recently argued that British TV has developed through a sequence of distinct periods: from *'scarcity'*, through *'availability'* to *'plenty'*. And plenty – or *excess* – is undeniably the defining – and hybrid – television condition of the moment.

If we do indeed now live in an age when we can effortlessly 'Rearrange television around our life', it may seem perverse to look back to a period when domestic life was, in fact, decisively *rearranged by* the arrival of television. Such perversity may, however, be required to produce a more complete account of the crucial 'take-off' of television; crudely, to explain more adequately how television got to where it is today.

MEMORIES OF TELEVISION: UNTOLD STORIES?

In the late 1980s I became interested in the ways in which historical accounts of television in Britain were marked by a relative absence of reference to, or, at least, engagement with, the 'domestic' dimension of television. This interest was partly the product of a kind of personal nostalgia and memory but was also motivated by admittedly vague, naive ideas that condensed around the notion of the *'domestication'* of TV (see Berker et al., 2006, Boddy, 1985, 2004, and Spigel, 1992): an 'untold' set of stories and issues that concerned the conditions under which television entered and became assimilated into the British home and how these homes, in response, domesticated TV. In part, I was interested in an 'everyday' oral history of TV (see O'Sullivan, 1991, Clayton, Harding and Lewis, 1995, and Moores, 1988): one that shifted, and even reversed, attention, from histories of television *supply*, institution and production to an emphasis on TV *demand*, domestic reception and the rise of the viewing culture. This switch of focus also has implications for how we might study the currency in this relationship – the television 'text', programme or genre (see Gray, 1987, and O'Shea, 1989). In particular, I became preoccupied with trying to do justice to the complex sets of social variables and cultural factors in the so-called 'take-off' of television in Britain. I date this vital, almost 'missing', period from the 1943 appointment of the Hankey Committee[7] up until 1960 or thereabouts. At least two factors may be relevant to this periodisation. The first concerns the spread and availability of television in the British home. In March 1947 there were fewer than 20,000 television sets capable of operating in the United Kingdom, the great majority of them in the London area – less than 1 per cent of the total population of adults *could* be viewers. By the early 1960s, in contrast, over 85 per cent of the population had access to domestic sets (5 per cent a single channel, 80 per cent two channels) (Silvey, 1974: 187). The BBC and ITV provided 10.5 million licence holders with about 16 hours of programming per day, available to the great majority of the UK audience/viewing culture. The second factor is that the 1960s began with the appointment of the Pilkington Committee, with its 'watershed' brief to appraise the performance of post-1955 competition and to advise on future organisation, with particular regard to a third channel (what emerged as BBC2 in April 1964).

During this period, 'television suffused the private domain with a new order of experience', argued Todd Gitlin (1982: 203), and, not surprisingly, most people from the immediate post-war generations have *memories* of their early encounters with TV. There are some key issues concerning generation and identity at work in the interviews I conducted with people who were old enough to remember 'life before' and 'life after' television in the late 1940s and the 1950s.[8] For many of the interviewees, the television set itself was an 'invisible apparatus'. Memories initially focus much more on programmes and the novel shared experiences of early TV viewing. Live television events (including particular reference to the 1953 Coronation and various sporting spectacles, etc.) were singled out as if 'punctuating' a kind of instant, participatory, *visible* television history. Nonetheless, these were also memories and markers anchored in recollections of particular places and people, of biography and situated culture.[9]

When pressed to recall the circumstances involved in the acquisition of their first set, interviewees related their first sights of television, usually at friends' or relatives' homes but also in non-domestic settings, such as retailers' demonstrations or even railway stations and cinema foyers. Most respondents remembered their first television as a considerable financial investment – with a marked ambivalence to early hire purchase, rental or credit schemes. In retrospect, the interviews suggest that it was the men in the household who tended to take 'technical ownership' of early sets and that the first television was more generally regarded as an exciting status symbol, part of 'being modern': 'You could tell from the aerials who had, and who hadn't got sets. I remember that we were one of the first three in the road to get one. If you had a car and a TV set, you'd really arrived' (O'Sullivan, 1991: 166). Other, less gendered pre-definitions of the cultural value or cachet of acquiring a set in this early phase foregrounded notions of an experience akin to a 'private cinema', as well as motives concerning the educational value of television for children in the home (see Oswell, 2002).

The interviews also suggest how the development of the television viewing culture had significant implications for domestic space, time and other routine arrangements as TV 'colonised' home life, 'challenged' the centrality of the hearth, the wireless and the parlour and restructured the pre-existing flows of domestic leisure culture, inside and outside the home. In 1955, for instance, only 40 per cent of the UK population watched TV, for an average of one and a half hours per evening (Silvey, 1974). Nevertheless, contemporary memories tend to index early anxieties, with indiscriminate, or 'too much', 'unplanned' viewing, resulting in the 'square eyes' syndrome. They also encompass matters relating to the changing design aesthetics and functional size of the TV screen, TV cabinets and 'doors', nine- to 14-inch screens, etc. At a more general level, the interviews also provide insights into the ways in which people became, at least in part, distinguished by their TV favourites, their 'must-sees' of the 'television week' – with 'good nights in on TV' – and the associated anticipations and expectations, such that one could talk about last night's television much in the same, shared, experiential and supposedly neutral way that one might talk about the weather, or yesterday's news. Memories of the rise of television celebrities and presenters (likes and dislikes) coexist uneasily with tales of guilt-tinged cultural displacement – cards, hobbies, pianos, radio listening and cinema-going; all had to make adjustments, as television negotiated its space and place.

If, as some commentators have argued persuasively, the rise of the TV-viewing culture was part and parcel of a more general realignment of public and private spheres – the withdrawal into 'interior space' (Moores, 2000: 95) – the interviews also offers an insight into matters concerning the 'habitus' and issues inextricably linked to dispositions of social class, class mobility and cultural capital.[10] The novelty of television in this early stage was counterbalanced by questions of its social and cultural *value* (as has been the case ever since?). These began with the object and product of the viewing culture, the television experience. Recollections index the ways in which, especially in middle-class homes, television was regarded as vulgar and unnecessary; for some, initially, an unwarranted and unwanted intrusion into private domesticity. This volatile, sectional and highly charged environment of cultural suspicion was in part, however, undermined and compromised by the rapid growth of the viewing culture[11] – although it was also given a new impetus by the launch of ITV in 1955 (recently a cause for anniversary celebration itself: see Johnson and Turnock, 2005), which redefined the 'vulgar', for some in more tangible, commercial and identifiably American terms. All the same, early BBC Television broadcasts are remembered by some as 'far too highbrow', as excessively formal, mannered and deferential on occasions, 'out of touch' with the times.[12] For households with children, even in the era of the 'toddlers' truce',[13] parents singled out key dilemmas in managing their television relationships – anxieties about the exposure to 'risqué' content, juxtaposed against the 'educational' merits of the new medium. Living with 'the box' in this early period more generally stimulates memories of shared and separate masculine and feminine domestic leisure, of 'television time', and these are interwoven with the recognition of TV both as a source of (virtual) companionship and as a genuine accompaniment to home work and routine.[14]

MAPPING THE CONDITIONS OF DEMAND: FROM 1946

> Whilst sound broadcasting settled down to consolidate its war-time gains, television began again from nowhere and suddenly revealed itself as a power to be reckoned with. Between 1945 and 1950 it passed from being a scientific achievement, a futuristic novelty, into being a successful rival to the older medium as a source of entertainment for the modern home. […] The future had changed hands. The fact was that people wanted to look as well as listen. (Gorham, 1952: 234)

In seeking to develop the initial work on memories of television, I recognised that the recollections provided and elicited by my interviews gave an important, personal, but ultimately only partial series of insights into the domestication of television in Britain. While I have continued, in both formal and less formal settings, to talk with people of those generations about their television memories of the time,[15] two issues have also prompted me to adopt a more questioning perspective that also attempts to situate their stories.

The first concerns the ways in which their memories tend to replay a kind of dominant, mythic and nostalgic television orthodoxy, and, understandably, reproduce a rather one-dimensional version of events, conforming to and conditioned by television's own history of itself[16] – a simple, celebratory story of unquestioned technical and social progress tinged with themes of later social disintegration and change. Second, interview material of this nature always requires wider contextualisation if it is to make a meaningful contribution to the bigger, historical picture. These two themes have resulted in a concern to map and capture more effectively and accurately the shifting conditions of demand for television in the 15 or so years from June 1946, and to identify the factors that might have been influential in this complex equation.

In a direct sense, we need to know more about the basic, geographical growth of technical transmission facilities, the broadcasting infrastructure that allowed the cultural development of a national, fully networked, regional television service and audience. There are a limited number of useful studies from the 1950s and early 1960s that provide worthwhile statistical summaries of the growth and development of the viewing culture. In addition to the groundbreaking work undertaken by the BBC Audience Research Department, under the direction of Robert Silvey (managing the sometimes fraught shift from 'listeners' to 'viewers'), studies by B.P. Emmett (1956), Political and Economic Planning (1958), William A. Belson (1959) and Andrew D. Bain (1962) provide significant contemporary accounts of this post-war history, mapping the geographical and social spread of television acquisition and demand and the emergence of what rapidly became known as the 'television public'. For Bain, for instance, there were four key features of the immediate post-war history: 'The geographical coverage was extended; a choice of programmes was provided; there were improvements, in transmission and reception; and television owners, being drawn initially from the wealthier classes, gradually became more representative of the whole population' (1962: 145–146). Related to these accounts are a number of other blind spots and neglected issues, concerning the growth of television retailing and domestic installation, and the industrial *mass production* and design of television sets. Keith Geddes and Gordon Bussey (1991) offer a valuable, if rather lonely, history of the British radio and television industries in the period. There are also some museum and specialist collections of televisions of the time, which deserve attention and visits.[17]

A number of perhaps less obvious archives and sources relevant to post-war culture and television also provide useful and revealing material. Two significant and illustrative examples are worthy of brief note here. The first concerns the attempts to document everyday life in Britain carried out by the Mass-Observation movement from 1937 onwards. In their project to produce an 'anthropology (or science) of our selves', the work of Charles Madge, Humphrey Jennings and Tom Harrisson and their network of intellectuals, artists, volunteer diarists, panellists and observers provides a rich and diverse account of British cultural life and adjustment to social change.[18] Their studies of 'Worktown' (Bolton, Lancashire), and more particularly of cinema-going (Richards and Sheridan, 1987), are acknowledged and distinctive historical sources, principally relating to the immediate pre-war, wartime and immediate post-war experience. In April 1949, however, they produced a fascinating and groundbreaking survey of public attitudes towards the new medium of television.[19] Two key questions were put to the M-O National Panel ('a predominantly middle class group, generally above average in intelligence and education') in January of that year: 'How do you feel about having television in your own home?' and 'If you had a television set how do you think it would affect your home leisure pursuits?'. Interestingly, of the 684 people who replied to the survey, only 2 per cent actually owned a television set, and about 10 per cent lived in areas where television was 'not yet visible'. Almost 40 per cent of the M-O National Panel respondents had *never seen* television and a further 20 per cent reported having seen TV only once – 'before the war'. In spite of this, the report offers rich insights – 'thick descriptions' – of how television was 'imagined' at the time by *potential* viewers/buyers. In fact, about a half of the panel members were strongly committed to having a set in their own home, typically on grounds of enhanced domestic entertainment and educational facilities, but status aspirations are also evident in many of the responses: 'If I could afford it I should certainly like to have a set in the same way as I should certainly like to have a car, a private swimming pool and other good things of life!' (27-year-old housewife).[20]

Against such positive, if wishful, dreams of luxury, about one-third of the respondents were, by contrast, definitely hostile to the thought of television in their own home, citing the cost of investment in an as yet unproven apparatus as the principal reason. Related 'drawbacks' to television in the home were perceived in its ability to demand and draw attention and concentration away from other, more 'worthwhile' pursuits or activities ('a colossal waste of money and time'), and its destabilising impact on the existing 'hub' of household arrangements with what, for many, was identified as 'synthetic entertainment':

> I have no desire whatsoever to have a set myself. I think it encourages the growing tendency for passive pastimes, and that this tendency should be prevented if possible. Since television involves a semi-darkened room and concentration of eyes and ears, it is particularly crippling for any other activity; and it is unnecessary as pleasure for our ears and eyes are already well catered for, with wireless, concerts, cinemas, theatres, etc. I myself would far rather do something more actively creative with my spare time than sit and look at what is given out to us on a television set. (24-year-old research chemist)[21]

Perhaps this is why responses to questions about the future development of television were overwhelmingly in favour of more outside broadcasts, for more television of respectable record, a seemingly unmediated mirror, the 'window on the world', whereby TV simply seemed to replace the eye at the live event. Having a television in the home was also identified as an obvious reason for decreased wireless listening, and cinema-going was also expected to suffer. Other home pursuits predicted to be most affected were reading and knitting. Home life – as it was known – would be in chaos:

> I believe that television makes family home life almost impossible. For 2–3 hours every evening the family must sit in darkness gazing at the screen – mother cannot knit, father cannot read, the children skimp through their homework and stay up late. No one can have a conversation, no letters get written, and friends calling are not welcomed since they break the sequence.[22]

For others, however, the promise of television transcended its perceived problematic presence in the home: 'I should like to have a television set in my home, whilst admitting it has some drawbacks: e.g. it demands an undivided attention and a darkened room for perfect viewing. It nevertheless possesses the power of providing me with the *otherwise unattainable*' (32-year-old commercial traveller; emphasis added).[23]

The second example of contemporary research into the early impact of television on the British home in the period is found in the work of the social anthropologist Geoffrey Gorer.[24] Some ten years after the M-O Panel Report, Gorer was commissioned in 1957 by *The Sunday Times* to conduct a survey provisionally entitled 'Television and the English'. He was given access to the services of a major advertising and market research agency to design and carry out a large-scale questionnaire and interview-based project.[25] The results, taken from a representative sample of 2,000 respondents, provided a rich diversity of insights into the steady march of television and its rapid domestication in the home. Although Gorer intended to publish a two-volume account of the research, this never transpired. What emerged from the research was compressed into four feature-length articles in *The Sunday Times*.[26] Whereas the earlier M-O work dealt largely in speculation about *what it would be like* to live with a TV set, by contrast, ten years later, Gorer starts his first feature by noting that in 1958 '[i]n England today television is installed in slightly more than six houses out of every ten...' [...] '[O]n a typical Sunday evening this last winter, two out of every five English people were watching a television set.' [...] '[N]o other Sunday evening occupation claimed anything like the same allegiance' (Gorer, 1958a: 14).

From this base he proceeded to map and to explore the ways in which participation in the television-viewing culture had displaced other pursuits, both inside and outside the home. His analysis is sensitive to dimensions of class, gender and generation, but he also found that television was becoming an omnipresent, cross-cutting focus for domestic relaxation and leisure. The metaphors of television '*addicts*' are interestingly contrasted with those of television '*abstainers*'. Television is reported as having either a 'hypnoidal', trance-inducing influence or as acting as a novel stimulant within the home. His discussion gives special emphasis to the relationships between children and TV – an issue that had, tellingly, already begun to attract widespread public debate and concern.[27] Overall, he argues: 'The major changes produced by the acquisition of television can be summed up in a single sentence: people stay at home much more, and tend to abandon the pastimes, hobbies and other occupations which had previously filled their evenings' (Gorer, 1958b). Future work will provide more detailed accounts of the M-O and Gorer archives, but, for now, I want to acknowledge them as examples of resources that have yet to be fully tapped into for the purposes of understanding the rise of the viewing culture.

If we need to know more about, and have a clearer picture of, the actual statistical spread of TV reception in the United Kingdom in order to understand more fully the conditions and formation of television demand at the time, we also need to come to terms more effectively with the ways in which television was itself 'imaged' and mediated to potential audiences in the period: in short, the 'hand in glove' of how television was culturally framed and represented and how the demand for television was 'cultivated'. This includes early national, and local, press coverage of TV – when (the sight of) television was itself newsworthy.[28]

This research cannot avoid consideration of the ways in which television was advertised in the period. It should also engage with the many ways in which television 'leaked' into films,[29] literature, plays, magazines and other cultural forms of the period – either as despised 'alien-propagandist-invader' or as aspired-to 'technical novelty', but then as 'naturalised referent': *the* sign of the indispensable, taken-for-granted domestic furniture and generalised social background.

In *Saturday Night and Sunday Morning*, for instance, first published as a novel by Alan Sillitoe in 1958, later a celebrated film (Karel Reisz, 1960), the hero, Arthur Seaton, early in the narrative takes his father to task for his TV habits: 'You'll go blind one day, dad, ...sittin' in front of the TV. You stick to it like glue from six to eleven every night. It can't be good for yer. You'll go blind one day.' Later, his father muses: 'Arthur teased him a lot, but in a way he was glad to see the TV standing in the corner of the living room, a glossy panelled box, looking, he thought, like something plundered from a space-ship' (Sillitoe, 1976: 19–20). In order that we avoid the pitfalls of producing 'a history of the context without the text' (Corner, 2003a: 277), we also need to know much more about the development of television 'flow' in this early, formative period:[30] where programmes came from, their generic or hybrid formations and how they were assembled into an expanding schedule. The rise of early television personalities and celebrities and the emergence of television criticism and TV magazines (for instance, *TV Mirror*) provide two additional but related lines of enquiry.

CONCLUDING REMARKS

> Doing television history raises a set of quite specific questions not only about available resources but also about how the multi-faceted object of study, television, connected as it is to a whole set of contested issues of *value*, is located within the account. (Corner, 2003a: 273)

In this recent and helpful account of the issues and challenges currently confronting British television history, John Corner has also noted a number of different aspects that comprise this 'multi-faceted' object of study. He documents what he sees as the key problems facing research. These begin with questions concerning access to historical data, but they also encompass the development of appropriate 'analytical schemes and discursive means'. As he notes, these span problems of periodisation, of longitudinal and lateral connections, of historical narrative and of dealing with existing normative schemes. In this brief discussion, I have given consideration to some of the 'blind spots' and gaps that seem to characterise our current knowledge and thinking about television history in Britain, in its key, formative moments of development, its expansion and, most importantly, its domestication. In considering the current state of TV historiography, I have suggested that we have to be careful not to (re)produce a 'lopsided' history of television in the United Kingdom: an account or orthodoxy that tends to focus on supply factors as opposed to those associated with demand. Most obviously, this is made manifest in an emphasis on institutional and production factors as opposed to those related to TV consumption or reception. In short, we need to know more about the complex conditions and dynamics that resulted in the television 'viewing culture' and how this became a historical agent in its own right. There are a number of related issues raised here. Has too much attention been devoted to pre-war television? To the BBC and related institutional biographies? To 'great', regulation and policy moments? We may also need to be wary of easy myths of 'displacement', and of the immediate post-war years and of the 1950s in general.

The texture of watching television is nearly always smoothed to over-simplification by everybody, from historians to TV critics. The story of what it is like to grow up watching television deserves to be told with more sensitivity and understanding than it has been (Jeffries, 2000: xxi).

ACKNOWLEDGEMENT

I would like to acknowledge support from the School of Media and Cultural Production Research Committee at De Montfort University, in enabling me to visit the archives referred to in this chapter. Colleagues at the British Library and at the Mass-Observation Archive at Sussex University also provided helpful assistance.

12 Writing the history of television audiences

The Coronation in the Mass-Observation Archive

Henrik Örnebring

Within the field of media history, historical accounts of the development of the press, radio and television are commonly written from an institutional perspective. The history of the media is, by and large, the history of media institutions: of corporations and government organisations, the political battles surrounding them, the changes within the institutions and the careers of important people. If the audience is covered at all in these histories, it is done adopting the same perspective on the audience as the media institutions themselves: the audience as an aggregate mass that can and should be measured, the audience as students to be taught, as errant children that need to be controlled, as citizens to be informed, as customers to be catered to, etc. – i.e. a view of the audience based mostly on what audiences *should* do, according to the media institutions. Tim O'Sullivan refers in the following way to studies of British television: 'Available historical accounts of the development of television in Britain have generally neglected the experiences and contexts of television viewing. Studies of viewers and the domestic conditions under which television was acquired and watched have been largely absent from the picture' (1991: 159).

O'Sullivan's point is applicable to media history as a whole; while there has been a great amount of insightful scholarship on institutional and organisational aspects, as well as textual aspects of media history, the historical perspective has seldom been applied to media audiences, except from the point of view of institutions and/or possible effects.[1] For example, in their comprehensive study of the early social history of British broadcasting, Paddy Scannell and David Cardiff write about the calendrical and community-building effects of early broadcasting:

> Nothing so well illustrates the noiseless manner in which the BBC became
> perhaps the central agent of the national culture as its calendrical role; the

cyclical reproduction, year in year out, of an orderly and regular progression of festivities, rituals and celebrations – major and minor, civil and sacred – that marked the unfolding of the broadcast year. [...] [The BBC] not only coordinates social life, but gives it renewable content, anticipatory pleasures, a horizon of expectations. (1991: 278–279)

Moreover, referring specifically to the royal Christmas broadcasts: 'It set a crowning seal on the role of broadcasting in binding the nation together, giving it a particular form and content: the family audience, the royal family, the nation as family' (Scannell and Cardiff, 1991: 280). While there is no reason to doubt the importance of broadcasting in fostering a sense of national belonging and national continuity, there seems to be present an implicit assumption that all members of the audience will react to these broadcasts in a similar way, that the content will have fairly uniform 'effects' on the audience, and that the audience in general will accept the efforts of the broadcasting institution to incorporate them into a 'national family' (see Moores, 2000: 56, for criticisms similar to those I advance here). It is perhaps a bit unfair to single out Scannell and Cardiff's work for critical attention in this regard, since they go much further than many in incorporating the audience in their history of broadcasting. It is, indeed, very difficult to avoid some measure of institutional bias when studying audiences historically, since what little empirical material one can get hold of often has been collected and collated by the media institutions, and thus subjected to particular institutional sets of biases.[2] Scannell and Cardiff rely largely on material from the BBC's own audience studies, letters to the BBC and material from *The Listener*, for example.

In all fairness, it must be said that one important reason for the neglect of the historical study of media audiences is one of simple methodology. How can we study audiences that do not exist anymore? For the most part, media audiences are ephemeral, fleeting collectives that do not leave any records of their activities – except, as was pointed out previously, in the form of quantitative information collected by the media institutions themselves. To some extent, the neglect of historical audiences is due to the scarcity of empirical material; but scarce is not the same as non-existent. In my own ongoing research project about the 1953 Coronation of Queen Elizabeth II as a media event, I was fortunate to find that rich material on the audience reception of this media event had been collected in the Mass-Observation Archive at the University of Sussex. It is this material that this chapter is based on.

THE 1953 CORONATION IN THE MASS-OBSERVATION ARCHIVE

One of Mass-Observation's last efforts before it closed down in the mid-1950s was the organisation of a major study of the Coronation – specifically, how the Coronation was received, celebrated and reacted to by 'ordinary people' in their everyday life, this subject area being Mass-Observation's very *raison d'être*. The materials from this study are collected in the Mass-Observation Archive as a part of Topic Collection 69: Royalty.[3] As in all their studies, Mass-Observation used a variety of methods to achieve their goal of writing a 'people's history'. The methodological cornerstone was the so-called 'directive replies': answers to open-ended questionnaires sent to the members of the Mass-Observation National Panel. The main material I have used comes from the directive replies on pre-Coronation and Coronation Day activities from 150 Panel members. Beyond the directive replies, Mass-Observation researchers showed a remarkable methodological inventiveness. Another major part of the study were three more traditional survey studies (two made before the Coronation, in February and May 1953, and one about five months afterwards, in October 1953) based on a quota sample of 2,000 individuals with a reply frequency of about 67 per cent (M-O A TC69/2/A). I have used these surveys mostly as background material, to provide context for my interpretations.

In addition to this, Mass-Observation sent out observers in the months before the Coronation to make detailed notes about Coronation decorations in shop windows and in people's homes. Observers were also employed to 'listen in' on people's everyday conversations in the streets and on public transportation (so-called 'overheards'), in order to catalogue public opinion, Coronation jokes and anecdotes, etc. Mass-Observation collected souvenirs and other Coronation paraphernalia. A separate case study of 'street parties' (i.e. Coronation celebrations in which people in a neighbourhood came together to organise and finance Coronation Day celebrations) was carried out in Fulham, south London. Mass-Observation also studied media coverage of the Coronation: among other things is a report (never published, only sketched) titled *The Coronation in Papers of Mass Appeal*, a summary of what popular weekly and monthly magazines had featured about the Coronation, both in terms of advertising and editorial material (M-O A: TC69/5/A).

The Mass-Observation investigators were also sent out to different parts of London, both along the Coronation procession route and elsewhere, to observe the behaviour of crowds and individuals during Coronation Day itself. Finally, at different times during the Coronation preparations, members of the public were invited to write to Mass-Observation about their observations and preparations relating to the Coronation. The plan was that this extensive study would result in a major book on public responses to the Coronation, a companion volume to the earlier Mass-Observation study of the Coronation of George VI in 1937 (Jennings and Madge, 1937). This was the first coronation to be covered by the BBC, both on radio and television (albeit the latter in a very limited fashion).

The material collected by Mass-Observation on the 1953 Coronation was not done for the specific purpose of studying television audiences, of course, but, as I shall show, there is a fair amount of information in the material that deals with television, both directly and indirectly. Soon after the Coronation data gathering was completed, Mass-Observation ceased its operations and would not be resurrected until the 1980s. Thus, the results of the study were never made public, although later scholars have used it (most notably Harrisson, 1961, Harris, 1966, and Ziegler, 1978), but never to provide a full account of the Coronation itself (the most complete account of the Coronation based on this material is probably to be found in Ziegler, 1978).

This study is based on the above-mentioned Panel replies and the results of the two pre-Coronation surveys. Much of the documentation from the survey is missing, but, from what I (and others) have been able to piece together, the sample seems to be representative and the surveys methodologically sound. The Panel replies are not, of course, representative in any statistical sense; indeed, they were not intended to be: the ideological basis for the whole Mass-Observation project was to allow for the idiosyncrasies and unique perspectives of 'ordinary people' to become available for social and historical study. Thus, in a more general sense, they are clearly representative of everyday life and public opinion in the United Kingdom at this time, since it can be assumed that non-Panel members in many instances held similar views to those expressed in the directive replies. Nevertheless, one has to be careful when generalising from this type of data. I have tried to use the directive replies mainly to indicate the existence or non-existence of some viewpoints, and, when possible, to support my conclusions with the material gathered from the surveys (for a more detailed discussion of the nature of the materials in the Mass-Observation Archive, and the key methodological issues involved in using this material, see Bloome, Sheridan and Street, 1993).

THE TV AUDIENCE IN 1953: DOMESTICATING A NEW MEDIUM

In this chapter I wish to focus on one particular aspect of the history of the television audience: the integration of television into the everyday lives of its viewers. The relationship between the media (television in particular) and everyday life has generated a vast amount of scholarship during the last two decades, but surprisingly little of this work has been historical in character. My aim here is thus not only to add audiences to the study of media history but also to add history to the study of media audiences.

One of the most salient features of television in the early 1950s was that it was a *new* medium. It was not yet the self-evident part of our everyday lives that it is today. On the other hand, it was not completely new to the audience, as experiments with television technology had taken place since the 1930s. The limits of technology and the high price of television sets had set a slow pace for the diffusion of television. In the 1930s TV transmissions did not reach outside London and the total number of television sets in the country numbered in the thousands. The BBC's television service was interrupted during the war, and when it was resumed again in 1946 the popularity and availability of the new medium started to grow (see also Crisell, 1997: 72). By the 1950s television was in some respects something extraordinary, and in other respects already well on its way to becoming an element of the everyday life of its audience. This becomes particularly clear when we look at the reception of the Coronation. The Coronation was a festive occasion, a nationwide celebration of great magnitude, and therefore clearly extraordinary. The everyday is always present in the extraordinary, however: the Coronation celebrations had to be planned in advance, and in some cases financed. Coronation parties in the home with friends and family had to be integrated with everyday routines. I use the concept of *domestication* to understand this dialectic between the extraordinary and the everyday in the reception of the Coronation as a television event.

THREE ASPECTS OF DOMESTICATION

The word 'domestication' originally refers to the process of humans (or humanity) bringing something from the wild under control and integrating it with existing living practices. In the case of media being integrated into everyday life, the metaphor of domestication is taken to mean the following:

> The domestication of technology refers to the capacity of a social group (a household, a family, but also an organization) to appropriate technological artifacts and delivery systems into its own culture – its own spaces and times, its own aesthetic and its own functioning – to control them, and to render them more or less 'invisible' within the daily routines of daily life. (Silverstone, 1994: 98)

Following Daniel Miller (1987), Roger Silverstone goes on to suggest that domestication is 'elastic' – that is, a process, or a scale, incorporating many different ways of integrating the technology in question into daily life, from enthusiastic introduction to reluctant acceptance. Since domestication is a process, it is also necessary historical, as Silverstone points out (Silverstone, 1994: 99). At the time of the Coronation, television was at the beginning of its domestication process, with radio (by this time more or less 'fully' domesticated) already present in the media landscape, providing a template for everyday media consumption. Moreover, even though this study centres on the household or family, we must remember that other social institutions are involved in the domestication process as well, most importantly the media organisations themselves. Programme planning and scheduling becomes a key way of integrating the new medium and disciplining the audience – teaching them to become viewers. Viewing domestication as a process, I have identified three main aspects of this process in the empirical material: *non-domestication, anti-domestication* and *extraordinary domestication*.

By *non-domestication*, I refer to the fact that television in its infancy was decidedly *not* a domestic medium. It was in some ways considered by people to be more similar to film than to radio, because, just as with film, television was often viewed in public – in pubs, clubs or even in cinemas. In 1953 the number of privately owned television sets was relatively low, although rising, and public viewing still formed an important part of audience experiences of the new medium. Television was both a domestic and a public medium. Broadcasts reached the whole of England as well as Scotland and Wales, and Northern Ireland and the Channel Islands were incorporated into the UK network in 1955.

Anti-domestication refers to a reluctance vis-à-vis the new medium of television – sometimes even a very critical approach. Some members of the audience clearly resisted the influences of television, and in various degrees recognised that a domestication process was going on – and that this domestication process was intrusive, even threatening. The introduction of television was a cause of concern for many – concern on moral, medical, social, cultural and economical grounds (see, for example, Spigel, 1992).

Extraordinary domestication, finally, refers to the particular kind of domesticating practices that occurred in conjunction with the Coronation – domesticating practices that seem to be similar for all big, celebratory events of this type. The television of the Coronation represented a contrast to the humdrum routines of everyday life: it was a festive, extraordinary ingredient in a non-everyday celebration. Coronation Day, 2 June, was declared a national holiday and most people had the day off work. In this way, television became associated with a break from the everyday – both connected to the holiday nature of the event, and as a fascinating technology in itself. Coronation TV was non-everyday TV – but it still had to be integrated into the home, special routines and accommodations had to be made, and the home viewing took place in the presence of many familiar everyday elements: the relationships of family and friends, the space of the living room, domestic leisure time, the routines of meal preparation, etc.

THE AUDIENCE SPEAKS

It is self-evident that the reception of a major event such as the Coronation was multifaceted – if nothing else, the sheer size of the audience indicates this. Even though this seems to be stating the obvious, however, it is interesting to note that key works on media events (such as Dayan and Katz, 1992 and Shils and Young, 1956) implicitly assume a mostly homogeneous audience response to events. Nick Couldry rightly cautions that it is easy to assume homogeneity in audience reception of media events if one looks at the media coverage of the event, which is indeed often very homogeneous (Couldry, 2002: 55). I have explored similar issues in an earlier article on the Coronation (Örnebring, 2004), and this criticism is also advanced by James Thomas (2002) in his work about the mourning and funeral of Diana, the Princess of Wales.

Thus, another important aim for this study is simply to bring attention to the fact that audience reception is not homogeneous, and that there were many diverse responses to the event and the televising of it – not all of them positive. As both Daniel Dayan and Elihu Katz (1992) and Ed Shils and Michael Young (1956) focus on the positive, integrative effects of media events (Shils and Young focus specifically on the Coronation), I think it is important to show and acknowledge that not everyone was an enthusiastic celebrant of the Coronation as a media event. In this regard, I wish in some small way to follow the suggestion made by Annette Kuhn (2002) and actually give space and voice to the audience itself when studying it. Some of my quotes are lengthy precisely because I think that letting the audience speak for itself deepens our understanding of viewing practices and viewing contexts, particularly when it comes to the process of domestication.

NON-DOMESTICATION: TELEVISION AS PUBLIC MEDIUM

Considering that the number of television licences in the United Kingdom was above 2 million in 1953,[4] the television viewing figures of the Coronation were very impressive (numbers taken from Briggs, 1979: 429; percentages calculated by the author): according to the BBC's own audience research, 53 per cent of the adult population (over 19 million) viewed the Coronation procession to Westminster Abbey, and 56 per cent (almost 20 million) viewed the Coronation service. The audience for the service was split as follows: 40 per cent (or 7,800,000) watched in their own home, 53 per cent viewed it in the homes of friends or family, and 8 per cent (or 1,500,000) viewed it in public places such as cinemas, public halls and public houses.[5] About one in 13 was thus not viewing television in a domestic context. In this aspect, the 150 Panel members of the Mass-Observation would seem to be a fairly representative sample: 55 per cent (or 83) report viewing the Coronation on television, and 7 per cent (or ten) of the television viewers report viewing it in public. As a point of comparison, the viewing audience outnumbered the listening (radio) audience all over the United Kingdom apart from in the west, and in the London and Midland regions the viewing audience was nearly three times the size of the listening audience (Briggs, 1979: 429).

Judging from television licence numbers, television in 1953 was well on its way to becoming domesticated. With just under 1 million licences in 1951, around 1.7 million in 1952 and hitting the 2 million mark and more in 1953, the number of sets was steadily growing. If we look at the number of new licences bought around these years, we can see that the Coronation (being the only major television event in 1953) probably stimulated the growth of television: while the number of new licences bought in 1950 was 400,000, growing to 700,000 in 1951 and 1952, it leapt to 1,100,000 in 1953. This relatively rapid integration of television into everyday life parallels the integration of radio some 25 years earlier. Viewing in the home was, in 1953, the dominant form of reception, even though it should be noted that the largest portion of viewers did not watch the Coronation in their own home.

Lack of television ownership was not the only reason to view television in public. The Panel members who did so mentioned the practical advantages of doing so: one could actually see more of the procession than one would being physically present, one did not have to deal with the crowds, and it was comfortable to view the Coronation in a pub with convenient access to beer and food (M-O A TC69/7/A, 4398 and unnumbered). Of these reasons, the two first could, of course, be said to apply to viewing the event on television in general as well as the specific watching of television in public. These same two Panel members also mentioned the factor of companionship – viewing in public allowed one to take part in the event in the presence of others.

Mass mediation in some sense implies a loss of control on the part of the broadcaster, since the reception contexts of the individual audience members are impossible to predict or control: they may ignore the event altogether, or view it while doing other things. Indeed, leading religious representatives were initially very reluctant to broadcast the Coronation on television, since this would diminish the solemnity of the occasion and intrude on the religious ceremony (Scannell, 1996: 80) as the necessary reverent behaviour on the part of the viewers could not be ensured. That this was not an unfounded fear is demonstrated in the report of one Mass-Observation investigator dispatched to study pub behaviour on Coronation Day: the investigator was present in a pub when the Coronation was broadcast on television, and commented on the often irreverent and loud (though generally good-natured) audience commentary – for example, after the anointing (the climax of the Westminster Abbey service): 'All hoped the Queen would be able to have a "quick one"[6] as she deserved it' (M-O A TC 69/6/C). Meanwhile, for the predominantly working-class audience who viewed the Coronation in an ice cream parlour in a poor London area, the ceremony became fodder for everyday conversation and good-natured patter as well as reverence:

A (a woman of 25): 'Look at the Queen. She's like a plum pudding by now, they've put so many dresses on her.'
B (woman of 45): 'She's got enough sceptres and things to keep her going.'
C (man of 35): 'They won't show us the actual anointing; it's been forbidden.'
D: (woman of 35): 'It's very moving.'
B: 'Makes you proud to be British.'
C: 'Those Yanks ain't got nothing like this.'
(M-O A TC 69/6/C, also quoted in Ziegler, 1978: 117)

Though an extraordinary event, the Coronation was clearly brought closer to everyday concerns and conversations by television. The same type of somewhat irreverent commentary present at public viewings can be noted in the collective viewing that took place in the home, as discussed in the later section on extraordinary domestication.

From the many accounts of Coronation Day preparations (particularly of street parties and other communal celebrations) present in the Mass-Observation Archive, it is clear that providing public access to television was viewed as important and a natural part of the preparation – most often motivated by the fact that those without TV sets at home also ought to be able to view the Coronation ceremony. This is a very simple indicator of how TV even at this early stage was viewed mostly as a 'naturally' domestic medium, whose context of consumption is the home – and that public viewing was more of a complement to the domestic viewing context. Television had taken the first steps towards domestication.

ANTI-DOMESTICATION: CRITIQUE AND 'OPTING OUT'

It is well known that the introduction of every new medium always brings its share of naysayers: people who, for some reason or other, are critical towards the new medium. In connection with a major media event such as the Coronation, accompanied as it was by saturating media coverage long before the actual event, it is hardly surprising to find people critical towards the media hoopla in general and the role played by television in particular. Criticism of new media ranges from those based on traditional notions about popular culture and high culture, to a general fear of a perceived decline in traditional values and norms, to seldom supported claims about the effects of the new medium on physical and mental health, to astute and reasonable predictions about the consequences of the new medium, and a keen if not always fully articulated sense of the disciplining efforts of the media institutions: not everyone likes being made into a member of a mass audience.

The types of criticism I have focused on in this study can all, to various extents, be interpreted as viewing the integration of television into everyday life as a kind of intrusion; domestication understood as an encroachment of home and everyday activities. For example, one audience member disapproved of television on the grounds of its inferior quality – as well, it would seem, as its lack of cultural prestige:

> I did not fancy accepting any of the numerous invitations to TV as I regard it as a very inferior cinema and I felt the conversation would be inane. [Later] I just did not feel like TV this day and spent it walking over the moors which is always my favourite pastime and I felt a very wise move as I go on a walking holiday next Friday. (M-O A TC 69/ 7/E, 059)

It should be noted that, in spite of his negative attitude, this Panel member nevertheless ended up watching television for a short time at a friend's house. Another audience member explicitly mentioned the contribution of television to the general Coronation publicity:

> I've nothing against it, I think she's very nice, but there's been so much about it on Television and in Woolworth's – I said to myself it's like the way they put

out X-mas cards the moment you come back from holidays. X-mas is stale before you get there and I feel the Coronation is like that too. Woolworth's is full of it far too long in advance. (M-O A TC69/2/A)

A few audience members commented on the hype and publicity surrounding the Coronation, and chose to opt out of the Coronation celebrations altogether – staying away from all media coverage, broadcast and otherwise. This strategy was explicitly mentioned in eight Panel responses (5 per cent of the total) – and all these apart from one remark on the virtual impossibility of avoiding the Coronation, especially because it is being mediated by radio and television. The determination and success of those opting out varied: one person listened briefly to the radio in the morning, but then preferred to have 'peace and quiet' (M-O A TC69/7/B, 1865), and another did his best to avoid mediations of the Coronation during the day but overheard a radio summary when he went to the cinema in the evening. The two respondents most decisively opting out were, first, one who went walking in Dartmoor with a group of friends, 'determined to avoid at all costs any news and activity connected with the Coronation' (M-O A TC69/7/H, 4378), and, second, one who resisted both media intrusion and the ideology of the Coronation itself by arranging a republican party with a group of friends (M-O A TC69/7/H, 1731). At this party, republican songs were sung, the Queen symbolically executed and various anti-royalist parlour games played. While none of this, of course, represents a specific resistance to or criticism towards television, it is nevertheless a curious and somewhat extreme example of people not at all accepting the celebratory mood prescribed by the media in general.

Another type of response is a bit harder to interpret; it is not outright criticism of television but, rather, a refusal to be impressed or influenced by it. Some Panel members and members of the public reported that the television broadcast, in fact, did not intrude on their everyday routines in any particular way. Others reported that they found the television broadcast unimpressive or even boring. It is, of course, difficult to say whether this was because of individual differences in preferences, or a sign that television was so domesticated that these viewers were not particularly fascinated by the technological achievement itself, or whether the dismissive attitude towards television was a sign of resistance to domestication and an implicit criticism. One thing is clear: many audience members made it clear that they were not very engaged in what is happening on the television screen (at least not initially): 'Inv.[7] hostile to television until converted by the ceremony itself, was bored by the crowd reportage and lame bits of interviewing, and the three nightmare New Zealanders who the commentator seemed unable to get rid of' (M-O A TC 69/6/C). Four other directive replies similarly stated that they found the procession broadcast on TV 'boring' (M-O A TC 69/7/A, unnumbered, and TC 69/7/E, unnumbered, 676, 4250), and one Panel member even reported falling asleep during the broadcast (M-O A TC 69/7/F, 896). For one member of the public, watching the Coronation proceedings for an hour was enough, and even this seems to be somewhat incidental:

For the first part of the afternoon I did some shooting and at 3:30 pm I went to watch television at the home of Mr and Mrs [X], who had kindly extended an open invitation to all in the neighbourhood. The TV reception was excellent but everyone was disappointed about the rain which made the closing of the carriages necessary in the procession back. I left at about 4:30... (M-O A TC 69/6/D)

One thing mentioned by many scholars of the early history of (broadcast) media is the widespread fascination with the technology itself, rather than with the content it provides. At the time of the Coronation, television's honeymoon with the audience seems to be drawing towards its end – or at least the more critical audience members were eager to point out that they did not feel this fascination.

EXTRAORDINARY DOMESTICATION: TELEVISION PARTIES

The viewing figures quoted previously demonstrate that the most common way of viewing television was not in one's own home but in someone else's, commonly members of family or friends. The portion of television viewers attending a 'television party' (this came to be the accepted term for an informal gathering of people to watch television and celebrate the Coronation) was higher among the Mass-Observation Panel members than in the audience in general: 69 per cent (or 57 out of 83) of the television viewers providing Mass-Observation directive replies attend a television party, either as hosts or guests, whereas the national average (according to the BBC's own measures) was 53 per cent. A few replies mention that Panel members attended television parties mainly to report their impressions to Mass-Observation, so the higher party attendance rate among the Mass-Observation participants can in part, perhaps, be explained by their very status as Mass-Observation Panel members.

The television parties represented an integration of television into the domestic context and clearly showed the emergent structuring of everyday life and routines around the presence of television. Most directive replies, public replies and investigator's reports show great similarity in describing the television parties, from preparation through execution to the cleaning up afterwards. We are all probably familiar with how house parties entail everyday drudgery (planning, food preparations, cleaning the dishes, etc.) as well as an enjoyable break from the everyday in terms of companionship, good cheer, and so forth. The following (abbreviated) account by an investigator reporting from a television party in Bradford can be considered fairly representative: it shows the little trials and tribulations of interpersonal relations and the (mild) irritation when the party planning is interfered with by early arrivals, as well as the undisciplined nature of viewing television in a group and commentary on the limitations and possibilities of the new medium – all, by extension, providing an image of how the domestic proceedings were structured temporally and spatially by the presence of television, and of how television touched the lives of its viewers.

Household consists of M60B, F50B, their son M22B and his American wife, F25B, and a small baby; F18B, their daughter, now working for the B.Sc. Visitors were Inv. And M24B, who is F18B's boy-friend and heartily disliked by the rest of the household. M24B was on the doorstep just before ten a.m., when nobody had breakfasted. The sitting-room was hastily tidied, people snatched some breakfast, and by 10.30 most of the party was ready to abandon itself to television. [...] M22B had a bad cold and came down in his dressing-gown. People fidgeted around, the baby seemed surprised not to be the centre of interest but settled down on M60B's knee. Gradually attention settled on the screen. Everything was punctuated by the young American's, 'Oh Gee', 'Oh Gosh', 'Gee, but you couldn't see that in America.' [...] Seeing the shot of the peeresses, somebody said 'They're not very pretty.' Young American, enthusiastically, 'No, but my God, look at the load of ice on them!' At the appearance of the little prince Charles, my hostess said darkly, 'I bet they've doped him with bromide.' Somebody reported an American joke, 'What do they do when they crown the new President?' 'All the oil interests do homage.' [...] The sense of a great national tradition seemed to silence even F18B for awhile, though she has communist leanings, and as soon as the ceremony was over declared defiantly that she was going out swimming, though the weather was bitterly cold and rainy. [...] But as the ceremony proceeded, there was certainly a sense of growing national pride among the onlookers, punctuated by little squabbles as to how old the Regalia actually was, and then 'Hush.' Derogatory remarks were thrown out about America, Hollywood, Russia. Somebody said, 'This is the last dignified thing in the world.' The only criticisms were, that more of the Abbey itself should have been shown, that one got slight claustrophobic feelings after too much of that narrow stage, and that people felt tense at the time and tired at the end, having been full of apprehension in case anything should have gone wrong – the slightest mistake or bungling would have seemed a bad omen. Pleasure was expressed at the few watery gleams of sun in London. Several visitors dropped in at times. Somewhere between two and three [after the anointing had been broadcast; author's note], the family sat down to a square meal, leaving unpopular M24B to manipulate his sandwiches and thermos by himself. (M-O A TC69/6/C)

This account vividly illustrates both something of the resentment towards television (as betrayed in the phrase 'abandon itself to television') and the gradual immersion in the ceremony and identification with the principal actors – indeed, this account is the same as the one referenced earlier in the text, in which the investigator revealed that he initially was critical towards television but was converted by the Coronation ceremony. It also shows a certain amount of tension between the extraordinariness of participating in a major ritual through television and the everyday concerns of family relations and domestic routines and practices.

Another Panel member clearly preferred the television coverage while distancing herself from participating in the Coronation celebrations as a spectator in London: 'I wouldn't go if I was paid to, lot of snobbery really just to say you had been to the Coronation' (M-O A TC69/7/B, 596). The same Panel member observed with some discomfort how food had to be taken during pauses in the Coronation broadcast, and that most party guests ate with their plate in their lap while remain-ing concentrated on the television – showing that people adapted their routines to the schedule imposed by television rather than adapting television to the party.

Reverent silence was generally not observed at the television parties. The viewing in groups at the parties was carried out to the accompaniment of a running commentary on things high and low (as was the case with viewing in public, as demonstrated previously). The following quotes were all collected by an investigator present at a Coronation party at a farm in rural England:

> It's hard on the Queen making her walk as slowly as that. It's a dirty shame I call it (young man).
>
> It's a tiring day for her. Two and a half hours in the Abbey. It's a whole day really (middle-aged woman).
>
> I expect she packs herself up with a couple of sandwiches (middle-aged man).
>
> I wish one of the ladies-in-waiting would trip over [when walking backwards], give us a bit of fun (middle-aged man).
>
> Three thousand in the Abbey! Most of them won't be able to see anything, they'll be behind a pillar or something (middle-aged man).
>
> It's the women I want to see. Their dresses (woman).
>
> They put a canopy over her when she's anointed, that's nice for her (young woman).
>
> [When archbishop is speaking] I'd forget the words if I had to do it (young man).
>
> [When an usher moves into the gangway] Oi get back to your place. It's an usher. I expect he's dropped a handkerchief.
>
> (M-O A TC69/6/D)

The commentary includes good-humoured joshing; identification with and/or concern for the principal actors; engagement in, as well as detachment from, the rituals; as well as more general commentary on events and the proceedings broadcast. All the commentary is firmly rooted in everyday jargon and practice.

CONCLUDING REMARKS

None of the observations presented above are very surprising, perhaps. Since previous studies of the Coronation have generally concerned themselves with large-scale, collective and mostly abstract phenomena such as the creation of national community through television, however, it is nevertheless interesting to bring the concrete, almost banal details of everyday television viewing to attention. Many scholars, Benedict Anderson (1991), Dayan and Katz (1992) and Scannell (1996) among them, suggest that mass media, television in particular, are links to a national, abstract 'imagined community'. As is demonstrated by my results, however, television also links and reshapes our very concrete communities and social groups, those together with which we view television – family, friends, acquaintances.

My object here has been both to find patterns in the reception of the Coronation relating to the domestication of the television medium and to challenge the conventional accounts of this event (e.g. Shils and Young, 1956; Briggs, 1979) by presenting the unique, particular and sometimes dissenting views of some audience members. Strong patterns are difficult to find simply because they have not been established yet; what we can see in the accounts preserved in the Mass-Observation Archive is, rather, the gradual emergence of patterns in television viewing. Above all, the televising of the Coronation can be interpreted as a transitional event, with the medium of television on its way to becoming more domesticated: going from a public to a private medium, silencing its critics and, through temporal and spatial structuring, becoming more seamlessly integrated into the domestic contexts of everyday life.

ACKNOWLEDGEMENTS

The author wishes to acknowledge the Trustees of the Mass-Observation Archive, University of Sussex, for access to the Mass-Observation material, and the Swedish Foundation for International Cooperation in Research and Higher Education (STINT), whose generous grant made work on this project possible.

APPENDIX I: ARCHIVAL MATERIAL

All Mass-Observation material is drawn from the Mass-Observation Archive, Topic Collection 69: Royalty.
TC69/1/B – Coronation Surveys and Questionnaires
TC69/2/A – General Analysis of Survey Material
TC69/5/A – The Coronation and the Press
TC69/6/C – Coronation Day Accounts (investigators)
TC69/6/D – Coronation Day Accounts (public)
TC69/6/A-H – Coronation Day Panel Survey

13 Teenagers and television drama in Britain, 1968–1982

Rachel Moseley

The historical film and television audience are notoriously difficult to define, access and research.[1] For television researchers, the difficulty is magnified by the problem of the dispersal of both text (seemingly endless, with multiple and shifting address and generic identity) and audience (geographically, demographically). Identifying and researching with the 'actual' historical television audience is an enormous, and enormously important, project, but it is not the only way of imagining and conceptualising the audience in relation to television. The ways in which television itself – by which I mean its policy makers, writers, producers, publicists, and so on – has imagined its audience at particular socio-historical moments, in particular national contexts, are extraordinarily revealing. Exploring the ways in which particular social and cultural groups have been produced discursively by television – from policy to writing, to text to publicity – can illuminate important moments in the personal and shared national histories we have lived through television. In the introduction to this collection, the editor argues that text-, industrially/institutionally and viewer- (whether empirical or imagined) based histories of television are, and must be, interconnected. In what follows, then, I attempt to take account of the intertwined histories of institution, social context and text in order to think through the ways in which a particular sector of the television audience – the teenager – was imagined by the industry, its creative personnel and in television's ephemera – its publications, press and publicity.

The larger project, of which the research presented here is an early stage, is a critical account of key moments in the history of television produced for teenagers in the United Kingdom and the United States (Moseley, forthcoming). This work is intended to investigate a gap in television historiography, and to consider why television drama for teenagers has been sparse, remaining critically out of focus and unavailable to view, whilst other, related, areas have been brought into the

184

foreground of the research and teaching canon.[2] There is, for instance, a wealth of material on children's television in Britain (see, for instance, Buckingham et al., 1999, Home, 1993, and McGown and Docherty, 2003) and emerging work on pop music, music television and American teen television (for instance, Davis and Dickinson, 2004, Hill, 1991, Lury, 2001, McLuskie, 1998, and Moseley, forthcoming). In this chapter I focus on a period that I shall argue is particularly rich in relation to the conjunction of 'teenagers and television', and is especially resonant for thinking about the development of dramatic programming for the teenage audience in the British context: the late 1970s and early 1980s (via a brief detour, by way of comparison, back to the late 1960s).

The late 1970s saw a number of working parties and reports within and between British broadcasters and associated groups, which were followed by the publication, in 1979, of a study called *Broadcasting and Youth* (see Calouste Gulbenkian Foundation, 1979). This was a report jointly commissioned by the Calouste Gulbenkian Foundation, the Manpower Services Commission, the BBC and the IBA, to investigate and assess the relationship between British broadcasting provision and young adults in the United Kingdom. Soon afterwards, in the first years of the 1980s, as a direct result of the recommendations of that report, there was a small flurry of programmes commissioned especially to address the specific needs of the adolescent British audience. It was a short blossoming, but through it the seeds were sown – though they have not necessarily germinated – for the future of television provision for teenagers in Britain. Accordingly, I want to focus in, towards the end of this chapter, on a drama serial that resulted from the recommendations of the *Broadcasting and Youth* report: *Going Out* (1981), written for Southern Television by Phil Redmond and directed by Colin Nutley. This serial received critical acclaim in the press and is remembered fondly by those who watched it as teenagers as the only thing on television that felt as though it was really 'for them'. As colleagues in the Midlands Television Research Group have helpfully pointed out, this memory is no doubt intensified by the fact that *Going Out* was broadcast just prior to the advent of home VCR recording, and so could not be saved and re-viewed in the same way that viewers now do with their favourite 'teen' shows. Redmond sees his later work – *Tucker's Luck* (BBC, 1983–1985), *What Now?* (Mersey Television for Channel 4, 1986), *Brookside* (Mersey Television for Channel 4, 1982–2003) and, of course, *Hollyoaks* (Mersey Television for Channel 4, 1995–) – as stemming directly from *Going Out*, which he wrote as a post-*Grange Hill* (1978–) drama.[3]

I have two interlocking aims, then, in this chapter. First, I am interested in thinking about the way in which 'the teenager' has been discursively constructed as a figure in need of information, education and regulation, rather than entertainment, by British television across its history. To do so, I want to consider some instances of policy and programming through which we can trace this impetus, and the moment when it changed in 1979 with *Broadcasting and Youth*, and then with *Going Out*. In this respect, I hope to demonstrate that, through looking at the intersections of text and institutional history and policy making, we can begin to construct a picture of the intended addressee, the teen viewer, as constructed discursively by the programme makers at a specific moment in British broadcasting history. Second, I want to begin to offer a critical assessment of the significance of the programming that was produced in relation to that impetus and the transformation it produced: Redmond's drama *Going Out* and the BBC Scotland drama serial *Maggie*, adapted by Joan Lingard from her novels of the same name and broadcast on BBC2 in two seasons in 1981 and 1982. In thinking about the ways in which the British teenager has been addressed and constructed by and in relation to television, I begin by looking back, briefly, to the BBC Schools Drama strand *Scene*, which ran from 1968 to the mid-1990s – those educated in the United Kingdom in the 1970s cannot fail to remember it.[4] These dramas have not been written about critically to date, and so the intellectual project of this piece is one of historiographic inquiry and rediscovery as well as critical assessment. I shall begin, then, with the general problem of the relationship between teenagers and television in this period and beyond, moving on to situate this in relation to the particular industrial and socio-cultural context of the late 1970s, and finally to an analysis of *Maggie* and *Going Out*.

THE 'PROBLEM' OF THE TEENAGER AND THE DIFFICULTY OF THE 'IN-BETWEEN'

In 1967, in what seems to me a revealing shift given the cultural visibility of the discourse of the teenager in the 1950s and 1960s, the BBC's Family Programmes Department was redesignated the Children's Programmes Department. In that move from the notion of entertainment provided for a family group, including the adolescent, to provision for children, the teenager, symbolically, seemed to disappear, now safely ensconced and contained within the family unit. Where teenagers have *always* been present, however, across the history of British television (and perhaps, especially, BBC Television), has been through their discursive construction as being in particular need of education, information and guidance. This has been offered mainly through Television for Schools and Colleges on BBC and Independent Television; apart from this programming strand, British television has, historically, offered little specifically to the teenage audience. Seen as 'light' viewers compared to the rest of the population, they have either been considered part of the audience for children's television, or have otherwise been catered for almost exclusively through pop music programming (for instance, *Cool for Cats* (ITV, 1956–1961), *Six-Five Special* (BBC, 1957–1958), *Oh Boy!* (ITV, 1958–1959), *Boy Meets Girls* (ITV, 1959–1960); Karen Lury, 2001, and Peter McLuskie, 1998, provide discussion of more recent 'youth' and music television in Britain). Dramatic programming for the teenage audience has been scarce, with education and information having been the driving force in decisions made about provision for young adults in Britain. Furthermore, it has been suggested repeatedly by the BBC that teenagers have been well catered for by the 'general output' of light entertainment, and are not in need of further programming tailored to them as a group outside that provision.[5] Teenagers, it is argued, find their entertainment outside the home.[6]

The question is begged, however, and is also asked in *Broadcasting and Youth* (Calouste Gulbenkian Foundation, 1979: 99); could it be the case that teenagers have not simply been 'light viewers' but, rather, that they have been offered very little other than an educative and usually institutionally linked context? Phil Redmond, the key figure in British teen television since the 1970s, has also suggested this in relation to his impetus in writing for a teenage audience: 'It's this whole mantra of "teenagers don't watch television", and I have another mantra, which is "There's nothing for them to watch"! And, like Kevin Costner, if you build it, they will come...'[7] Indeed, one has only to think of the popularity of programming for the teenage audience offered in recent years (Phil Redmond's teen soap *Hollyoaks*, Channel 4's *T4* strand, including, of course, bought-in American dramas such as *Dawson's Creek* (Outerbank/Columbia Tristar, 1998–2003), *The O.C.* (WB/Wonderland/College Hill, for Fox, 2003–) and, on BBC2 and Sky One, *Buffy the Vampire Slayer* (20th Century Fox/Mutant Enemy/Kuzui/Sandollar, 1997–2003) to see that, undoubtedly, the experience of recent years suggests that, if relevant dramatic formats are offered, teenagers – and the extended audience for teen programming – will watch (Davis and Dickinson, 2004: 11–12). Certainly, the questionnaires I have looked at that were used to produce the information on which such assessments and policy decisions have been made do indicate that either the question has not been asked or that, when it has been asked, the answers have not been used.[8] Drama has been shown repeatedly in research to be a favourite programme format amongst teenagers, and yet has been rarely provided specifically for them (Calouste Gulbenkian Foundation, 1979: 43).

'Teenage-ness' is, quite literally, a time both of 'in-between-ness' and of possibility: physically (between child and adult, school and work, dependence and independence), emotionally and, unquestionably, in relation to television, in production and scheduling terms, as the 'teen slot', between 6 p.m. and 7 p.m., which quite literally marks the moment between children's and general output, was originally a gap in the schedules – the 'toddlers' truce' until the BBC's music show *Six-Five Special* began in 1957 (Hill, 1991: 90). I suggest, then, that it is this 'in-between-ness' (between production departments, schedules and audience sectors), in conjunction with rapidly decreasing drama budgets, as documents at the BBC's Written Archives Centre demonstrate,[9] that has generated the long-standing scarcity of dramatic programming for teenagers in the history of British television.

Scene is a fascinating instance of dramatic programming for teenagers in Britain; it was devised as entertaining education to be viewed in an institutional setting, and thus offers a revealing picture of the discursive production of the British teenager in and through television. A long-running series (1968–) of specially commissioned 30-minute dramas and documentaries for use in the classroom, *Scene* was part of BBC Schools' output for 14- to 16-year-olds studying English and the humanities and was a replacement for the current affairs programme *Spotlight* (1961–1967). Whereas dramatic programming for young people up to this point had focused on the classics, *Scene* was especially commissioned drama *for* television, *for* young people, by contemporary playwrights such as Fay Weldon, Alan Plater, Tom Stoppard and Willy Russell, to name but a few.[10] It was designed to be shown by teachers in order to stimulate discussion on a range of topics and issues seen as relevant to contemporary teenagers (such as race, disability, work, unemployment, sexual relationships, crime and the community), and became part of the 'Preparation for Adult Life' campaign that was part of middle and secondary school education in the United Kingdom in the 1970s and 1980s. While *Scene* was made as educational rather than entertainment programming for schools, it attracted a great deal of critical esteem, as well as controversy, as most programming for teenagers has tended to do. Peter Fiddick, writing in the *Guardian* (2 August 1979), remarked, for instance, that 'performances and production are as good as you could wish… [T]his may be schools drama, but it most certainly is not child's play.' Jasper Rees, writing in the *Independent*, argued late in *Scene's* life (24 September 1994) that the series should find a family-friendly evening slot. Similarly, Thomas Sutcliffe in the *Independent* praised the series in the context of the extinction of the one-off drama in mainstream broadcasting, arguing that 'either it's disgraceful that writers of this calibre are reduced to schools programming to get single dramas on screen, or we should throw up a cheer that our children are being nourished by the best available' (24 October 1994). Indicative, here, of the broad-based anxiety around teenagers and television, I think, is the sense that Sutcliffe is unsure how to express the coming together of excellent television drama and the teenage audience.

In trying to think about how the relationship between television and teenagers has been constructed, it is revealing to look at the reports submitted to the Schools Broadcasting Council by their Education Officers, who regularly attended screenings of *Scene* in schools. For example, John Robottom, a Midlands Education Officer attending a screening of *Scene* in a classroom in Moseley Comprehensive School in Birmingham in 1976, commented the following:

> A typical Friday afternoon *Scene* viewing, then – or one of the possible typicalities: a quiet, and in the teachers' language 'dull' group of children responsive in an inarticulate sort of way to a programme which they appreciated as being for them and not quite able to say what they felt which was that they had been treated to *a very rich example of television at its best*. (emphasis added)[11]

This may well be an accurate description of the classroom dynamic, but it is suggestive, again, that there is a perceived disjunction between the provision of excellent drama for teenagers and their ability to receive it, quite aside from the assumption of 'what they were feeling'. Helpfully for the argument I want to make here about the relationship between education and entertainment in programming for teenagers, another Education Officer reports teachers seeing *Scene* as 'an excellent "containerization" series for those children where staff seem to be at a loss to discipline them *and* entertain them before they leave school' (emphasis added).[12]

There is evidence, then, to suggest both the importance of television drama in addressing a teenage audience, whether in a wholly educational or entertainment context, and the perceived quality of much of the drama that has been offered to them. Certain plays in the *Scene* series were shifted in the schedules, both to children's *and* to the general output schedule as stand-alone drama. Many were also repeated in the 1990s as part of BBC2's late-night *DEF II* teenage zone. An early example, written by Alan Plater, was 'Terry' (1969), starring a young Dennis Waterman; this episode offers a flavour of the way in which television drama for teenagers operated prior to the watershed of *Going Out*. Thematically they are similar: *Going Out* addresses youth unemployment and follows six teenagers for the first six weeks after they leave school. 'Terry', ten years earlier, focuses on a young man two years out of school and still moving rapidly from job to job, looking for his place in life, and on the ways in which those around him see him. Each drama's treatment of its subject, however, differs in significant ways. The scripts for *Scene* were published with an account of production techniques and 'talking points', both for use in the classroom; here are some of those proposed for 'Terry'

(1) 'Being happy, that's what counts!' says Terry. Is it?
(2) Are his hopes possible or unreasonable? Do you blame Janie for ditching Terry?
(3) Are many jobs as bad as Terry thinks? Are many people as dissatisfied with them as Terry? Are there any ways in which jobs could be made more interesting? (Marland, 1972: 182)

This contextual material suggests that the key issues to be discussed centre on personal relationships and citizenship – precisely those addressed in *Going Out*, more than a decade later – and suggests too, perhaps, that the concerns around teenage identity are perceived as unchanging, although, as I shall argue, in the context of the early 1980s they are given a particular resonance.

'Terry' is marked by its use of distinctive audio-visual devices that break apart the diegetic world and offer the drama to its audience as innovative and exciting. Waterman, as Terry, explicitly addresses the camera and the teenage audience, offering a direct access to his thoughts, concerns and attitudes to those around him, and thus providing a significantly attention-grabbing 'way in' to the text. The drama nods throughout to cinematic devices likely to be perceived as 'modern', such as the use of jarring cuts, the way in which Terry walks casually from one shot into another (between diegetic spaces and times) while commenting

on the action, and the use of visual framing devices. The distanciation produced
by these stylistic devices seems intended to make the piece feel relevant and
contemporary to its intended audience, as well as to provoke discussion. Moreover,
in 'Terry' studio space and editing are used creatively, in order to draw a distinction
between the stifling entrapment of the family living room and the relative
youthfulness and liveliness of the coffee bar. Significant creative figures in British
television were involved in *Scene*; Plater, for instance, has written a great deal
for television, including many episodes of *Z Cars* (BBC, 1962–1978) and *Flambards*
(Yorkshire Television, 1979), and 'Terry's director, Michael Simpson, went on to
direct television dramas such as *Rumpole of the Bailey* (Thames Television,
1978–1992) and *The Bill* (Fremantle Media Ltd/Thames Television, 1984–). It
is likely that *Scene* has remained out of view to date because it was part of BBC
Schools' output, but, while didactic, the series also offered thought-provoking
drama in a non-condescending form, and represents some of the only dedicated
television drama, before the 1980s, for a British teenage audience.

UNEMPLOYMENT AND ANXIETY

Turning to the specific context for *Going Out*, and the moment of the late 1970s
in the United Kingdom, it is clear from an examination of press and television
publications such as the *Radio Times* and *TV Times* that the teenager was, at this
moment, being constructed discursively as a 'problem' in a way that reinforced
and reproduced the already existing and dominant profile of the teenager as an
object of anxiety in need of education, information and guidance. This
construction, through a new set of circumstances, significantly shaped the
relationship between teenagers and television in this period. In late 1970s Britain,
'antisocial' punk and related teenage subcultural activity was both prominent
and highly visible in the media, and especially on television. In addition, the
recession and the collapse of traditional industries in the country had led to
spiralling unemployment.

Against this backdrop, 'youth' was a particular object of anxiety, as signalled
by the then Prime Minister James Callaghan's 'Ruskin Hall' speech on educational
standards in 1976, the subsequent 'Great Debate' and the House of Commons
inquiry into 'The Attainment of the School Leaver', the Holland Report on Young
People and Work (Manpower Services Commission, 1978) and YOPS – the
Youth Opportunities Programme introduced by the Labour government for
unemployed school leavers in 1977. With unemployment affecting young people
in particular, and with projections suggesting that levels would continue to rise
into the 1980s, the school leaver, and particularly the school leaver without
qualifications or prospects, became the focus of social anxiety. This was not a
new discourse, as we have seen from 'Terry', but it was significantly reinvigorated
at that moment. This anxiety is reflected in the way in which the figure of the

teenager appears on and in relation to television in this period; a consideration of this relationship provides a useful background, against which the significance of the drama I want to discuss comes into strong relief.

TEENAGERS ON TELEVISION

In an examination of the *Radio Times* and *TV Times* in this period, significant trends emerge around teenagers and their (non-)relationship with television in the late 1970s and early 1980s. There was virtually no dedicated programming for them apart from television for schools and colleges – in other words, other than for those in full- or part-time education. Programming under this aegis focused on school subjects and on general educational and personal development issues – health, sexual relationships, the community, etc. Dominating, however, was programming aimed at the school leaver, within television for schools and colleges on both ITV and BBC, about work – or, rather, about unemployment: for instance, the BBC's *Going to Work* (1979) and ITV's *Making a Living* (Yorkshire Television, 1979). There were also many examples of what was described as 'older children's' drama about enterprising youngsters setting up their own businesses (for instance, *Four Idle Hands* (ATV, 1976) and *A Bunch of Fives* (ATV, 1977–1978)), and there was also a glut of programming *about* teenagers – and, more specifically, the problem of the teenager.

These programmes often had accompanying articles in TV listings guides (about, for instance, teenage homelessness, unemployment and drugs use) and were clearly addressed to parents. Programmes ranged from daytime 'help' programming for parents (e.g. BBC2's 1979 *Signs of Trouble*, a series for parents on 'Aspects of delinquency' with Laurie Taylor, Professor of Sociology at the University of York, and in May 1978 Granada's *Parents' Day*: 'What happens if your youngster doesn't want to stay on at school, but can't get a job?') to a wide range of prime-time television drama, about, but not really addressed to, teenagers and their problems. London Weekend Television's *Kids* (1979), broadcast on ITV on Friday nights at 9 p.m., is a key instance here: an anthology drama series that looked at the problems faced by children living in a care home, putting them in 'adult situations'. This went out alongside a Saturday night series of four programmes, *Two People* (LWT), broadcast at 10 p.m., which addressed the parent–teenager relationship as experienced by four television stars giving the parental view and described in the accompanying article by Jane Ennis (1979) as '[a] four-star guide to bringing up teenagers'. Interestingly, many of these programmes emerged in the wake of the recommendations made in internal industry reports and *Broadcasting and Youth*, that more programmes that might help adults understand the problems faced by teenagers today should be provided,[13] but it is revealing that there was still little evidence of similar programming being provided specifically for those teenagers in question. Again, the teenager was constructed as a problem to be addressed and to be educated, but is rarely the focus of specific provision (apart from pop and rock music programming) other than this remit.

INDUSTRY AND POLICY: THE REPORTS

This, then, very broadly, is the context that saw the formation, in 1978, of a series of working parties and reports on television provision for the teenager – both inside the British television industry, and with outside organisations – that aimed to investigate broadcast provision for this troubled age group. Rather predictably, most of them were concerned entirely with educational broadcasting, but they still had interesting things to say about general television output for this age range. Some key reports were as follows.

- ITC (Independent Television Commission): Report of the 16–19 Working Party on the Period of Transition from School to Work.
- BBC: SBC (Schools Broadcasting Council)/FEBC (Further Education Broadcasting Council) 1978 Joint Working Party on Educational Broadcasting for the 15–19 Age Group.[14]
- BBC: Report for the GAC (General Advisory Council), *The BBC's Programme Responsibilities towards Adolescents and Young Adults*.[15]
- The Gulbenkian/MSC (Manpower Services Commission)/BBC/ITC Young Adult Study,[16] later published as *Broadcasting and Youth*.

In short, all these reports, with the exception of the BBC's internal report to its own General Advisory Council, found that there was *limited to no* entertainment programming for teenagers in the United Kingdom, and recommended that entertainment formats be introduced, not just as the sugared coating on the bitter pill of education but also in and for its own sake. They all also highlighted the needs of girls and ethnic minorities in relation to television provision. These findings echoed those made in similar reports a decade earlier, and which, clearly, had not been acted upon. In fact, the BBC 1973 report *Children as Viewers and Listeners* mentioned, in an early draft, that *Scene* was the closest the BBC came to a youth drama programme; interestingly, however, this comment was omitted in the final version of the report as it was published.[17]

In contrast, the BBC's own 1978 report to its GAC found its provision for adolescents and young adults to be entirely adequate. As a press release shows,[18] the BBC were subsequently dismayed by the contradictions between their own findings and that of the *Broadcasting and Youth* study, which found that there was a serious lack of general output provision for the 14–21 age group (distinct, the report said, because, in spite of their heterogeneity, they nevertheless share a common emotional life and culture), and especially for those not in education: 'There is simply not enough programming for young people [...] [W]e are forced to conclude that general programming is not providing anything like the range of output appropriate to meet the needs of young people' (Calouste Gulbenkian Foundation, 1979: 86, 98). It highlighted the need to offer programming that dealt not just with work and employment but also with personal development, relationships and related issues within *entertainment and dramatic formats*. Dramatic forms, and particularly soap opera, were suggested as likely formats for reaching this age group (Calouste Gulbenkian Foundation, 1979: 101). The report also emphasised the importance of appropriate scheduling for such programming, suggesting 5–7 p.m. on weekday evenings, and Saturday mornings. In looking at planning within the BBC, 1980–1981 was seen as the time frame in which responses to the study might be implemented at the earliest. The BBC does not seem to have responded with enthusiasm to these recommendations, however, except with further educational output in magazine format.[19]

If we take into account the additional factor of the decreasing drama budget within the BBC, in conjunction with the apparent ongoing defensiveness and reluctance to recognise and cater for the teenage audience, we can begin to understand why, historically, there has been so little drama for teenagers on British television.[20]

BRITISH TEEN DRAMA

There have been a few significant exceptions to this trend, however, and, in many ways, the *Broadcasting and Youth* report was a watershed moment, in that it produced two drama serials commissioned specifically for teenagers – *Maggie* and *Going Out* – both of which were broadcast in 1981. While there is an argument for uncovering and writing these programmes back into television history simply from a historiographic point of view, and as an address to the contemporaneity of the current research and teaching canon in this area, certainly, in the case of *Going Out*, there is a further argument on the basis of innovation in television drama. Both serials are clearly informed by a concern to address the problems facing contemporary teenagers (and, indeed, to address the issue of girls and, to a limited extent, questions of ethnicity, as suggested in the report – and as Anna Home, who produced *Maggie*, confirms in looking back at this period[21]), but, unlike *Scene*, these programmes do not represent 'education by stealth'. Both serials focus on leaving school and the decisions to be made: *Maggie*, clearly aimed at a young teenage audience and with a teenage girl from a working-class family in Glasgow at its heart, centres on the dilemma of whether to stay on at school or to go to work; *Going Out* focuses on a group of teenagers from a comprehensive school on the south coast and follows their first six weeks after leaving, in six episodes, and the beginning of their life on the dole. These programmes used the particular pleasures of the serial drama form, with its development of familiarity and suspense, to address its audience in their own terms.

Set and filmed on location in Glasgow as well as in the studio, *Maggie* is the story of a teenage girl whose family have been moved from their tenement building into a high-rise block, and her struggles with school, family and work. Whilst parochial in setting, it deals in universal, as well as regionally specific, themes: adolescence, school, love and social class. Made by BBC Scotland with the Scottish Youth Theatre and Glasgow Drama Workshop, it was broadcast in the 'teen' slot recommended by the *Broadcasting and Youth* report (at around 6 p.m. on Tuesdays and Thursdays) on BBC2. It was unusual in this period for its serious focus on teenage girlhood, which was highlighted particularly by the report as a deficiency in current broadcast provision.[22] Adapted from Joan Lingard's novels as a straightforward serial in nine parts, as with much low-budget drama of the period its studio portions are often stilted and non-dynamic, but, nonetheless, convey effectively the sense of entrapment that Maggie experiences at home.[23] Its use of location filming and ambient sound give it a tough, naturalist edge, however, which is now most unusual in dominant constructions of adolescent girlhood. Further, there is a historically specific feminist discourse running through this serial and the audio-visual construction of its main character, in costuming, content and theme tune. Maggie typically wears a post-punk pop combination of drainpipe jeans with shirt, tie and cardigan, an outfit that has feminist connotations in its appropriation of male attire (think Chrissy Hind and Debbie Harry in the period in question).

Focusing on Maggie's attempt not to be drawn into factory work and early marriage, the adaptation charts the struggle of a working-class girl's desires for academic achievement and success, her romance with a middle-class boy, her attempts to encourage her father into self-employment, and the impact these conflicting aims have on her own life and planning for the future. The serial also places her squarely in a line of strong and independent Scottish women. The theme tune, 'Maggie', by B.A. Robertson, accompanies a title sequence of teen-magazine-style graphics over location shots of a run-down Glasgow tenement in the process of demolition, and has lyrics that give a flavour of the serial's tone: 'She's a rebel of sorts, she's inclined academically, she won't be a teenage bride, she won't dance or work in a factory, though her parents think she should.' I argue that this programme is a rare and important instance of British television drama addressed specifically to an adolescent, female teenage audience, and that, seen as the production of a very particular set of circumstances (social, institutional, creative[24]), it offers insight into the discursive construction of the teenager – and, specifically, the teenage girl – in British television culture in the early 1980s.

Similarly, *Going Out* explores the decision to be made about staying on at school at a time of high youth unemployment, but its focus is most clearly on the nature of unemployed existence for the young. Written by Phil Redmond and made by Southern Television using, largely, young actors from Anna Scher's Theatre Workshop, the six-part serial, filmed on location in Portsmouth, follows the first six weeks of a group of teenagers after leaving school. The tagline for the series was 'What's it like to be 16, with no job, no girlfriend and no future?'. Elkan Allan, writing in *The Times* (1981), begins his piece on *Going Out* thus: 'You will almost certainly be unaware that the best contemporary serial since *Grange Hill* is to be seen on ITV at present... Doubtless the honesty of the language will be cited as an excuse for the absurd late-night timings. It isn't good enough.' Despite the report's recommendations, ITV had appeared to 'chicken out' over the serial and scheduled it late at night, at times ranging from 10.30 in the Midlands ATV region to midnight in London, and on differing days across the regions. Redmond, however, points to the fact that, because Southern Television lost their ITV franchise at the same time that *Going Out* was to be transmitted, not only was there only one series, but it also had to be broadcast before 31 December 1981 in order for them to keep their tax breaks, and this is, in fact, part of the reason for the varied scheduling.[25] Later, Allan writes: 'As a direct result of *Going Out*, I feel that I can look across the generation gap for the first time in many years and begin to appreciate that the unruly tribe of often violent, frightening youngsters is made up of individuals with a range of personalities and problems' (Allan, 1981). While this serial was primarily intended as entertainment for a dispossessed generation of teenagers, in line with the recommendations of *Broadcasting and Youth* (Calouste Gulbenkian Foundation, 1979: 105), it also offered a different perspective on them to an adult audience.

One of the main achievements of this serial, though, in aesthetic terms, was its lively, engaging yet sophisticated articulation of the coexistent experiences of unemployment, boredom and empty time for its teenage characters. This is achieved at a number of levels and from a number of perspectives. First, in the writing, which gives the disaffected teenage protagonists a voice, through a great deal of repetition of phrases and a bouncing back and forth of the same phrases and words between characters ('Where are you going?' 'Going Out.' 'Out where?' 'Just out.'), creating a sense of purposelessness and boredom that pervades the text. On the visual level, the same spaces are repeated throughout each episode and across episodes, frequently from the same perspective, establishing the feeling that there is only a limited possibility for change and escape. In a similar way, the camera's frequent focus and long hold on empty spaces, and the constant framing of characters by the bleak, grey concrete landscape of Portsmouth (there is little impression that this is a coastal town), have a similar effect and suggest the tedium of the passing of time made empty by unemployment. There is a sense, then, that this existence is offered both through the characters but also as a discourse on them; in many ways, this serial could be described as an expressionist drama, in that it offers an external expression, through the mise en scène, of its characters' internal states, but is also at times impressionistic in its portrayal of empty time and barren space.

The serial's most significant device, though, is the successful dialectic produced between action and stasis in its representation of this particular historical experience of teenage time and space, and this dialectic can be traced, as a visual trope, throughout the text. The title sequence, which is identical at the beginning of each of the six episodes, begins this thematic through its contrasting of different types of movement within the frame, and the lyrics of the theme song underline the tension produced in the opening images. The lyrics constantly repeat the phrase 'I'm going out', and highlight the entrapment and restlessness of teenage experience: 'So many things I've been wanting to do, so many things I've been itching to do, but I can't do them when I'm stuck in here with you, I'm going out.' They also point, ironically, to teenagers finding their entertainment away from television: 'Keep your telly, I'm going out.'

The title sequence shows the main characters, virtually in silhouette, animatedly fooling about with each other on the banks of a river, in a setting signalled as relatively industrial. Their dynamic movement, however, like the theme song, is repetitive, is rooted to one place and takes them nowhere (and, of course, it is repeated exactly each week). Literally, despite the title, they are going 'nowhere'. In contrast, however, is the movement in and out of the frame of the cars on the distant bridge, which serves to highlight the aimlessness – though also the vibrancy – of their movement on the shore. The two forms of movement sit productively in tension with each other, given that the theme of the serial is the lack of possibility and change in their lives, and this is also in tension with the vaguely romantic use of colour (a hazy, muted orange) and silhouette in this sequence. This tension, between movement and stasis, recurs throughout the serial. In the first episode, on the last day of school, the characters meet at the final school dance, and as they arrive in the school hall the camera tracks through the crowd, emphasising its similarly vibrant, but aimless, movement ('rockers' headbanging) as it follows the main characters to their place against the wall. The dialogue, spoken by Dikey (played indolently yet engagingly by Peter Hugo Daley), a character who left school in the previous year, emphasises its repetitive nature: 'Still going?' he says as he joins in.

It is notable that the camera's sweeping movement across the bleak urban environment in *Going Out* serves perfectly to highlight its bleakness and to frame the characters repeatedly against and within its limits. At the same time, these moments of dynamism (of the characters and of the camera) are tied to fighting, dancing – and borderline vandalism – and other forms of goal-less but time-filling, affect-producing, movement, and as a result they give a sense of what it might be like to try to fill time and focus solely on the present moment. In the second episode, the characters move upwards in a spiral through one of their frequently revisited spaces, a concrete staircase on the outside of a car park; spirals are frequent in *Going Out* and are a good instance of convoluted, non-directional movement. The camera cranes, tracks and pans in one long take to follow them as they circle the inside of the car park in their 'borrowed' car, expressing well the excitement, but aimlessness, of their activity.

Going Out frequently uses diegetic snippets of contemporary pop music to speak to its audience in a less than heavy-handed nod to their own culture. Redmond says of his writing for *Going Out* that not only was he inspired by *Saturday Night Fever* (John Badham, 1977) but that he saw it as 'a sort of take on Britain then, almost as if I wanted to hold up a mirror to society, so in a sense there was no manipulation of the image, it was just "Here it is"'. What is significant about this comment, and others such as 'The actors thought they were adlibbing, but in fact they weren't' and 'We might think about show, not tell', is that they clearly highlight the naturalist agenda that underpinned the conceptualisation and writing of *Going Out*.[26] It is the distinctive conjunction of this impulse with what is often a mannered aesthetic (exemplified by the baroque movement within a long take described above) in which the achievement of this serial resides, and, indeed, which contemporary British teen dramas, including Redmond's own *Hollyoaks* but also *As If*, have inherited.

CONCLUSION

British teenagers had been fairly thoroughly informed, educated, regulated and contained by television, but less often entertained by television drama, until the watershed of 1981 and two programmes in the wake of *Broadcasting and Youth* that aimed to address British teenagers in an entertaining but serious fashion. While I think that they must be seen as paving the way for a broader address to the teenage television audience in Britain, partly, of course, in relation to industrial and technological changes in the television landscape over the past 20 years, they also, perhaps, offer a glimpse of what might have been. *Going Out* was well received critically and is fondly held in popular memory as an important moment for teenage viewers in the early 1980s, but the brevity of its moment was the result of industrial factors (Southern Television's loss of its franchise), the resulting late night scheduling, and questions of censorship and the moral guardianship of the nation's youth. Had *Going Out* appeared post-VCR and at a time when TVs in teenagers' bedrooms were more common, its impact might have been more widely felt and a more significant tradition of serious teen-oriented drama in Britain might have emerged in its wake. As it is, *Going Out* and *Maggie*, considered in their particular historical and industrial context, allow us a glimpse of the British television industry's perception of its teenage audience, and of what can happen when creative personnel take teenagers seriously.

Appendix

Directory of Key Research Resources for Television History in the United Kingdom[1]

ARCHIVES[2]

BBC Information and Archives – BBC Television Centre, Wood Lane, London, W12 7RJ. Email: research-central@bbc.co.uk. Phone: 020 8225 7193. Website: www.bbcresearchcentral.com[3]

BBC Written Archives Centre – Peppard Road, Caversham Park, Reading, RG4 8TZ. Email: heritage@bbc.co.uk. Phone: 0118 948 6281. Website: www.bbc.co.uk/heritage/more/wac.shtml

BFI National Library – British Film Institute, 21 Stephen Street, London, W1T 1LN. Phone: 020 7255 1444. Website: www.bfi.org.uk/filmtvinfo/library/index.html

Border Television News and Archive Library – Border Television plc, Television Centre, Harraby Industrial Estate, Carlisle, Cumbria, CA1 3NT. Email: dutyoffice@itv.com. Phone: 01228 525101. Website: www.itvregions.com/border

British Universities Film and Video Council – 77 Wells Street, London, W1T 3QJ. Phone: 020 7393 1500. Website: www.bufvc.ac.uk

Canal + Image UK Ltd – Pinewood Studios, Pinewood Road, Iver, Buckinghamshire, SL0 0NH. Phone: 01753 631111

Channel Television – The Television Centre, La Pouquelaye, St Helier, Jersey, JE2 3ZD. Email: broadcast@channeltv.co.uk. Phone: 01534 816816. Website: www.channeltv.co.uk

East Anglian Film Archive – East Anglian Film Archive (UEA), The Archive Centre, Martineau Lane, Norwich, NR1 2DQ. Email: eafa@uea.ac.uk. Phone: 01603 592664. Website: www.uea.ac.uk/eafa/

Granada Media Clip Sales[4] – c/o: ITN Archive, 200 Grays Inn Road, London, WC1X 8XZ. Email: sales@itnarchive.com. Phone: 020 7430 4480. Website: www.itnsource.com

Imperial War Museum – Keeper of the Film and Video Archive, Imperial War Museum, Lambeth Road, London, SE1 6HZ. Email: film@iwm.org.uk. Phone: 020 7416 5291. Website: www.iwm.org.uk/

Independent Television News Archive – ITN Archive, 200 Grays Inn Road, London, WC1X 8XZ. Email: sales@itnarchive.com. Phone: 020 7430 4480. Website: www.itnsource.com

Mass-Observation Archive – University of Sussex Library, Brighton, BN1 9QL. Email: library.specialcoll@sussex.ac.uk. Phone: 01273 678157. Website: www.massobs.org.uk/

Media Archive of Central England – The University of Leicester, Salisbury Road, Leicester, LE1 7QR. Email: macearchive@le.ac.uk. Phone: 0116 252 5066. Website: www.macearchive.org

National Film and Television Archive – BFI Archive Enquiries, 21 Stephen Street, London, W17 1LN. Phone: 020 7957 4726. Website: www.bfi.org.uk/nftva/

National Museum of Photography, Film and Television – Bradford, West Yorkshire, BD1 1NQ. Email: talk.nmpft@nmsi.ac.uk. Phone: 0870 70 10 201. Website: www.nationalmediamuseum.org.uk/Television/ExperienceTV.asp

National Screen and Sound Archive of Wales – National Library of Wales, Aberystwyth, Ceredigion, SY23 3BU. Email: agssc@llgc.org.uk. Phone: 01970 632828. Website: screenandsound.llgc.org.uk/

North West Film Archive – Manchester Metropolitan University, Minshull House, 47–49 Chorlton Street, Manchester, M1 3EU. Email: n.w.filmarchive@mmu.ac.uk. Phone: 0161 247 3097. Website: www.nwfa.mmu.ac.uk

Northern Region Film and Television Archive – School of Arts and Media, University of Teesside, Middlesborough, TS1 3BA. Phone: 0191 277 2250. Website: www.nrfta.org.uk

Royal Television Society Library and Archive – 100 Grays Inn Road, London, WC12X 8AL. Phone: 020 7430 1000. Website: www.rts.org.uk

Scottish Screen Archive – 1 Bowmont Gardens, Glasgow, G12 9LR. Email: archive@scottishscreen.com. Phone: 0141 337 7400. Website: www.scottish-screen.com/home/

Scottish Television Film and Videotape Library – Scottish TV, 200 Renfield Street, Glasgow, Scotland, G2 3PR. Email: footage.sales@smg.plc.uk. Phone: 0141 300 3122. Website: www.stv.tv

The South West Film and Television Archive – Melville Building, Royal William Yard, Stonehouse, Plymouth, PL1 3RP. Email: enquiries@tswfta.co.uk. Phone: 01752 202650. Website: www.tswfta.co.uk

Ulster Television Film Library – Ulster Television Limited, Havelock House, Ormeau Road, Belfast, BT7 1EB. Phone: 028 9026 2147. Website: www.u.tv/

Voice of the Listener and Viewer – 101 Kings Drive, Gravesend, Kent, DA12 5BQ. Email: info@vlv.org.uk. Phone: 01474 352835. Website: www.vlv.org.uk

Wessex Film and Sound Archive – Hampshire Record Office, Sussex Street, Winchester, SO23 8TH. Email: david.lee@hants.gov.uk. Phone: 01962 847742. Website: www.hants.gov.uk/record-office/film/index.html

Yorkshire Film Archive – York St John College, Lord Mayors Walk, York, YO31 7EX. Email: info@yorkshirefilmarchive.com. Phone: 01904 716550. Website: www.yorkshirefilmarchive.com

INTERNET-BASED ARCHIVES AND OTHER RESOURCES

ARKive: www.arkive.org/

Newsfilm Online: www.bufvc.ac.uk/newsfilmonline/

Screenonline: www.screenonline.org.uk/index.html

TV Times Project: tvtip.bufvc.ac.uk/index.php

Notes

INTRODUCTION

1. For example: 'Did ITV Revolutionise British Television?' (Bournemouth University, begun 1999); 'Cultures of British Television Drama, 1960–1982' (University of Reading, begun 2002); 'British TV Drama and Acquired US Programmes, 1970–2000' (University of Reading, begun 2005).

2. For example: 'TV Times Digitisation Project' (Bournemouth University, begun 2001); 'Database and Catalogued Archive Relating to the ITV Current Affairs Programme *This Week*, 1956–1992' (Bournemouth University, begun 2004).

3. For example, the International Association for Media and History (www.iamhist.org/) and the 'Media history and history in the media' conferences held by the University of Wales in 2005 and 2007, or indeed the symposia and conferences on television history that initiated this volume, held at the University of Reading between 2003 and 2005 as an outcome of the research project 'Cultures of British Television Drama, 1960–1982'.

4. For example, the Screen studies conference held in Glasgow attracted three papers on television history in 2004, seven in 2005 and 21 in 2006.

5. Jason Jacobs' account of researching in the television archive offers a vivid account of the imaginative and pleasurable processes of historical research, for example (see Jacobs, 2006a).

6. Similarly, calls for multi-methodological studies of television have been made within non-historical television studies (see Born, 2000, and Frith, 2000). As Simon Frith has argued: 'These three strands [production studies, textual analysis and cultural-studies-based audience ethnography] need to be woven together in ways they have not yet been... What is now needed...is a television culture research network...a means to encourage dialogue between all the quite different kinds of researchers who are concerned to make sense of what is happening inside that black box' (2000: 49–50).

7. 'Television for Women in Britain: a Critical, Industrial and Reception History Workshop', 5–6 July 2004, University of Warwick (organisers: Rachel Moseley, Helen Wheatley and Helen Wood).

8. Research projects led by Jason Jacobs ('Early Television Drama in Australia, Great Britain and the USA – a Three-Year ARC Discovery Project, 2003–2005') and Jonathan Bignell ('British TV Drama and Acquired US Programmes, 1970–2000') have sought to address these factors; I am grateful to Jacobs for sharing his thoughts on the internationalisation of television history with me.

9. See Jamie Medhurst in this volume, for example.

10.   See Su Holmes, Lez Cooke, Darrell Newton and Rachel Moseley in this book for examples of this critical reinterpretation.

11.   Emma Sandon offers an eloquent discussion of this process in her chapter in this book.

12.   I am grateful to all the participants of the symposium 'Reconsidering the Canon: Popular British Television Drama in the 1960s and '70s' (19 September 2003 – University of Reading) for providing stimulating debate on this subject, an event that, in part, inspired the production of this collection.

CHAPTER 1

1.   The distinction I am making here is not new. It is used, for example, by Theodor Adorno in the distinction between immanent and transcendent criticism (both seen as impossible in their purest form) that he makes in *Prisms* (1981).

2.   Francis Watson is Professor of New Testament Exegesis, University of Aberdeen.

3.   Watson's criticism of textual-historicism runs the risk of conflating the endurance of faiths over millennia with the text that is at their centre; of confusing beliefs with the book. Behind his nervousness in the face of a historical interpretation lies a view that historical interpretation diminishes not the text so much as the institutions of faith that use it. But a textual-historical view of that text simply tries to provide an account of the concrete process that brought the text into being. It would be another history entirely to explain why the faiths that used this book have endured.

4.   Of the two, the TV is more prominently displayed and more often used. Both claim to be everyday textual arrays, but their address to the everyday is rather different.

5.   As opposed to the public form of TV developed to an advanced level in Nazi Germany in the late 1930s, for example, when TV was shown in small cinema-like television halls. These were originally public but during the Second World War were increasingly used for military audiences. The technology used was 'intermediate film', producing a TV image from scanning film material still wet from development. A considerable amount of this material survived in the East German film archive (see Knut Hickethier's (1990) work on this).

6.   One minor problem of interpretation for material from the first period of TV history, running to the mid-1970s or even the 1980s in Europe, is the fact that TV transmissions were limited to certain times of the day. So TV, though present every day, tended to have an event status in some households, and programmes might have been regarded less as part of a flow (as in 'I will watch TV') and more as single texts (as in 'I will watch this particular programme').

7.   Ofcom Review of Public Service Broadcasting, 21 April 2004, table 22, specifies that analogue homes watch an average of 3.4 hours per week and digital homes 3.8 hours (derived from Broadcasters' Audience Research Board (BARB) research).

8. *Desperate Housewives* (Touchstone Television for ABC, 2004–); *Heartbeat* (Yorkshire TV/Granada for ITV, 1991–); *Rosemary and Thyme* (Carnival Films for ITV, 2003–2006).
9. For a consideration of the changing levels of spending on TV drama, see Ellis (2005).
10. See also Wheatley (2007) for a discussion of this episode and its survival. The Screenonline entry is found at www.screenonline.org.uk/tv/id/579165/index.html.
11. Though the Ampex system was used, the drama would have been recorded 'as live'. Since video editing did not really exist, the only option for correcting mistakes would have been to re-record the whole 'act' again; and the *Armchair Theatre* schedule, let alone that of the actors, would have permitted that only in extremis. Much of this technical detail is explored in the 1987 documentary produced by Paul Madden, directed by Laurens Postma for Microcraze Productions/Channel 4, when this programme was retransmitted.
12. The Robbins Report of 1963 unleashed a wave of foundations of new universities, such as Warwick, York, Keele, Sussex, Kent, Exeter and Stirling. It was the beginning of a half-century of continual expansion of the university sector, with the result that '[t]he UK now has more postgraduate students (about 300,000) than there were undergraduates in the early 1960s (about 270,000); and the proportion of women students has doubled from under 25 per cent to 50 per cent' (Williams, 1997: 4).
13. Cited in *Theories of Authorship* (Caughie, 1981: 29). This book is a very useful starting point for understanding debates around authorship in film studies. It should be supplemented by examination of the third edition of Geoffrey Nowell-Smith's book *Luchino Visconti* (2003), especially pages 209 to 223.
14. See, for instance, John R. Cook, *Dennis Potter: A Life on Screen* (1995).
15. See, for instance, Michael Balcon on the making of *Scott of the Antarctic* (1948): 'In those days, with our eye on the American market, we used to submit our scripts in advance to the appropriate authority in Hollywood' (Balcon, 1969: 174).
16. See Ellis (2000b).

CHAPTER 2

1. This section draws on the longer analysis of publication on television drama in Bignell (2005b).
2. See Máire Messenger-Davies' chapter in this book for a discussion of this phenomenon.
3. This point is, necessarily, a generalisation, but it does apply to the books identified as introductory texts in the lists of publishers such as McGraw-Hill, Palgrave and Routledge.
4. By spring 2007 volumes published comprised: Bignell and O'Day (2004), Morgan-Russell (2004), Cardwell (2005), Hallam (2005a), Rolinson (2005), Tulloch (2007) and Cooke (2007), with a further volume forthcoming on Tony Garnett.
5. See Lez Cooke's chapter in this collection, for example.

6. Leonard White, unpublished contribution to the symposium 'Producing Popular Television Drama, 1960–1982', interviewed by Helen Wheatley at the University of Reading, October 2004.

CHAPTER 3

1. See Davies (2000) for a fuller discussion of the issues raised by this problem.
2. Just how unsung can be seen from its omission from a useful and otherwise comprehensive book, *British Television Drama: A History*, by Lez Cooke, published in 2003 by the BFI, which mentions *Clayhanger* but does not mention a single children's drama, apart from a passing reference to *Grange Hill* in the context of the career in adult drama of Phil Redmond. It's arguable that *Grange Hill* may turn out to be a more enduring example of Redmond's importance to TV drama than *Hollyoaks* or even *Brookside*.
3. In a chapter on ITV's *Upstairs Downstairs* (2005), Helen Wheatley draws attention to another possible reason for the disappearance of series such as *Clayhanger*: the critical disdain towards and invisibility of studio-based costume dramas.
4. See, for instance, Steven Kline's *Out of the Garden: Toys and Children's Culture in the Age of TV Marketing* (1993).
5. See also Catherine Johnson's chapter on historiography and evaluation in this volume.
6. See also Jacobs, 2001, Geraghty, 2003, Jancovich and Lyons, 2003, and the forthcoming collected edition on high-quality television by Janet McCabe and Kim Akass. This debate also raged at a recent conference at the University of Reading, entitled 'Cultures of British Television Drama' (September 2005).
7. For a sceptical view of these developments, see also Gripsrud, 2004; Jostein Gripsrud argues that, despite the increasing prevalence of digital libraries, DVDs, downloading, etc., 'broadcasting's provision of a more or less shared cultural menu is still a highly important element in people's construction of their social identities, their sense of selfhood and their experience of community... [T]he only major advantage of digital television is that movie channels transmit the same movies three times in the same evening' (213–215).

CHAPTER 4

1. See the chapters by Jonathan Bignell, John Ellis and Máire Messenger Davies in this collection, for example.
2. John Caughie (2000) is perhaps an exception to this in his exploration and evaluation of the golden age of British television in the 1960s, which will be discussed in more detail below.
3. Such hesitancy is also apparent in Robert J. Thompson's book on US quality television, *Television's Second Golden Age* (1997), which, despite its title, is cautious of the evaluative power of the term 'golden age'.

4. It also raises the question of the definition of creativity and artistry, and its relationship to other criteria of evaluation, which will be discussed below.

5. Sue Harper and Vincent Porter's (2005) special journal edition on visual style in British film and television would seem to fulfil the kind of aesthetic history called for by Allen and Gomery.

6. Of course, taste is also contingent; see Pierre Bourdieu (1984).

7. Máire Messenger Davies' discussion of evaluating *Clayhanger* in this volume illustrates precisely the difficulty of categorisation for historians.

8. I will return later in this chapter to the issue of distinguishing between judgements of artistic value and of quality.

9. *The Quatermass Experiment* (BBC, 1953), *Quatermass II* (BBC, 1955), and *Quatermass and the Pit* (BBC, 1958–1959) were all six-part serials that were written by Nigel Kneale and produced/directed by Rudolph Cartier. They were all adapted for film, and were followed by a further production in the late 1970s made for both film and television (see Johnson, 2005).

10. A response that is similar to that described by Helen Wheatley (2005) above in relation to the studio costume drama.

11. As Jonathan Bignell argues, the pressures on research into British television have tended 'to lend legitimacy to writing and teaching in the UK about television drama that centres on a social realist aesthetic, and values formal complexity, reflexivity, the importance of authorship, and an engagement with contemporary issues that are recognizable from non-dramatic forms' (2005b: 19; see also his chapter in this collection).

12. There is an issue here about canonisation that is beyond the scope of this chapter. It is worth noting, however, that, while evaluation cannot simply be equated with the imposition of timeless criteria onto works of art, evaluative judgements are certainly shaped by the contexts within which they are made. Hence, the criteria by which works are already considered valuable are likely to shape the ways in which works are evaluated in the future; see Herrnstein Smith, 1988: 46–47, and Máire Messenger Davies (in this volume), who discusses some of the reasons why certain television programmes become canonised. As will be argued below, engaging in evaluations of old programmes can be one way of challenging the evaluative criteria of such canonisation.

13. While there is the occasional 'special event' live television drama, these are rare exceptions. Indeed, it is noticeable that the 2005 remake of *The Quatermass Experiment* (BBC, 2005), which was transmitted live, actually ran 20 minutes under time, suggesting that the skills of producing and directing live television drama are ones that have largely dissipated in contemporary television production.

14. Indeed, in the four years that I have been teaching the *Quatermass* serials to undergraduates, I have only ever encountered one student who knew who Kneale and Cartier were in advance of the class.

15. See, for example, Siegel, 1984, and Johnson-Smith, 2005.

16. Bruce Berman, 1976, makes a fascinating attempt to examine these issues, arguing that different sports require different stylistic approaches and that it is possible to examine the artistry of live television sports.

17. A number of fascinating papers at the 'Screen studies' conference in July 2006 suggest that the relative lack of historical work on popular television is beginning to be challenged. Helen Wheatley examined natural history programmes from the 1950s, Rachel Moseley looked at Marguerite Patten's early cookery programmes, Su Holmes explored the 1950s soap opera *The Grove Family* and Emma Sandon explored light entertainment from the 1940s and 1950s.

CHAPTER 5

1. Viewer Research Report, *Picture Parade*, 12 June 1956, T6/400/1 (BBC Written Archives Centre [BBC WAC hereafter]).
2. Viewer Research Report, *Picture Parade*, 2 June 1958, R9/7/34 (BBC WAC).
3. Whether from the BBC or ITV, however, none of the existing shows contain the film excerpts themselves. In this respect, none of them are entirely complete.
4. Memorandum by Director of Talks 10 April 1946, R51/173/4 (BBC WAC).
5. Memorandum on 'Film', 23 October 1936, R51/173/1 (BBC WAC).
6. Michael Bell to CT, 31 August 1949, R51/173/5 (BBC WAC).
7. Harman Grisewood to CT 6 July 1949, R51/173/4 (BBC WAC).
8. Precisely because of its apparent lack of critical autonomy, this can be contextualised within a much longer history of critical disdain for the cinema programme. For a contemporary discussion, see Kerr (1996).
9. Meeting between BBC and CEA/KRS, 1 June 1950, T6/ 104/1 (BBC WAC).
10. 'Current release notes', W. Farquarson Small, 26 September 1951, T6/104/1 (BBC WAC).
11. Cecil Madden to Cecil McGivern, 2 January 1956, T6/240/1 (BBC WAC).
12. 11 January 1956, *Today's Cinema*, 11.
13. This clearly also raises the issue of gender in the developing conventions of television presenting, and the cinema programme in particular. Although a wider analysis of this is beyond the scope of this chapter, the cinema programme in the 1950s was resolutely dominated by male presenters, and there seemed to be the suggestion that – despite the entertainment basis of the series – a woman would not carry the necessary authority and 'weight'. For a broader discussion of women as television presenters at this time, see Leman (1987).
14. The last two categories clearly apply more to the BBC programmes, again foregrounding the difficultly of reconstructing the ITV shows.
15. Cecil McGivern to John Dennett, 19 March 1951, T6/104/1 (BBC WAC).
16. Cecil McGivern to W. Farquarson Small, 27 March 1952, T6/104/2 (BBC WAC).
17. Indeed, archival research into the early television quiz shows in Britain also questions the dichotomous construction of the channels. Although the quiz show is often foregrounded as the epitome of the differences between the BBC and ITV (with the latter's emphasis on prize-giving, commercialism and 'gambling'), a more sustained analysis blurs these contrasts (see Holmes, forthcoming).

CHAPTER 6

1. The exceptions include Alvarado and Stewart (1985) and Ward (2004).
2. One further play – 'Club Havana' (BBC2, 25 October 1975) – survives in the form of unedited material, while for another – 'Atrocity' (BBC2, 15 March 1973) – only 11 minutes of filmed footage remain. I am grateful to Kathleen Dickson at the British Film Institute and to Christine Slattery at the BBC Film Library for their assistance in enabling me to view all the surviving half-hour plays produced by BBC English Regions Drama.
3. David Rose, telephone message to the author, 10 October 2003.
4. Audience Research Report for 'That Quiet Earth', 22 March 1972, BBC.
5. David Rose, interviewed by the author, 23 February 2003.
6. See *In Two Minds* (BBC1, 1 March 1967), directed by Ken Loach.
7. Peter Ansorge, interviewed by the author, 2 June 2005.
8. Peter Ansorge, interviewed by the author, 2 June 2005. Ansorge is referring here to the camera rehearsal and recording all being done on one day in the studio. Prior to going into the studio the director would spend five days rehearsing with the actors.
9. Television Weekly Programme Review Minutes, 27 February 1974, 12, BBC WAC.
10. In fact, 'The Actual Woman' was not in 'the last series' of *Second City Firsts* to be shown (which would have been series four) but the second series. Three plays from the first two series were repeated between series four and five, in May and October 1975: 'Girl' and 'The Actual Woman' from series two, and 'Mrs Pool's Preserves' (also directed by Philip Saville) from the first series.
11. Neville Smith had previously written a contribution for *Wednesday Play*, directed by Ken Loach, called 'The Golden Vision' (BBC1, 17 April 1968), a drama-documentary about Everton FC in which Smith played an Everton supporter, which he was.
12. Only 11 minutes of film sequences survive.
13. First shown as a *Thirty-Minute Theatre* play (BBC2, 13 March 1972).
14. Exists only in the form of unedited studio takes.

CHAPTER 7

1. For a fuller account, see Sandon (2004).
2. See also the television programmes *Auntie: The Inside Story of the BBC: The House that Reith Built* (BBC, 1997), *Birth of Television* (BBC, 1976), *Magic Rays of Light* (BBC, 1981), *We Bring You Live Pictures* (BBC, 1984) and *Television* (Granada, 1984).
3. The Alexandra Palace studios continued to be used once the BBC Television Service was moved to the Lime Grove studios, by the producers of BBC television newsreel, then the Open University, until the 1970s.
4. See the APTS website: www.apts.org.uk.

5. Michael Henderson, Newsletter to members, 29 September 1993.
6. A full list of recordings and submissions is held in the APTS archive.
7. For example, *A Night in with the Girls* (BFI/BBC, 1996) raised complaints from the APTS members involved: June Averill, Joy Leman and Yvonne Littlewood.
8. See, for example, Michael Grade's 'Foreword' to Vahimagi (1994) and Norden, Harper and Gilbert (1985).
9. See Barry (1992) and Jacobs (2000) for accounts of early television drama.
10. See also Scannell (1979) for a discussion of current affairs in this early period.
11. Oral sources have also been used for historical assessments of television from a viewer/consumer point for view. Audience studies, drawing as they do on ethnographic methodologies, have been more attuned to the subjectivity of oral sources (see Tim O'Sullivan and Henrik Örnebring in this collection, and also O'Sullivan, 1991).
12. The BECTU oral history project collection is housed in the British Film Institute library. See www.bfi.org.uk, www.uea.ac.uk/eas/britcin/ and www.bectu.org.uk/about/hisproj/hisproj.html.
13. For a general, and extremely useful, introduction to oral history techniques, see Raleigh Yow (1994).
14. Interviewees: Basil Adams, studio manager; Philip Bate, producer; Barrie Edgar, producer; Bimbi Harris, vision mixer; Yvonne Littlewood, producer; Elizabeth MacGregor, grams operator; Robin Nash, producer; Ian Orr-Ewing, producer; Lionel Salter, accompanist; John Vernon, producer; Bill Ward, producer.
15. Interview with Bill Ward, 30 September 1996.
16. Interview with Lionel Salter, 5 December 1995.
17. APTS recording no. 8.
18. APTS recording no. 7.
19. APTS recording no. 13.
20. Interview with Bill Ward, 30 September 1996.
21. See the documentary *Auntie: The Inside Story of the BBC* (BBC, 1997).
22. Interview with Bill Ward, 30 September 1996.
23. Interview with Bill Ward, 30 September 1996.
24. Interview with Bill Ward, 30 September 1996.
25. APTS recording no. 7.
26. Interview with Basil Adams, 14 November 1995.
27. Interview with Philip Bate, 5 December 1995.
28. Bimbi Harris and Gladys Davies, APTS recording no. 23.
29. APTS recording no. 8.
30. Interview with Bill Ward, 30 September 1996.
31. Interview with Ian Orr-Ewing, 4 April 1996.
32. APTS recording no. 7.
33. Interview with Elizabeth MacGregor, 8 December 1995.
34. Interview with Lionel Salter, 5 December 1995.
35. See the documentary *Auntie: The Inside Story of the BBC* (BBC, 1997).
36. See the documentary *Fools on the Hill* (BBC, 1986).
37. See Su Holmes in this collection for an account of the light entertainment cinema programme.

CHAPTER 8

1. BBC Programme as Broadcast Record, *Television Newsreel* programme no. 50, 25 June 1948.

2. BBC Programme as Broadcast Record, *BBC and Pathé News*, 17 January 1955.

3. The work referred to is the dissertation *Beyond the Black Atlantic: West Indian Imagery, Cultural Production and BBC Television*, by Darrell Mottley Newton, 2002. Briefly, the project examines BBC Television policies as they related to West Indian immigrants and their appearance in BBC Television programming from the 1950s to the 1990s.

4. The only available example of ITV programming that directly addressed racial assimilation at the time of this study was an excerpt from the programme *People in Trouble* (ITV, 1958), as featured on the historical documentary *Black and White in Colour* (BBC, 1992), a programme that examined the perceived dangers of miscegenation and the subsequent 'mongrelisation' of the British people through interracial marriage. Because it was only excerpts of this ITV docudrama that were featured in the documentary, it was impossible to determine the ultimate narrative emphasis of the programme. The fact that I was unable to find complete copies of the programme reinforces concerns about the social myopia often inherent in historical television programming, which, after being edited, is offered as no more than a snippet within a frame constructed by contemporary documentary television.

5. *BBC Variety Programmes Policy Guide*, 1948.

6. Cecil McGivern, memorandum, 24 August 1951, T16/175/1 (BBC WAC).

7. There is a record of Pathé Film showing West Indians disembarking at Tilbury in a BBC Programme as Broadcast Record for *Television Newsreel*, programme no. 50, 25 June 1948.

8. Mrs M. Adams, memorandum for George H. Noordhof, 5 January 1952, T32/209/1 (BBC WAC).

9. Draft script, *Race and Colour*, 10 November 1952, T32/209/1 (BBC WAC).

10. George H. Noordhof, memorandum on caption requirements for the production of *Race and Colour*, 10 November 1952, T32/209/2 (BBC WAC).

11. James Bredin, memorandum to Grace Wyndham Goldie, 15 October 1952, T32/209/1 (BBC WAC).

12. Sir David Attenborough began working in 1952 in the BBC Television Talks Department at Alexandra Palace. As well as pioneering the BBC's wildlife programming, he also served as a host for archaeological, political and religious programmes.

13. Draft script, 1952, T32/209/1 (BBC WAC).

14. BBC Audience Research Department, Viewer Research Report for *Race and Colour: A Scientific Introduction to the Problem of Race Relations*, 26 November 1952, VR/52/513 (BBC WAC).

15. Viewer Research Report, 1952.

16. Peter Stone, production notes to Anthony de Lotheniere about filming at the Hockley garage, 11 November 1954, T4/55/1 (BBC WAC).

17. Production notes for *Special Enquiry – Third Year No. 3: The Colour Bar* – Second Background Information, T16/175/1 (BBC WAC).

18. Anthony de Lotheniere, letter to Doctor Kenneth Little, 6 December 1954, T4/55/1 (BBC WAC).

19. Anthony de Lotheniere, letter to Harry Green, Transport and General Workers' Union, 14 January 1955, T4/55/1 (BBC WAC).

20. Rough Outline Treatment, *Special Enquiry No. 3: The Colour Bar*, 14 December 1954, T4/55/1 (BBC WAC).

21. Rough Outline Treatment, *Special Enquiry No. 3: The Colour Bar*, 14 December 1954, T4/55/1 (BBC WAC).

22. As also shown on the BBC series *Black and White in Colour* (BBC, 1992).

23. David Martin, memorandum to Norman Swallow, 31 July 1958, T16/175/2 (BBC WAC).

24. BBC Audience Research Department, Viewer Research Report for *A Question of Colour: Second Enquiry into Some of Britain's Social Problems*, 14 November 1958, T4/55 (BBC WAC).

25. David Martin, memorandum to Norman Swallow, 31 July 1958, T16/175/2 (BBC WAC).

26. Norman Swallow, memorandum to David Martin, 2 August 1958, T16/175/2 (BBC WAC).

27. Norman Swallow, memorandum to David Martin, 2 August 1958, T16/175/2 (BBC WAC).

28. BBC Audience Research Department, Viewer Research Report for *A Question of Colour: Second Enquiry into Some of Britain's Social Problems*, 14 November 1958, T4/55 (BBC WAC).

29. Robert McCall, memorandum to Norman Swallow, 29 December 1958, T16/175/2 (BBC WAC).

30. Oliver Hunkin, memorandum to Norman Swallow, 1 January 1959, T16/175/2 (BBC WAC).

31. Minute 41 from the Director General's meeting with Regional Controllers, 8 March 1965, N/25/175/1 (BBC WAC).

32. Minute 41 from the Director General's meeting with Regional Controllers, 8 March 1965, N/25/175/1 (BBC WAC).

33. Press announcement from BBC Evening Press Officer Dulcie J. Marshall to various press organisations, 6 July 1965, N/25/175/1 (BBC WAC).

34. Meeting notes from the Council Chamber, Broadcasting House, for the 'Programmes for immigrants' meeting held with members of the West Indian community in London, 13 July 1965, N/25/175/1 (BBC WAC).

35. Memorandum from Further Education regarding West Indian organisations identified as research contacts, 21 November 1956, T16/175/2 (BBC WAC).

36. N/25/175/1 (BBC WAC).

37. N/25/175/1 (BBC WAC).

38. N/25/175/1 (BBC WAC).

39. N/25/175/1 (BBC WAC).

40. R/31/104 (BBC WAC).

CHAPTER 9

1. Teledu Cymru translates literally as 'Wales Television'. For an account of the company's origins and demise, see Medhurst (2005).
2. For example, the Welsh historian John Davies has argued that 'broadcasting has played a central role, both positive and negative, in the development of the concept of a national community' (1994: ix). Likewise, Aled Jones states that 'the belief that forms of communication materially affect both social consciousness and behaviour remains deeply rooted in the political culture as well as in the historiography of Wales' (1993: 3).
3. For a study of the notion of television as 'alien visitor', see Sconce (2000).
4. The footage is located at the ITV Wales Film and Television Archive in Cardiff.
5. Paperwork giving, *inter alia*, recording and transmission details of the programme.
6. Interview with Wyn Roberts (now Lord Roberts of Conwy), 18 August 1999.
7. T. I. Ellis Diaries. 10 May 1962.
8. T. I. Ellis Diaries. 30 July 1962.
9. See chapter by Erin Bell and Ann Gray in this volume.

CHAPTER 10

1. A version of this chapter appears in the 'Televising history' special issue of the European Journal of Cultural Studies, 10, 1 (2007).
2. See www.history.ac.uk/ihr/resources/teachers.inst.html for HE history teachers in the United Kingdom.
3. See Judd (2005).
4. This can be seen on the DVD A *History of Britain*, BBC Worldwide Ltd, 2002.
5. This can be seen on the DVD case of A *History of Britain*, BBC Worldwide Ltd, 2002.
6. See John Oliver's biography of Taylor, at www.screenonline.org.uk/people/id/838462/.
7. 13 weeks conveniently fitted into a quarter of the annual schedule. Sir David Attenborough on the making of *Civilisation* on DVD: *Civilisation*, BBC Worldwide Ltd, 2005.
8. 'History and the media', Institute of Historical Research and the History Channel, Institute for Historical Research, University of London, December 2002.
9. See Wood's Maya Vision International website for further press quotes: www.mayavisionint.com.
10. This can be seen on the DVD A *History of Britain*, BBC Worldwide Ltd, 2002.
11. This framework resonates with the active/passive figures identified in television audience research by John Fiske (1987).
12. Interview with Simon Schama by Mark Lawson, on the DVD of A *History of Britain*, BBC Worldwide Ltd, 2002.

CHAPTER 11

1. A modern version and logical extension of 'Film studies'? See, for instance, Brunsdon (1998) and Corner (1997).
2. See Jenkins (1991) and Iggers (1997) for useful exploratory accounts.
3. As I have suggested elsewhere, 'TV began as a medium without a memory and with little regard for the value of archiving or systematically storing and preserving its output' (O'Sullivan, 1998: 201). In the DVD, hard-drive, digital age it is still also instructive to note the assessment of Bryant (1989).
4. I am interested here in how the television has mutated as a domestic apparatus: see Morley (1995). In the week that I finished writing this chapter, Dixons, the popular UK high street retailer of electrical goods, announced that in 2006 it would cease selling the traditional cathode ray tube television sets in favour of exclusively stocking flat-screen televisions.
5. This is taken from a MORI poll of viewing habits reported in Leonard (2001).
6. For development of these themes, see Gauntlett and Hill (1999), Morley (2000), Livingstone (2002) and Moores (2000).
7. The Hankey Committee (named after its chair, Lord Maurice Hankey) was appointed in September 1943 to consider 'the re-instatement and development of the television service'. The committee met over 30 times and operated in secret until January 1944. It took evidence from pre-war television technical experts, BBC and industry representatives and other interested parties – for example, J. Arthur Rank. Its deliberations and recommendations were published as *The Hankey Report* in March 1945: 'Our general conclusions are that television has come to stay...' (para. 378). Some of its key recommendations concerned the rapid, planned expansion of a post-war technical infrastructure capable of enabling *national* television reception. See Briggs (1979, chap. 3) and also BBC (1946).
8. For useful discussions, see Misztal (2003), Grainge (2003), Middleton and Edwards (1990) and Breakwell and Hammond (1990).
9. The 'defining moments' of the modern age, according to the ITN archives, draw heavily on televised events. The 'top three' include the first Moon walk in 1969, the assassination of JFK in 1963 and the more recent 11 September attacks on the World Trade Center in 2001 (see Leonard, 2003). Television has provided a site for the intersection of public and private memories, as one of the people I interviewed remarked: 'Well, I remember that someone was doing my hair when President Kennedy was shot' (O'Sullivan, 1991: 172). See also Morley (2000).
10. See Bourdieu (1984); see also Silvey (1974) and Political and Economic Planning (1958) for relevant commentaries on social class and television set acquisition.
11. As Maurice Gorham, Head of the Television Service from 1946, noted in his account of the late 1940s and early 1950s: 'There was no such thing as "sales resistance" in those early years; every dealer had waiting lists and every set that left the manufacturers found its way into a home, but supply fell far short of demand' (1952: 237).
12. See Su Holmes in this collection for further discussion of the remembering and 'misremembering' of the BBC and ITV.

13. The 'toddlers' truce' referred to the 6–7 p.m. slot in the BBC schedule during which time there were no programmes transmitted, in part on the assumption that this made it easier for parents to get their young children off to bed. The 'truce' ended in 1957, when, under pressure from the ITV alternative, BBC introduced *Tonight*, the long-running current affairs news magazine programme. See Wyndham Goldie (1977).

14. These themes are developed in a later study by Morley (1986).

15. Generation is a significant issue here. Those who can remember 'life before television' are now in their 70s or 80s and are a diminishing population.

16. A number of television histories that have looked at television in the period would include, for instance, *Television* (ITV, 1985), *Open the Box* (Channel 4, 1986) and *The People's Century* (BBC, 1995), as well as recent celebrations of the first 50 years of ITV.

17. See the National Museum of Photography, Film and Television, Bradford, www.nmsi.ac.uk/NMPFT/, and, especially, the British Vintage Wireless and Television Museum, West Dulwich, London, www.bvwm.org.uk.

18. The Mass-Observation Archive is housed in the Special Collections section of the library at the University of Sussex, Brighton, United Kingdom: see www.massobs.org.uk. For useful references, see also Mass-Observation (1939), Calder and Sheridan (1984), Jeffrey (1978) and Henrik Örnebring in this collection.

19. M-O Archive: File 3106, 'Mass-Observation's Panel on Television', April 1949. It is interesting also to note Tom Harrisson's reflections on the changing status of television some ten years later, in 'The telly: how important?', chapter 12 in Harrisson (1961).

20. M-O Panel on Television, 3.

21. M-O Panel on Television, 6.

22. M-O Panel on Television, 28.

23. M-O Panel on Television, 6.

24. Geoffrey Gorer (1905–1985) was a social anthropologist who studied with Margaret Mead in 1935 and published a number of studies of national characteristics (for example, 1955). His collected papers are also housed in the Special Collections section of the University of Sussex Library. For a useful commentary, see Stanton (2000).

25. For methodological details, see Gorer Papers: 'TV & the English', Box GM 62: File 4A, University of Sussex, Special Collections.

26. *The Sunday Times*: 13 April 1958, 'Television in our lives', 14–15; 20 April 1958, 'Is it a drug or stimulant?', 12; 27 April 1958, 'Home life, habits and hobbies', 9; 4 May 1958, 'TV & the growing child', 13.

27. See, for instance, BBC (1959) and Himmelweit, Oppenheim and Vince (1958).

28. In the late 1940s, and into the 1950s, television was an increasingly regular news item in national and local newspapers. *The Leicester Mercury*, for instance, reported on the televised Victory Parade of 8 June 1946 and had a headline 'Leicester woman sees daughter on TV' on 19 July 1946. Such news items by the late 1940s were also accompanied by a massive increase in newspaper copy devoted to advertising and promoting television sets. *The Leicester Mercury* did

not feature a daily television schedule until 1951, when it initially appeared as a minor adjunct to the radio schedule.

29. A number of British and American films of the period focus on the domestic arrival of television and the chaos it causes: *Meet Mr Lucifer* (Anthony Pelissier, 1953) and *Happy Anniversary* (David Miller, 1959) are two of the most celebrated examples, but television begins to appear in many other films of the time. See Stokes (1999) for useful discussion of this phenomenon.

30. In his celebrated analysis, Raymond Williams notes that 'the central television experience is the fact of flow' (1974: 95). See also Laing (1991).

CHAPTER 12

1. See Rachel Moseley in this collection, for example.

2. See Darrell Newton in this collection for a discussion of the BBC's Audience Research Reports as historiographic source material, for example.

3. All archival material is referenced in short form in this text, using the notation 'M-O A TC69/X/Y'. References to directive replies from Panel members are also followed by the number of the panel member, or by the designation 'unnumbered' when this is the case.

4. All data on television licences come from the Annual Abstract of Statistics 1950–1953.

5. This sums to 101 per cent because of rounding up.

6. I.e. a quick drink; author's note.

7. Inv. = investigator, i.e. the writer himself; author's note.

CHAPTER 13

1. See, for instance, Ang (1985), Stacey (1994) and Moseley (2002) for accounts of the difficulties of empirical audience research.

2. The texts I discuss in this chapter are a case in point. *Going Out* is not available to view in the National Film and Television Archive; I was supplied with copies by the writer, Phil Redmond. *Maggie* is available to researchers to view, but is difficult to access for teaching purposes.

3. *Grange Hill* is the long-running children's programme, set in a London comprehensive school, for which Redmond was best known – perhaps infamous – at the time. As Alistair McGown and Mark Docherty suggest, it has 'been the most watched and the most consistently controversial within the genre [of children's drama] bar none' (2003: 113). *Tucker's Luck*, which followed the fortunes of one of the serial's popular characters after leaving school, would be broadcast in the Thursday 6 p.m. BBC2 slot occupied by *Maggie*, between 1983 and 1985, and shared the preoccupations of both this serial and Redmond's earlier *Going Out* and subsequent *What Now?*.

4. I am thus looking specifically at the television that was provided for the teenage audience, rather than at what the actual social audience might have mainly

been watching – for example, *Starsky and Hutch* (Spelling-Goldberg Productions, 1975–1979) on the BBC or *The Professionals* (LWT, 1977–1983) and *Charlie's Angels* (Spelling-Goldberg Productions, 1976–1981) on ITV (Calouste Gulbenkian Foundation, 1979: 44).

5. *The BBC's Programme Responsibilities towards Adolescents and Young People*, 22 March 1978, GAC/543/7 (BBC WAC). The ongoing dearth of dramatic programming for teenagers on BBC Television suggests that this feeling persists, but it remains to be seen, when later years of policy documentation are made available at the WAC, how the institution has framed this in recent history.

6. SBC/FEAC Joint Working Party on Educational Broadcasting for the 15–19 Age Group, 1978, WAC R99/210/1/19; 1978, WAC GAC/543; Oswell, 1998: 44; David Gauntlet and Annette Hill's findings are slightly different (1999, 82).

7. Phil Redmond, personal interview, March 2004.

8. In a fascinating appendix to the BBC's report to its General Advisory Council (*The BBC's Programme Responsibilities towards Adolescents and Young People*, 22 March 1978, GAC/543/15), the questionnaire used by the BBC Audience Research Department to produce the survey upon which the report was based is given. Questions 71 and 72 are 'In general, what kinds of television programme would you like to see more of?' and 'less of?' respectively. The answers to these questions are not given, and this is difficult for the media historian to interpret, given that the report argues that the present general output of the BBC meets the needs of the teenage audience. Maybe the questions were not, in practice, asked? Perhaps they were asked, but the answers not used because they did not meet the BBC's agenda? Maybe this is simply an incomplete document? Similarly, question 9 asks whether respondents felt that BBC and ITV television 'make a special effort to show programmes which will interest people in your age group'. While the majority of teenage respondents answered in the negative, this does not seem to be reflected in the report as published.

9. 9 April 1973, WAC R78/1, 840/1.

10. 'Break In', which looks at teenage vandalism in schools, was probably Russell's most well-known and controversial play for this series.

11. 30 September 1977, WAC R99/104/1.

12. Memorandum from Hilda Wurr, Education Officer, East, 30 September 1977, WAC R99/104/1.

13. Memorandum on the SBC/FEAC 1978 Joint Working Party on Educational Broadcasting for the 15–19 Age Group, WAC R103/13/1.

14. WAC R103/13/1.

15. 22 March 1978, WAC GAC/543.

16. 1979, WAC R78/2, 095/1.

17. WAC R78/1, 840/1/18.

18. February 1979, WAC R78/2, 095/1.

19. Magazine and current affairs programming for young adults did increase and develop as a result of the report, however, with the BBC's Community Programmes Unit's *Something Else* (1978) and LWT's *The London Weekend Show* (1975–1979) being joined in 1981 by *The Oxford Roadshow* and *16 Up* (1981) on BBC2.

20. A case in point is offered by producer Anna Home's struggle to prevent the

cancellation of *The Changes*, the 1975 eco-sci-fi drama for older children based on Peter Dickinson's novels, which eventually attracted controversy through its address to questions of race, belonging, violence and morality.

21. Anna Home, personal interview, January 2005.
22. In an interesting shift, contemporary teen drama on British television (both indigenously produced and imported) is predominantly addressed to a young female audience.
23. This is an argument also made recently by Helen Wheatley in relation to the studio setting of *Upstairs Downstairs* (Wheatley, 2005).
24. Anna Home has talked about her particular concern to offer relevant dramatic programming addressing young women (personal interview, January 2005).
25. Phil Redmond, personal interview, March 2004.
26. Phil Redmond, personal interview, March 2004.

APPENDIX

1. This appendix offers contact details for archives and other key research resources for British television history only. For a more inclusive database of archives and holdings, see the BUFVC's indispensable *Researcher's Guide Online* (http://joseph.bufvc.ac.uk/RGO/index.html). Another useful research portal with full descriptions of all the key archives can be found on the website *Moving History* (www.movinghistory.ac.uk/index.html).
2. Although many of these archives are entitled 'Film Archives' they all contain substantial television holdings. This list includes all the relevant public sector archives, plus key commercial archives offering access to academic researchers.
3. NB. Scholarly use of moving image material from the BBC's Film and Television Archive is accessed through the National Film and Television Archive at the British Film Institute (see above). Otherwise external research is charged at commercial rates.
4. NB. Granada holds the largest archive of commercial television programmes in the United Kingdom.

Bibliography

Adorno, T. (1981) *Prisms*, Cambridge, MA: MIT Press.

Allan, E. (1981) 'Teleview: looking across the generation gap', *Times*, 24 October: 11.

Allen, R. C. (ed.) (1992) *Channels of Discourse: Reassembled*, Carolina: University of North Carolina Press.

Allen, R. C., and Gomery, D. (1985) *Film History: Theory and Practice*, New York: McGraw-Hill.

Alvarado, M., and Stewart, J. (1985) *Made for Television: Euston Films Limited*, London: British Film Institute.

Anderson, B. (1991) *Imagined Communities*, London: Verso.

Anderson, C. (1994) *Hollywood TV: The Studio System in the Fifties*, Austin: University of Texas Press.

Ang, I. (1985) *Watching Dallas: Soap Opera and the Melodramatic Imagination*, London: Methuen.

Apple, M. (ed.) (1982) *Cultural and Economic Reproduction in Education*, London: Routledge.

Ashby, J., and Higson, A. (eds) (2000) *British Cinema, Past and Present*, London: Routledge.

Attenborough, D. (2002) *Life on Air*, London: BBC Books.

Attie, J. (1992) 'Illusions of history: a review of the Civil War', *Radical History Review*, 52: 95–104.

Baehr, H., and Dyer, G. (eds) (1987) *Boxed In: Women and Television*, London: Pandora Press.

Bain, A. D. (1962) 'The growth of television ownership in the United Kingdom', *International Economic Review*, 3, 2: 145–167.

Balcon, M. (1969) *Michael Balcon Presents…: A Lifetime of Films*, London: Hutchinson.

Barker, D. L., and Allen, S. (eds) (1976) *Dependence and Exploitation in Work and Marriage*, London: Longman.

Barlow, D., Mitchell, P., and O'Malley, T. (2005) *The Media in Wales: Voices of a Small Nation*, Cardiff: University of Wales Press.

Barnouw, E. (1982) *Tube of Plenty: The Evolution of American Television*, Oxford: Oxford University Press.

Barr, C. (1997) '"They think it's all over": the dramatic legacy of live television', in J. Hill and M. McLoone (eds) *Big Picture, Small Screen: The Relations between Film and Television*, 47–75.

Barry, M. (1992) *From the Palace to the Grove*, London: Royal Television Society.

BBC (1946) *The BBC Year Book*, London: British Broadcasting Corporation.

— (1959) *Television and the Family* (the Knight Report), London: British Broadcasting Corporation.

— (1969) *Broadcasting in the Seventies*, London: British Broadcasting Corporation.

— (1972) *BBC Handbook 1973*, London: British Broadcasting Corporation.

BBC News: Education (2002) 'Schama attacks school history', 10 October: http://news.bbc.co.uk/1/hi/education/2316Th891.stm.

Bell, D., and Hollows, J. (eds) (2005) *Ordinary Lifestyles: Popular Media, Consumption and Taste*, Maidenhead: Open University Press.

Bell, E. (1986) 'The origins of British television documentary: the BBC 1946–1955', in J. Corner (ed.) *Documentary and the Mass Media*, 65–80.

Belson, W. (1959) 'Effects of television on the interests and initiative of adult viewers in Greater London', *British Journal of Psychology*, 50, 2: 145–158.

Benjamin, W. (1973) *Illuminations*, London: Collins.

Bennett, A. (1989) *Clayhanger* [1919], London: Penguin.

Berker, T., Hartmann, M., Punie, Y., and Ward, K. (eds) (2006) *Domestication of Media and Technology*, Maidenhead: Open University Press.

Berman, B. (1976) 'TV sports auteurs', *Film Comment*, 12, 2: 34–35, 64.

Bevan, D. (1984) 'The mobilization of cultural minorities: the case of Sianel Pedwar Cymru', *Media, Culture and Society*, 6, 2: 103–117.

Bignell, J. (2004) *An Introduction to Television Studies*, London: Routledge.

— (2005a) 'And the rest is history: Lew Grade, creation narratives and television historiography', in C. Johnson and R. Turnock (eds) *ITV Cultures: Independent Television over Fifty Years*, 57–70.

— (2005b) 'Exemplarity, pedagogy and television history', *New Review of Film and Television Studies*, 3, 1: 15–32.

Bignell, J., and Lacey, S. (eds) (2005) *Popular Television Drama: Critical Perspectives*, Manchester: Manchester University Press.

Bignell, J., Lacey, S., and Macmurraugh-Kavanagh, M. K. (eds) (2000) *British Television Drama: Past, Present and Future*, Basingstoke: Palgrave Macmillan.

Bignell, J., and O'Day, A. (2004) *Terry Nation*, Manchester: Manchester University Press.

Bignell, J., and Orlebar, J. (2005) *The Television Handbook* (3rd edn), London: Routledge.

Billen, A. (2003) 'The man who made history sexy explains why it is also our freedom', *Times2*, 20 May: 14.

Black, L. (2005) 'Whose finger on the button? British television and the politics of cultural control', *Historical Journal of Film, Radio and Television*, 25, 4: 547–575.

Black, P. (1972) *The Mirror in the Corner: People's Television*, London: Hutchinson.

Bloome, D., Sheridan, D., and Street B. (1993) *Reading Mass-Observation Writing. Theoretical and Methodological Issues in Researching the Mass-Observation Archive*, Mass-Observation Archive Occasional Paper no. 1, Brighton: University of Sussex Library.

Boddy, W. (1985) 'The shining centre of the home: ontologies of television in the "Golden Age"', in P. Drummond and R. Patterson (eds) *Television in Transition*, 125–134.

— (1993) *Fifties Television: The Industry and its Critics*, Urbana and Chicago: University of Illinois Press.

— (2004) *New Media and Popular Imagination*, Oxford: Oxford University Press.

Bonner, F. (2003) *Ordinary Television*, London: Sage.

Born, G. (2000) 'Inside television: television studies and the sociology of culture', *Screen*, 41, 4: 404–424.

— (2004) *Uncertain Vision: Birt, Dyke and the Reinvention of the BBC*, London: Secker and Warburg.

Bourdieu, P. (1984) *Distinction: A Social Critique of the Judgement of Taste*, London: Routledge.

Bourne, S. (1998) *Black in the British Frame: Black People in British Film and Television 1896–1996*, London: Cassell.

— (1999) 'The Caribbean presence on BBC television and radio: a chronology 1948–98', *Urban Black and Caribbean Canadian Learning Resource Network*, 22 April: www.ccmacanada.org/urban/blackbrithistory/radioandtv.htm.

Boyle, A. (1972) *Only the Wind Will Listen: Reith of the BBC*, London: Hutchinson.

Brandt, G. (ed.) (1981) *British Television Drama*, Cambridge: Cambridge University Press.

— (ed.) (1993) *British Television Drama in the 1980s*, Cambridge: Cambridge University Press.

Branston, G. (1998) 'Histories of British television', in C. Geraghty and D. Lusted (eds) *The Television Studies Book*, 51–62.

Breakwell, I., and Hammond, P. (eds) (1990) *Seeing in the Dark: A Compendium of Cinemagoing*, London: Serpents Tail.

Bremner, I. (2001) 'History without archives: Simon Schama's *A History of Britain*', in G. Roberts and P. M. Taylor (eds) *The Historian, Television and Television History*, 63–75.

Briggs, A. (1960) *They Saw It Happen: An Anthology of Eye-Witnesses' Accounts of Events in British History, 1897–1940*, Oxford: Blackwell.

— (1965) *The History of Broadcasting in the United Kingdom*, vol. 2, *The Golden Age of Wireless*, Oxford: Oxford University Press.

— (1979) *The History of Broadcasting in the United Kingdom*, vol. 4, *Sound and Vision*, Oxford: Oxford University Press.

— (1980) 'Problems and possibilities in the writing of broadcasting history', *Media, Culture and Society*, 2, 1: 5–13.

Brunsdon, C. (1997) *Screen Tastes: Soap Opera to Satellite Dishes*, London: Routledge.

— (1998) 'What is the television of television studies?', in C. Geraghty and D. Lusted (eds) *The Television Studies Book*, 95–113.

— (2002) *The Feminist, the Housewife, and the Soap Opera*, Oxford: Clarendon Press.

Brunsdon, C., D'Acci, J., and Spigel, L. (eds) *Feminist Television Criticism*, Oxford: Oxford University Press.

Bryant, S. (1989) *The Television Heritage*, London: British Film Institute.

Buckingham, D., Davies, H., Jones, K., and Kelley, P. (1999) *Children's Television in Britain: History, Discourse and Policy*, London: British Film Institute.

Burnett, F. H. (1886) *Little Lord Fauntleroy*, London: Warne.

— (1978) *The Secret Garden* [1911], London: Penguin.

Burns, T. (1977) *The BBC: Public Institution and Private World*, Basingstoke: Macmillan.

Buscombe, E. (1973) 'Ideas of authorship', *Screen*, 14, 3: 75–85.

— (1980) 'Broadcasting from above', *Screen Education*, 37: 73–78.

— (1991) 'All bark and no bite: the film industry's response to television', in J. Corner (ed.), *Popular Television in Britain: Studies in Cultural History*, 197–209.

— (ed.) (2000) *British Television: A Reader*, Oxford: Oxford University Press.

Butt Philip, A. (1975) *The Welsh Question: Nationalism and Welsh Politics 1945–1970*, Cardiff: University of Wales Press.

Calder, A., and Sheridan, D. (eds) (1984) *Speak for Yourself: A Mass-Observation Anthology, 1937–49*, London: Jonathan Cape.

Calouste Gulbenkian Foundation (1979) *Broadcasting and Youth: A Study Commissioned by the British Broadcasting Corporation, the Calouste Gulbenkian Foundation, the Independent Broadcasting Authority and the Manpower Services Commission*, London: Calouste Gulbenkian Foundation.

Cannadine, D. (ed.) (2004) *History and the Media*, Basingstoke: Palgrave Macmillan.

Cardwell, S. (2005) *Andrew Davies*, Manchester: Manchester University Press.

Carr, E. H. (1990) *What Is History?* [1961], Basingstoke: Macmillan.

Carroll, N. (2000) 'Introducing film evaluation', in C. Gledhill and L. Williams (eds) *Reinventing Film Studies*, 265–278.

Carter, C., Branston, G., and Allen, S. (eds) (1998) *News, Gender and Power*, London: Routledge.

Caughie, J. (ed.) (1981) *Theories of Authorship*, London: Routledge.

— (1991) 'Before the Golden Age: early television drama', in J. Corner (ed.) *Popular Television in Britain: Studies in Cultural History*, 30–40.

— (2000) *Television Drama: Realism, Modernism and British Culture*, Oxford: Oxford University Press.

Central Statistical Office (1950) *Annual Abstract of Statistics*, London: HMSO.

— (1951) *Annual Abstract of Statistics*, London: HMSO.

— (1952) *Annual Abstract of Statistics*, London: HMSO.

— (1953) *Annual Abstract of Statistics*, London: HMSO.

Champion, J. (2003) 'Seeing the past: Simon Schama's *A History of Britain* and public history', *History Workshop Journal*, 56: 153–174.

Chapman, J. (2001) '*The World at War*: television, documentary, history', in G. Roberts and P. M. Taylor (eds) *The Historian, Television and Television History*, 127–144.

— (2002) *Saints and Avengers: British Adventure Series of the 1960s*, London: I.B.Tauris.

Clayton, I., Harding, C., and Lewis, B. (eds) (1995) *Opening the Box: The Popular Experience of Television*, Castleford and Bradford: Yorkshire Art Circus/National Museum of Photography, Film and Television.

Collingwood, R. G. (1994) *The Idea of History* (rev. edn) [1946], Oxford: Oxford University Press.

Cook, J. R. (1995) *Dennis Potter: A Life on Screen*, Manchester: Manchester University Press.

Cooke, L. (2003) *British Television Drama: A History*, London: British Film Institute.

— (2007) *Troy Kennedy Martin*, Manchester: Manchester Univrsity Press.

Corner, J. (ed.) (1986) *Documentary and the Mass Media*, London: Arnold.

— (ed.) (1991a) *Popular Television in Britain: Studies in Cultural History*, London: British Film Institute.

— (1991b) 'General introduction: television and British society in the 1950s', in J. Corner (ed.) *Popular Television in Britain: Studies in Cultural History*, 1–22.

— (1997) 'Television in theory', *Media, Culture and Society*, 19, 2: 247–262.

— (1999) *Critical Ideas in Television Studies*, Oxford: Clarendon Press.

— (2002) 'Finding data, reading patterns, telling stories: issues in the historiography of television', paper presented at 'Re:visions – broadcasting archaeologies, histories, impacts, futures' conference, University of Central Lancashire.

— (2003a) 'Finding data, reading patterns, telling stories: issues in the historiography of television', *Media, Culture and Society*, 25, 2: 273–280.

— (2003b) 'Television, documentary and the category of the aesthetic', *Screen*, 44, 1: 92–100.

Cottle, S. (2004) 'Producing nature(s): on the changing production ecology of natural history TV', *Media, Culture and Society*, 26, 1: 81–101.

Couldry, N. (2002) *Media Rituals: A Critical Approach*, London: Routledge.

Creeber, G. (ed.) (2004) *Fifty Key Television Programmes*, London: Arnold.

— (ed.) (2006) *Tele-Visions: An Introduction to Studying Television*, London: British Film Institute.

Crisell, A. (1997) *An Introductory History of British Broadcasting*, London: Routledge.

— (2002) *An Introductory History of British Broadcasting* (2nd edn), London: Routledge.

Culpitt, D. H. (1961) 'Yr oes olau hon', in *Blodau'r Ffair*, Cardiff: Urdd Gobaith Cymru.

Curran, C. (1970) 'A decade in prospect', in *BBC Handbook 1970*, London: British Broadcasting Corporation.

Curran, J., and Seaton, J. (1997) *Power Without Responsibility: The Press and Broadcasting in Britain* [3rd edn], London: Routledge.

Curtis, T. (ed.) (1986) *Wales – The Imagined Nation: Essays in Cultural and National Identity*, Bridgend: Poetry Wales Press.

Dahl, H. F. (1994) 'The pursuit of media history', *Media, Culture and Society*, 16, 4: 551–563.

Davies, J. (1992) *Hanes Cymru: A History of Wales in Welsh*, London: Penguin.

— (1994) *Broadcasting and the BBC in Wales*, Cardiff: University of Wales Press.

Davies, M. M. (2000) 'Must moving image culture die? Teaching television in a pre-digital Dark Age', in M. Deegan, J. Anderson and H. Short (eds) *Digital Resources for the Humanities 1998*, 63–75.

— (2001) '"A bit of earth": sexuality and the representation of childhood in text and screen versions of *The Secret Garden*', *The Velvet Light Trap: Critical Journal of Film and Television*, 48: 48–58.

— (2006) 'Production studies', *Critical Studies in Television*, 1, 1: 21–30.

Davies, S., and Paine, C. (2004) 'Talking about museums: the insider's voice', *Oral History*, 32: 54–62.

Davis, G., and Dickinson, K. (eds) (2004) *Teen Television: Genre Consumption and Identity*, London: British Film Institute.

Dayan, D., and Katz, E. (1992) *Media Events: The Live Broadcasting of History*, Cambridge, MA: Harvard University Press.

Dinsmore, U. (1998) 'Chaos, order and plastic boxes: the significance of videotapes for the people who collect them', in C. Geraghty and D. Lusted (eds) *The Television Studies Book*, 315–326.

Drummond, P., and Patterson, R. (eds) (1985) *Television in Transition*, London: British Film Institute.

Dyer, R., Geraghty, C., Jordan, M., Lovell, T., Paterson, R., and Stewart, J. (eds) (1981) *Coronation Street*, London: British Film Institute.

Eisenstein, E. (1993) *The Printing Revolution in Early Modern Europe*, Cambridge: Cambridge University Press.

Eitzen, D. (1995) 'Against the ivory tower: an apologia for "popular" historical documentaries', *Film-Historia* 5, 1, reprinted in A. Rosenthal and J. Corner (eds) (2005) *New Challenges for Documentary*, 409–418.

Ellis, J. (2000a) *Seeing Things: Television in the Age of Uncertainty*, London: I.B.Tauris.

— (2000b) 'British cinema as performance art: *Brief Encounter, Radio Parade of 1935* and the circumstances of film exhibition', in J. Ashby and A. Higson (eds) *British Cinema: Past and Present*, 95–109.

— (2005) 'Importance, significance, cost and value: is an ITV canon possible?', in C. Johnson and R. Turnock (eds) *ITV Cultures: Independent Television over Fifty Years*, 36–56.

Elton, G. R. (1969) *The Practice of History*, London: Fontana.

Emmett, B. P. (1956) 'The television audience in the United Kingdom', *Journal of the Royal Statistical Society*, 119, 3: 284–306.

Ennis, J. (1979) 'Two people', *TV Times* (ATV region), 8–14 December: 25.

Evans, G. (1964) *Rhagom i Ryddid*, Bangor: Plaid Cymru.

Evans, I. (1997a) 'Drunk on hopes and ideals: the failure of Wales Television, 1959–63', *Llafur: Journal of Welsh Labour History*, 7, 2: 81–93.

— (1997b) 'Teledu Cymru: an independent television service for Wales? 1959–63', unpublished MA dissertation, University of Wales.

Evans, R. J. (1997) *In Defence of History*, London: Granta.

Feuer, J. (1992) 'Genre studies and television', in R. C. Allen (ed.) *Channels of Discourse: Reassembled*, 138–161.

— (2003) 'Quality drama in the US: the new "golden age"?', in M. Hilmes (ed.) *The Television History Book*, 98–102.

Fiddy, D. (2001) *Missing Believed Wiped: Searching for the Lost Treasures of British Television*, London: British Film Institute.

Finch, J., Cox, M., and Giles, M. (eds) (2003) *Granada Television: The First Generation*, Manchester: Manchester University Press.

Fiske, J. (1987) *Television Culture*, London: Methuen.

Fiske, J., and Hartley, J. (1978) *Reading Television*, London: Methuen.

Frith, S. (2000) 'The black box: the value of television and the future of television research', *Screen*, 41, 1: 33–50.

Gauntlett, D., and Hill, A. (1999) *TV Living*, London: Routledge.

Geddes, K., and Bussey, G. (1991) *The Setmakers: A History of the Radio and Television Industry*, London: BREMA/John Libbey.

Geraghty, C. (2003) 'Aesthetics and quality in popular television drama', *International Journal of Cultural Studies*, 6: 25–45.

Geraghty, C., and Lusted, D. (eds) (1998) *The Television Studies Book*, London: Arnold.

Giddings, R. (2000) '*Pickwick Papers:* beyond that time and place', in R. Giddings and E. Sheen (eds) *The Classic Novel from Page to Screen*, 31–53.

Giddings, R., and Sheen, E. (eds) (2000) *The Classic Novel from Page to Screen*, Manchester: Manchester University Press

Gitlin, T. (1982) 'Televisions screens: hegemony in transition', in M. Apple (ed.) *Cultural and Economic Reproduction in Education*, 202–246.

Gledhill, C., and Williams, L. (eds) (2000) *Reinventing Film Studies*, London: Arnold.

Goodwin, A., and Whannel, G. (eds) (1990) *Understanding Television*, London: Routledge.

Gorer, G. (1955) *Exploring English Character*, London: Cresset Press.

— (1958a) 'Television in our lives', *Sunday Times*, 13 April: 14–15.

— (1958b) 'Home life, habits and hobbies', *Sunday Times*, 27 April: 9.

Gorham, M. (1952) *Broadcasting and Television: Since 1900*, London: Andrew Dakers.

Grainge, P. (ed.) (2003) *Memory and Popular Film*, Manchester: Manchester University Press.

Gray, A. (1987) 'Reading the audience', *Screen*, 28, 3: 24–35.

— (1997a) 'Behind closed doors: video recorders in the home', in C. Brunsdon, J. D'Acci and L. Spigel (eds) *Feminist Television Criticism*, 235–246.

— (1997b) 'Learning from experience: cultural studies and feminism', in J. McGuigan (ed.) *Cultural Methodologies*, 87–105.

Gray, A., Hermes, J., and Alasuutari, P. (2001) 'Introduction: history and cultural studies', *European Journal of Cultural Studies*, 4, 3: 259–260.

Gregory, C. (1997) *Be Seeing You…: Decoding The Prisoner*, Luton: University of Luton Press.

Green, H. (1929) *Living*, London: Harvill.

Gripsrud, J. (2004) 'Broadcast television: the chances of its survival in a digital age', in L. Spigel and J. Olsson (eds) *Television After TV: Essays on a Medium in Transition*, 210–223.

Hallam, J. (2005a) *Lynda La Plante*, Manchester: Manchester University Press.

— (2005b) 'Remembering *Butterflies*: the comic art of housework', in J. Bignell and S. Lacey (eds) *Popular Television Drama: Critical Perspectives*, 34–50.

Haralovich, M. B., and Rabinovitz, L. (eds) (1999) *Television, History, and American Culture*, Durham, NC: Duke University Press.

Harper, S., and Porter, V. (2005) 'Beyond media history: the challenge of visual style', *Journal of British Cinema and Television*, 2, 1: 1–17.

Harris, L. (1966) *Long to Reign over Us? The Status of the Royal Family in the Sixties*, London: Kimber.

Harrisson, T. (ed.) (1961) *Britain Revisited*, London: Victor Gollancz.

Hartley, J. (1992) *The Politics of Pictures: The Creation of the Public in the Age of Popular Media*, London: Routledge.

Herrnstein Smith, B. (1988) *Contingencies of Value: Alternative Perspectives for Critical Theory*, Cambridge, MA: Harvard University Press.

Hickethier, K. (1990) 'The television play in the Third Reich', *The Historical Journal of Film, Radio and Television*, 10, 2: 163–186.

Hill, A. (2004) *Reality TV*, London: Routledge.

Hill, J. (1991) 'Television and pop: the case of the 1950s', in J. Corner (ed.) *Popular Television in Britain: Studies in Cultural History*, 90–107.

Hill, J., and McLoone, M. (eds) (1996) *Big Picture, Small Screen: The Relations between Film and Television*, Luton: University of Luton Press.

Hilmes, M. (1990) *Hollywood and Broadcasting: From Radio and Cable*, Urbana and Chicago: University of Illinois Press.

— (ed.) (2003) *The Television History Book*, London: British Film Institute.

Himmelweit, H., Oppenheim, A., and Vince, P. (1958) *Television and the Child*, Oxford: Oxford University Press.

Hobsbawm, E. (1995) *Age of Extremes*, London: Abacus.

Hoggart, R. (1957) *The Uses of Literacy*, London: Chatto and Windus.

Holmes, S. (2001a) '"As they really are and in close-up": film stars on 1950s British television', *Screen*, 42, 2: 167–187.

— (2001b) '"The infant medium with the adult manner": television promotes the "X" film (1952–1962)', *The Historical Journal of Film, Radio, and Television*, 21, 4: 379–397.

— (2005) *British TV and Film Culture in the 1950s*, Bristol: Intellect.

— (2006) '"Neighbours to the nation": the BBC, *The Grove Family*, and the negotiation of popular appeal', paper presented at 'Screen studies' conference, University of Glasgow.

— (forthcoming) '"The 'give-away' shows – who is really paying?": "ordinary" people and the development of the British quiz show', *Journal of Popular British Cinema and Television*.

Holmes, S., and Jermyn, D. (eds) (2004) *Understanding Reality Television*, London: Routledge.

Holt, H. (1975) 'A play of many virtues', *Television Today*, 16 October: 13.

Home, A. (1993) *Into the Box of Delights: A History of Children's Television*, London: British Broadcasting Corporation.

Hood, S. (1980) *On Television*, London: Pluto Press.

Hunt, T. (2004) 'How does television enhance history?', in D. Cannadine (ed.) *History and the Media*, 88–102.

Iggers, G. (1997) *Historiography in the Twentieth Century*, Middletown, CT: Wesleyan University Press.

Isaacs, J. (2004) 'All our yesterdays', in D. Cannadine (ed.) *History and the Media*, 34–50.

Jacobs, J. (2000) *The Intimate Screen: Early British Television Drama*, Oxford: Oxford University Press.

— (2001) 'Issues of judgement and value in television studies', *International Journal of Cultural Studies*, 4, 4: 427–444.

— (2006a) 'Television aesthetics: an infantile disorder', *Journal of British Cinema and Television*, 3, 1: 19–33.

— (2006b). 'Television and history: investigating the past', in G. Creeber (ed.) *Tele-Visions: An Introduction to Studying Television*, 107–115.

— (2006c) 'The television archive: past, present, future', *Critical Studies in Television*, 1, 1: 13–20.

James, C. (1976) *Visions before Midnight*, London: Picador.

James, A., and Prout, A. (1990) *Constructing and Reconstructing Childhood: Contemporary Issues in the Sociological Study of Childhood*, London: Falmer Press.

Jancovich, M., and Lyons, J. (eds) (2003) *Quality Popular Television*, London: British Film Institute.

Jardine, L. (1996) *Reading Shakespeare Historically*, London: Routledge.

Jeffries, S. (2000) *Mrs Slocombe's Pussy: Growing up in Front of the Telly*, London: Flamingo.

Jeffrey, T. (1978) *Mass-Observation: A Short History*, CCCS Stencilled Occasional Paper no. 55, Birmingham: University of Birmingham.

Jenkins, G. H. (2002a) 'Clio and Wales: Welsh remembrances and historical writing', *Transactions of the Honourable Society of Cymmrodorion 2001*, 8: 119–136.

— (ed.) (2002b) *Cof Cenedl XVII*, Llandysul: Gomer.

Jenkins, K. (1991) *Re-Thinking History*, London: Routledge.

Jenks, C. (ed.) (1995) *Visual Culture*, London: Routledge.

Jennings, H., and Madge, C. (eds) (1937) *May The Twelfth: Mass-Observation Day-Surveys, 1937, by over Two Hundred Observers*, London: Faber and Faber.

Johnson, C. (2005) *Telefantasy*, London: British Film Institute.

Johnson, C., and Turnock R. (eds) (2005) *ITV Cultures: Independent Television over Fifty Years*, Maidenhead: Open University Press.

Johnson, R. (2001) 'Historical returns: transdisciplinarity, cultural studies and history', *European Journal of Cultural Studies*, 4, 3: 261–288.

Johnson-Smith, J. (2005) *American Science Fiction TV*, London: I.B.Tauris.

Jones, A. (1993) *Press, Politics and Society: A History of Journalism in Wales*, Cardiff: University of Wales Press.

Jones, P. H., and Rees, E. (1998) *A Nation and Its Books: A History of the Book in Wales*, Aberystwyth: National Library of Wales.

Judd, D. (2005) 'Thomas Babington Macauley', *BBC History*, 71: 95.

Kavanagh, J. (1999) 'The BBC's written archives as a source for media history', *Media History*, 5, 1: 81–86.

Kermode, F. (2001) *Shakespeare's Language*, London: Penguin.

Kershaw, I. (2004) 'The past on the box: strengths and weaknesses', in D. Cannadine (ed.) *History and the Media*, 118–123.

Kerr, P. (1996) 'Television programmes about the cinema: the making of moving pictures', in J. Hill and M. McLoone (eds) *Big Picture, Small Screen: The Relations between Film and Television*, 133–141.

Kline, S. (1993) *Out of the Garden: Toys and Children's Culture in the Age of TV Marketing*, London: Verso.

Kuehl, J. (1976) 'History on the public screen, II', in P. Smith (ed.) *The Historian and Film*, reprinted in A. Rosenthal and J. Corner (eds) (2005) *New Challenges for Documentary*, 177–185.

Kuhn, A. (2002) *An Everyday Magic: Cinema and Cultural Memory*, London: I.B.Tauris.

Lacey, S. (2006) 'Some thoughts on television history and historiography: a British perspective', *Critical Studies in Television*, 1, 1: 3–12.

Laing, S. (1991) 'Raymond Williams and the cultural analysis of television', *Media, Culture and Society*, 13, 2: 153–169.

Leman, J. (1987) 'Programmes for women in 1950s British television', in H. Baehr and G. Dyer (eds) *Boxed In: Women and Television*, 73–88.

Leonard, T. (2001) 'One in two Britons says life would be lonely without TV', *Daily Telegraph*, 28 August: 5.

— (2003) 'Moon walk is most memorable moment', *Daily Telegraph*, 3 September: 11.

Livingstone, S. (2002) *Young People and New Media*, London: Sage.

Lumley, R. (ed.) *The Museum Time Machine*, London: Routledge.

Lurie, A. (1990) *Don't Tell the Grownups: Subversive Children's Fiction*, London: Bloomsbury.

Lury, K. (2001) *British Youth Television: Cynicism and Enchantment*, Oxford: Oxford University Press.

MacArthur, C. (1980) *Television and History*, London: British Film Institute.

McCarthy, A. (2001) *Ambient Television: Visual Culture and Public Space*, Durham, NC: Duke University Press.

McEwan, I. (1981) *The Imitation Game: Three Plays for Television*, London: Jonathan Cape.

McGown, A. D., and Docherty, M. J. (2003) *The Hill and Beyond: Children's Television Drama – An Encyclopedia*, London: British Film Institute.

McGuigan, J. (ed.) (1997) *Cultural Methodologies*, London: Sage.

McLuskie, P. (1998) 'Youth television: history, genre and authenticity', unpublished PhD thesis, University of Warwick.

Manpower Services Commission (1978) *Young People and Work*, London: Manpower Services Commission.

Marland, M. (ed.) (1972) *Scene Scripts*, London: Longman.

Marwick, A. (2001) *The New Nature of History: Knowledge, Evidence, Language*, Basingstoke: Palgrave Macmillan.

Mass-Observation (1939) *Britain*, London: Penguin.

Medhurst, J. (2002a) 'Servant of two tongues: the demise of TWW', *Llafur: Journal of Welsh Labour History*, 8, 3: 79–87.

— (2002b) 'Teledu Cymru: menter gyffrous neu freuddwyd ffôl?', in G. H. Jenkins (ed.) *Cof Cenedl XVII*, 167–193.

— (2003) 'Competition and change in British television', in M. Hilmes (ed.) *The Television History Book*, 40–44.

— (2004a) 'Teledu Cymru – Teledu Mamon? Independent television in Wales, 1959–63', unpublished PhD thesis, University of Wales.

— (2004b) 'Wales Television – Mammon's television? ITV in Wales in the 1960s', *Media History*, 10, 2: 119–131.

— (2005) 'Mammon's television? ITV in Wales 1959–1963', in C. Johnson and R. Turnock (eds) *ITV Cultures: Independent Television over Fifty Years*, 88–107.

Meehan, E. (2003) 'Heads of household and ladies of the house: gender, genre and broadcast ratings, 1929–1990', in V. Nightingale and K. Ross (eds) *Critical Readings: Media and Audiences*, 196–214.

Mercer, D. (1967) *The Parachute, with Two More TV Plays: Let's Murder Vivaldi and In Two Minds*, London: Calder.

Middleton, D., and Edwards, D. (eds) (1990) *Collective Remembering*, London: Sage.

Milland, J. (2004) 'Courting Malvolio: the background to the Pilkington Committee on broadcasting, 1960–1962', *Contemporary British History*, 18, 2: 76–102.

Miller, D. (1987) *Material Culture and Mass Consumption*, Oxford: Blackwell.

Miller, T. (1997) *The Avengers*, London: British Film Institute.

Millington, B., and Nelson, R. (1986) *Boys from the Blackstuff: The Making of TV Drama*, London: Comedia.

Misztal, B. (2003) *Theories of Social Remembering*, Maidenhead: Open University Press.

Mittell, J. (2005) 'The loss of value (or the value of *Lost*)', *Flow*, 2, 5: http://idg.communication.utexas.edu/flow.

Moores, S. (1988) 'The box on the dresser: memories of early radio and everyday life', *Media, Culture and Society*, 10, 1: 23–40.

— (1990) 'Texts, readers and contexts of reading: developments in the study of media', *Media, Culture and Society*, 12, 1: 9–29.

— (2000) *Media and Everyday Life in Modern Society*, Edinburgh: Edinburgh University Press.

Morgan-Russell, S. (2004) *Jimmy Perry and David Croft*, Manchester: Manchester University Press.

Morley, D. (1986) *Family Television: Cultural Power and Domestic Leisure*, London: Comedia.

— (1995) 'Television: not so much a visual medium, more a visible object', in C. Jenks (ed.) *Visual Culture*, 170–189.

— (2000) *Home Territories*, London: Routledge.

Moscardo, G. (1996) 'Mindful visitors: heritage and tourism', *Annals of Tourism Research*, 23: 376–396.

Moseley, R. (2002) *Growing Up with Audrey Hepburn: Text, Audience, Resonance*, Manchester: Manchester University Press.

— (2006) 'Reconstructing early television for women in Britain: Marguerite Patten, television cookery and the production of domestic femininity', paper presented at 'Screen studies' conference, University of Glasgow.

— (forthcoming) *Television for Teenagers: Genre, Discourse and Identity*, London: I.B.Tauris.

Mulvey, L., and Sexton, J. (eds) (2007) *Experimental Television*, Manchester: Manchester University Press.

Nelson, R. (1997) *TV Drama in Transition: Forms, Values and Cultural Change*, Basingstoke: Macmillan.

Newton, D. M. (2002) 'Beyond the black Atlantic: West Indian imagery, cultural production and BBC Television', unpublished PhD thesis, University of Wisconsin.

Nichols, B. (1991) *Representing Reality: Issues and Concepts in Documentary*, Bloomington: Indiana University Press.

— (2001) *Introduction to Documentary*, Bloomington: Indiana University Press.

Nicholson-Lord, D. (1992) 'TV pioneers recall days of fun', *Independent*, 24 April: 3.

Nightingale, V., and Ross, K. (eds) *Critical Readings: Media and Audiences*, Maidenhead: Open University Press.

Norden, D., Harper, S., and Gilbert, N. (1985) *Coming to You Live! Behind the Screen Memories of 40s and 50s TV*, London: Methuen.

Nowell-Smith, G. (2003) *Luchino Visconti* (3rd edn), London: British Film Institute.

Open University (1981) *The Historical Development of Popular Culture in Britain*, vol. 2, Maidenhead: Open University Press.

Örnebring, H. (2004) 'Revisiting the Coronation: a critical perspective on the Coronation of Queen Elizabeth II in 1953', *Nordicom Review*, 25, 1–2: 175–196.

O'Shea, A. (1989) 'Television as culture: not just texts and readers', *Media, Culture and Society*, 11, 3: 373–379.

O'Sullivan, T. (1991) 'Television memories and cultures of viewing, 1950–1965', in J. Corner (ed.) *Popular Television in Britain*, 159–181.

— (1998) 'Nostalgia, revelation and intimacy: tendencies in the flow of modern popular television', in C. Geraghty and D. Lusted (eds) *The Television Studies Book*, 198–211.

— (2005) 'From television lifestyle to lifestyle television', in D. Bell and J. Hollows (eds) *Ordinary Lifestyles: Popular Media, Consumption and Taste*, 21–34.

Oswell, D. (1998) 'A question of belonging: television, youth and the domestic', in T. Skelton and G. Valentine (eds) *Cool Places: Geographies of Youth Cultures*, 35–49.

— (2002) *Television, Childhood and the Home: A History of the Making of the Child Television Audience in Britain*, Oxford: Oxford University Press.

Passerini, L. (1979) 'Work ideology under Italian fascism', *History Workshop Journal*, 8: 84–92.

Paulu, B. (1961) *British Broadcasting in Transition*, Minneapolis: University of Minnesota Press.

Perks, R., and Thomson, A. (eds) (1998) *The Oral History Reader*, London: Routledge.

Piccini, A. (2004) 'TV in BA', *British Archaeology*, 75: www.britarch.ac.uk/ba/ba75/column2.shtml.

Pines, J. (ed.) (1992) *Black and White in Colour: Black People in British Television Since 1936*, London: British Film Institute.

Political and Economic Planning (1958) 'Television in Britain', *Political and Economic Planning*, 24: 38–68.

Portelli, A. (1998) 'What makes oral history different', in R. Perks and A. Thomson (eds) *The Oral History Reader*, 63–74.

Porter, G. (1988) 'Putting your house in order: representations of women and domestic life', in R. Lumley (ed.) *The Museum Time Machine*, 102–127.

Porter, V. (2000) 'Outsiders in England: the films of ABPC, 1949–1958', in J. Ashby and A. Higson (eds) *British Cinema: Past and Present*, 152–166.

Prentice, R., Guerin, S., and McGugan, S. (1998) 'Visitor learning at a heritage attraction: a case study of Discovery as a media product', *Tourism Management*, 19: 5–23.

Raleigh Yow, V. (1994) *Recording Oral History: A Practical Guide for Social Scientists*, London: Sage.

Reith, J. C. W. (1924) *Broadcast over Britain*, London: Hodder and Stoughton.

Richards, J., and Sheridan, D. (eds) (1987) *Mass-Observation at the Movies*, London: Routledge.

Roberts, G. (2001) 'The historian and television: a methodological survey', in G. Roberts and P. M. Taylor (eds) *The Historian, Television and Television History*, 1–7.

Roberts, G., and Taylor, P. M. (eds) (2001) *The Historian, Television and Television History*, Luton: University of Luton Press.

Rolinson, D. (2005) *Alan Clarke*, Manchester: Manchester University Press.

Rosenthal, A., and Corner, J. (eds) (2005) *New Challenges for Documentary*, Manchester: Manchester University Press.

Ryan, M. (1986) 'Blocking the channels: TV and film in Wales', in T. Curtis (ed.) *Wales – The Imagined Nation: Essays in Cultural and National Identity*, 181–196.

Samuel, R. (ed.) (1981) *People's History and Socialist Theory*, London: Routledge.

— (2000) 'People's history', in J. Tosh (ed.) *Historians on History*, 110–118.

Sandford, J. (1967) *Cathy Come Home, together with Special Report by the Author: 'What I have written is true'*, London: Pan.

Sandon, E. (2004) 'From vision to mundanity: television at Alexandra Palace, London 1936–1952. Memories of production: an oral history approach to the reassessment of the early period of British television history', unpublished PhD thesis, University of Sussex.

— (2006) 'The aesthetics of entertainment in early television in Britain', paper presented at 'Screen Studies' conference, University of Glasgow.

Scannell, P. (1979) 'The social eye of television, 1946–1955', *Media, Culture and Society*, 1, 1: 97–106.

— (1990) 'Public service broadcasting: the history of a concept', in A. Goodwin and G. Whannel (eds) *Understanding Television*, 11–29.

— (1996) *Radio, Television and Modern Life*, Oxford: Blackwell.

Scannell, P., and Cardiff, D. (1981) 'Radio in World War II', in Open University, *The Historical Development of Popular Culture in Britain*, vol. 2, 32–77.

— (1991) *A Social History of British Broadcasting*, vol. 1, *1922–1939: Serving the Nation*, Oxford: Blackwell.

Schafer, E. (1998) *MsDirecting Shakespeare*, London: Women's Press.

Schama, S. (2004) 'Television and the trouble with history', in D. Cannadine (ed.) *History and the Media*, 20–33.

Sconce, J. (2000) *Haunted Media: Electronic Presence from Telegraphy to Television*, Durham, NC: Duke University Press.

Scott, J. W. (ed.) *Feminism and History*, Oxford: Oxford University Press.

Screen Education (1976) no. 20.

Seaton, J. (2004) 'Writing the history of broadcasting', in D. Cannadine (ed.) *History and the Media*, 141–159.

Selby, K., and Cowdery, R. (1995) *How to Study Television*, Basingstoke: Macmillan.

Sendall, B. (1982) *Independent Television in Britain*, vol. 1, *Origin and Foundation, 1946–62*, Basingstoke: Macmillan.

— (1983) *Independent Television in Britain*, vol. 2, *Expansion and Change, 1958–68*, Basingstoke: Macmillan.

Sennett, R. (1992) *The Fall of Public Man*, New York: Norton.

Shils, E. (1975) *Center and Periphery: Essays in Macrosociology*, Chicago: University of Chicago Press.

Shils, E., and Young, M. (1956) 'The meaning of the Coronation', in E. Shils (1975) *Center and Periphery: Essays in Macrosociology*, 135–152.

Siegel, M. (1984) 'Towards an aesthetics of science fiction television', *Extrapolation*, 24: 60–75.

Sillitoe, A. (1976) *Saturday Night and Sunday Morning*, London: Longman.

Silverstone, R. (1994) *Television and Everyday Life*, London: Routledge.

Silvey, R. (1974) *Who's Listening?*, London: Allen and Unwin.

Skelton, T., and Valentine, G. (eds) (1998) *Cool Places: Geographies of Youth Cultures*, London: Routledge.

Skutch, I. (ed.) (1998) *The Days of Live*, Lanham, MD: Scarecrow Press.

Smith, A. (ed.) (1998) *Television: An International History* (2nd edn), Oxford: Oxford University Press.

Smith, B. G. (1996) 'Historiography, objectivity, and the case of the abusive widow', in J. W. Scott (ed.) *Feminism and History*, 547–567.

Smith, D. (1999) *Wales: A Question for History*, Bridgend: Seren.

Smith, P. (1976) *The Historian and Film*, Cambridge: Cambridge University Press.

Smith Rosenberg, C. (1986) *Disorderly Conduct: Visions of Gender in Victorian America*, Oxford: Oxford University Press.

Spigel, L. (1992) *Make Room for TV: Television and the Family Ideal in Postwar America*, Chicago: University of Chicago Press.

— (1995) 'From the dark ages to the golden age: women's memories and television reruns', *Screen*, 36, 1: 16–33.

— (2001) *Welcome to the Dreamhouse: Popular Media and Postwar Suburbs*, Durham, NC: Duke University Press.

— (2005) 'TV's next season', *Cinema Journal*, 45, 1: 83–90.

Spigel, L., and Mann, D. (eds) (1992) *Private Screenings: Television and the Female Consumer*, Minneapolis: University of Minnesota Press.

Spigel, L., and Olsson, J. (eds) (2004) *Television after TV: Essays on a Medium in Transition*, Durham, NC: Duke University Press.

Stacey, J. (1994) *Star Gazing: Hollywood Cinema and Female Spectatorship*, London: Routledge.

Stanton, G. (2000) 'Gorer's gaze: aspects of the inauguration of audience studies in British television', *Goldsmiths Anthropology Research Papers*, 1.

Startt, J. D., and Sloan, W. D. (1989) *Historical Methods in Mass Communications*, Hillsdale, NJ: Erlbaum.

Stokes, J. (1999) *On Screen Rivals: Cinema and Television in the United States and Britain*, Basingstoke: Macmillan.

Street, S. (2006) *Crossing the Ether: British Public Service Radio and Commercial Competition 1922–1945*, Eastleigh: John Libbey.

Sturcken, F. (1990) *Live Television: The Golden Age of 1946–1958 in New York*, Jefferson, NC: McFarland.

Talfan Davies, A. (1972) *Darlledu a'r Genedl*, London: British Broadcasting Corporation.

Taylor, A. J. P. (1967) *The First World War* [1963], London: Penguin.

— (1969) *The Trouble Makers* [1957], London: Panther History.

Taylor, P. M. (2001) 'Television and the future historian', in G. Roberts and P. M. Taylor (eds) *The Historian, Television and Television History*, 171–177.

Thomas, J. (2002) *Diana's Mourning: A People's History*, Cardiff: University of Wales Press.

Thomas, M. W. (ed.) (2002) *Emyr Humphreys: Conversations and Reflections*, Cardiff: University of Wales Press.

Thompson, J. B. (1995) *The Media and Modernity*, Cambridge: Polity Press.

Thompson, R. J. (1997) *Television's Second Golden Age: From Hill Street Blues to ER*, Syracuse, NY: Syracuse University Press.

Thomson, A. (1994) *Anzac Memories: Living with the Legend*, Oxford: Oxford University Press.

Thornham, S., and Purvis, T. (2005) *Television Drama: Theories and Identities*, Basingstoke: Palgrave Macmillan.

Thumim, J. (1998) 'Mrs Knight *must* be balanced: methodological problems in researching early British television', in C. Carter, G. Branston and S. Allen (eds) *News, Gender and Power*, 91–104.

— (ed.) (2002) *Small Screen, Big Ideas: Television in the 1950s*, London: I.B.Tauris.

Tosh, J. (2000a) *The Pursuit of History* (3rd edn), London: Longman.

— (ed.) (2000b) *Historians on History*, London: Longman.

Trevelyan, G. M. (1978) *English Social History: A Survey of Six Centuries from Chaucer to Queen Victoria* [1942], London: Longman.

Tulloch, J. (1990) *Television Drama: Agency, Audience and Myth*, London: Routledge.

— (2007) *Trevor Griffiths*, Manchester: Manchester University Press.

Tulloch, J., and Alvarado, M. (1983) *Doctor Who: The Unfolding Text*, Basingstoke: Macmillan.

Vahimagi, T. (1994) *British Television*, London: British Film Institute.

Ward, M. (2004) *Out of the Unknown: A Guide to the Legendary BBC Series*, Bristol: Kaleidoscope.

Watson, F. (2003) 'Review of *The Biblical World* ed. John Barton', *Times Higher Education Supplement*, 16 May: 30–31.

Watt, D. (1976) 'History on the public screen, I', in P. Smith (ed.) *The Historian and Film*, reprinted in A Rosenthal and J. Corner (eds) (2005) *New Challenges for Documentary*, 363–371.

Wells, S. (1966) *Shakespeare: A Dramatic Life*, London: Sinclair-Stevenson.

Wheatley, H. (2003) 'ITV 1955–89: populism and experimentation', in M. Hilmes (ed.) *The Television History Book*, 76–81.

— (2004) 'Putting the *Mystery* back into *Armchair Theatre*', *Journal of British Film and Television*, 1, 2: 197–210.

— (2005) 'Rooms within rooms: *Upstairs Downstairs* and the studio costume drama of the 1970s', in C. Johnson and R. Turnock (eds) *ITV Cultures: Independent Television over Fifty Years*, 143–158.

— (2006a) 'Colonial spectacle, domestic space: natural history television in the 1950s', paper presented at 'Screen Studies' conference, University of Glasgow.

— (2006b) *Gothic Television*, Manchester: Manchester University Press.

— (2007) '"And now for your Sunday night experimental drama…": experimentation and *Armchair Theatre*', in L. Mulvey and J. Sexton (eds) *Experimental Television*, 31–47.

Whitehead, A. (1976) 'Sexual antagonism in Herefordshire', in D. L. Barker and S. Allen (eds) *Dependence and Exploitation in Work and Marriage*, 169–203.

Whittaker, C. (2001) 'How the BBC pictured itself' in G. Roberts and P. M. Taylor (eds) *The Historian, Television and Television History*, 145–156.

Williams, G. (1997) 'Editorial', *Higher Education Quarterly*, 51, 1: 1–5.

Williams, K. (1988) *Get Me a Murder a Day: A History of Mass Communications in Britain*, London: Arnold.

Williams, R. (1974) *Television: Technology and Cultural Form*, London: Fontana.

— (1977) *Marxism and Culture*, Oxford: Oxford University Press.

— (1984) *The Long Revolution* [1961], London: Penguin.

Winston, B. (1998) *Media, Technology and Society: A History from the Telegraph to the Internet*, London: Routledge.

Wood, N. (1992) 'Vichy memories', *New Formations*, 17: 148–152.

Wyndham Goldie, G. (1977) *Facing the Nation*, London: Bodley Head.

Ytreberg, E. (2002) 'Ideal types in public service television: paternalists and bureaucrats, charismatics and avant-gardists', *Media, Culture and Society*, 24, 6: 759–774.

Ziegler, P. (1978) *Crown and People*, London: Collins.

Index

Abigail's Party 90, 92
'Actual Woman, The' 89, 94, 209n10
Adams, Basil 106, 107, 210n14
Adorno, Theodor 204n1
Africa Series: Scientific Programme 116
Akass, Kim 206n6
Alexandra Palace Television Society 99–112, 209n4, 210n6, 210n7
Allan, Elkan 195
Allen, Robert C. 57–60, 207n5
Alvarado, Manuel 38, 209n1
Ampex 205n11
Anderson, Benedict 183
Anderson, Christopher 70
Andrews, Harry 41, 51
Ang, Ien 216n1
Angelis, Michael 85
Angelis, Paul 85
Anglo-Caribbean Club, 123
Ansorge, Peter 87, 209n7, 209n8
Apted, Michael 85, 88
ARKive 201
Armchair Theatre 20–23, 25, 26, 37–38, 39, 136, 205n11 – see also individual episode titles
Arne, Peter 76
Arnold Bennett Society, 42, 43, 44, 47, 49, 51–52
Arts and Humanities Research Council (AHRC) 1, 36, 39, 95, 155
Ascent of Man, The 147, 149
As If 197
Asimov, Isaac 39
Associated British Corporation (ABC) 20, 39, 70, 73, 74–76, 78
Associated British Pathé 74, 114
Associated British Picture Corporation (ABPC) 74–76, 80

Associated Television (ATV) 41, 42, 43, 44, 45, 51, 70, 195
Atkins, Ian 106
'Atrocity' 93, 209n2
Attenborough, David 117, 146–147, 211n12, 213n7
Attie, Jeanie 148
Atwell, Winifred 113
Auntie: The Inside Story of the BBC 110, 209n2, 210n21, 210n35
Avengers, The 37, 39
Averill, June 210n7

Bain, Andrew D. 165
Balcon, Michael 205n15
Bal Creole 116
Bardot, Brigitte 78
Barlow, David 130
Barnouw, Erik 7
Barr, Charles 56
Barry, Michael 210n9
Bate, Philip 107, 109, 210n14
BBC Written Archives Centre (WAC) 6, 69, 72, 83, 114–115, 135, 137, 187, 199, 217n5
Bean, Charles, 103
Bell, Elaine 101
Bell, Erin 98, 142–155, 213n9
Bell, Michael 208n6
Belson, William A. 165
Benjamin, Walter 3, 40, 41
Bennett, Arnold 41, 42, 43, 44, 46, 48–49, 50–51
Benny Hill Show, The 25
Berker, Thomas 161
Berman, Bruce 207n16
Bevan, David 132–133
Beveridge Committee, 113, 133, 139
Bible 16–18

Big Brother 61

Bignell, Jonathan 1, 3, 11, 27–39, 203n8, 205n1, 205n4, 206n1, 207n11

Bill, The 190

Billen, Andrew 148

Birt, John 110

Birth of Television, The 209n2

Black, Lawrence 8

Black, Peter 67, 71, 79

Black and White in Colour 211n4, 212n22

Blair, Les 90, 91

Blakely, Colin 20, 85

Bleasdale, Alan 90, 92, 94

Bloome, David 173

Boddy, William 5, 7, 56, 161

Bold, James 109

Bond, Derek 67, 76–77, 80

Bonner, Frances 65, 68

Border Television 199

Born, Georgina 7, 97, 203n6

Bourdieu, Pierre 207n6, 214n10

Bourne, Stephen 116

Boy Meets Girls 186

Boys from the Blackstuff 92

Brandt, George 28–29

Branston, Gill 1, 3, 127

'Break-in' 217n10

Breakwell, Ian 214n8

Bredin, James 116–117

Bremner, Ian 144, 147, 149

Brideshead Revisited 52, 87

Briggs, Asa 4, 7, 68, 71, 79, 99, 100, 105–106, 107, 135, 176, 183, 214n7

British Broadcasting Corporation (BBC) 4, 6, 7, 9, 37, 41–46, 50, 52, 53–54, 67–81, 82–95, 97–112, 113–126, 128, 130–135, 139–140, 144, 146–147, 149, 162, 163–164, 165, 170–171, 185, 186–188, 191, 192–194, 199, 208n3, 208n9, 208n14, 208n17, 209n2, 209n3, 211n3, 211n12, 214n7, 214n12, 215n13, 217n5, 217n8, 218n3

British Film Institute (BFI) 20, 32–33, 35, 43, 44, 47, 137, 199, 200, 206n2, 209n2, 210n12, 218n3

British Universities Film and Video Council (BUFVC) 199, 218n1

British Vintage Wireless and Television Museum 215n17

Broadcasters' Audience Research Board (BARB) 204n7

Broadcasting Act, the (1981) 135

Broadcasting Entertainment and Cinematographic Theatre Union (BECTU) 102, 109, 210n12

Bronowski, Jacob 147

Brookside 29, 185, 206n2

Brown, Alan 92, 95

Brunsdon, Charlotte 2, 29, 48, 55, 59, 65, 214n1

Bryant, Steve 214n3

Buck and Bubbles 113

Buckingham, David 185

Buffy the Vampire Slayer 187

Bunch of Fives, A 191

Burnett, Frances Hodgson 41, 46, 50

Burns, Ken 148

Burns, Tom 101, 105

Buscombe, Edward 23, 57, 70, 71, 100, 111

Bussey, Gordon 165

Butterworth, Eric D. 124

Butt Philip, Alan 132–133

Bygraves, Max 136

Calder, Angus 215n18

Calder, Gilchrist (Ritchie) 104–105, 109, 117

Callaghan, James 190

Calouste Gulbenkian Foundation 185, 187, 192–193, 195

Cambrian Television 139

Cambrian (North and West Wales) Television 139

Canal + Image UK Limited 199

Cardiff, David 2, 72, 101, 170–171

Cardwell, Sarah 35, 205n4

Carlton International 43, 45

Carol, Martine 78

Carpenter, Paul 76

Carr, Edward Hallet 5, 7, 10, 138

Caribbean Cabaret 116

Carroll, Noël 59

Cartier, Rudolph 62, 207n9, 207n14

Cathy Come Home 15, 32, 61

Caughie, John 7, 20, 23, 30, 63–65, 68, 69, 79, 104, 127, 205n13, 206n2
Central 43, 45
Champion, Justin 65, 144–145
Changes, The 218n20
Channel Four 145, 147, 149, 187
Channel Television 199
Chapman, James 38, 56, 144
Charlie's Angels 217n4
Cheeseman, Peter 90, 94
Christian, Angela 122
Christmas Carol, A 77
Cinderella 46
Civilisation: A Personal View by Lord Clark 146–147, 149, 213n7
Civil War, The 148
Clark, Kenneth 146–147, 151, 154
Clarke, Alan 85, 91
Clarke, Sheila 116
Clayhanger 11–12, 41–52, 206n2, 206n3, 207n7
Clayton, Ian 161
Clive of India 103
'Club Havana' 92, 94, 209n2
Coast 149
Cock, Gerald 113
Collingwood, Robin George 12
Colour in Britain 122
Connor, Edric 116
Constantine, Sir Learie 122
Cook, John R. 205n14
Cooke, Alastair 147
Cooke, Lez 6, 7, 20, 30–31, 39, 41, 53–54, 82–95, 97, 204n10, 205n4, 205n5, 206n2
Cool for Cats 186
Cooper, Edward 115
Corner, John 1, 2–3, 4, 7, 8, 69, 80, 98, 145, 151, 152, 153, 159, 168, 214n1
Coronation broadcasts 110, 157, 162, 171–183
Coronation Street 32, 48
Cottle, Simon 7
Couldry, Nick 175
Courts of Justice, The 106
Cowdery, Ron 34
Cox, Harold 109
Cox, Michael 97
Creeber, Glen 2, 11, 15, 31, 57–58, 61

Cregan, David 87, 93
Crisell, Andrew 2, 71, 72, 174
Culpitt, D.H. 129
Curran, Charles 84
Curran, James 2
Current Release 68–71, 73–74, 79–80

Dad's Army 25, 42
Dahl, Hans Fredrik 2, 9, 128–129
Dallas 61
Davies, Aneirin Talfan 128, 130
Davies, Gladys 108
Davies, Hannah 185
Davies, Islwyn 140
Davies, John (1934) 41, 51
Davies, John (1938) 128, 130, 133, 135, 213n2
Davies, Máire Messenger 11–12, 40–52, 98, 205n2, 206n1, 206n1, 207n7, 207n12
Davies, S. Kenneth 140
Davies, Stuart 142–143
Davis, Glyn 185, 187
Dawson's Creek 187
Day, Frances 115
Dayan, Daniel 175–176, 183
DEF II 189
De Lotheniere, Anthony 118–120
De Maupassant, Guy 49
Dennett, John 208n15
Desperate Housewives 18, 205n8
Dewch I Mewn 136, 139
Dick, Philip K. 39
Dickinson, Kay 185, 187
Dickinson, Peter 218n20
Dickson, Kathleen 209n2
Dinsmore, Uma 42
Dobbs, Mattiwalda 121
Docherty, Mark 185, 216n3
Doctor Who 38
'Dumb Waiter' 39
Dyer, Richard 32

'Early to Bed' 90, 94
East Anglian Film Archive 199
EastEnders 49
Edgar, Barrie 109, 210n14
Edwards, Derek 214n8
Eisenstein, Elizabeth 40

Eitzen, Dirk 151
Elliott, Denholm 51
Ellis, John 2, 3, 10, 11, 15–26, 39, 161, 205n9, 205n16, 206n1
Ellis, Thomas Iowerth 137, 140
Elton, Geoffrey Rudolph 5
Elvey, Maurice 77
Emmett, B.P. 165
Ennis, Jane 191
English by Radio 122
Evans, Gwynfor 128, 129, 140
Evans, Ifan Gwynfil 128, 132–133
Evans, Lady Olwen Carey 140
Evans, Richard J. 6, 9, 138

Farquarson Small, W. 208n10, 208n16
Fawlty Towers 34
Ferguson, Niall 145–146
Feuer, Jane 56, 77
Fiddick, Peter 188
Fiddy, Dick 136
Fields, Barbara 148
'Fight for Shelton Bar' 90, 92, 94
Film Fanfare 68, 70–71, 73–80
Filmtime 73
Finch, John 97
First Love, Last Rites 91
'Fishing Party, The' 86
Fiske, John 155, 213n11
Fitzgerald, John 73, 76, 79
Flambards 190
Flying Doctors, The 29
Fools on the Hill 110, 210n36
Forbes, Scott 20
Ford, John 23
Four Idle Hands 191
Four Weddings and a Funeral 91
Frances, Myra 89
Frankfurt School 40
'Frank Crank Story, The' 91, 94
Fraser, Sir Robert 139
Frears, Stephen 89, 91
Freedman, Maurice 117
Frith, Simon 203n6
Fulton, Nora 88
Further Education Broadcasting Council 192

Galbraith, John Kenneth 147
Garnett, Tony 205n4
Gaumont British News 113
Gauntlett, David 214n6, 217n4
Geddes, Keith 165
Georgeson, Valerie 88
Geraghty, Christine 55–56, 59, 206n6
Giddens, Anthony 153
Giddings, Robert 49, 50
Gilbert, Norma 210n8
Giles, Marjorie 97
'Girl' 88–89, 93, 209n10
Gitlin, Todd 162
Glasgow Drama Workshop 194
Glover, Brian 88, 93, 94
Gnanamuthu, Vedaneyagon 122
Going Out 158, 185, 189, 190, 193–197, 216n2, 216n3
Going to Work 191
'Golden Vision, The' 209n11
Gomery, Douglas 57–60, 207n5
Good Life, The 25
Gorer, Geoffrey 167, 215n24
Gorham, Maurice 164, 214n11
Grade, Michael 210n8
Grainge, Paul 214n8
Granada 52, 74, 132, 136, 139, 191, 199, 218n4
Granada Television Archive 137
Grange Hill 185, 195, 206n2, 216n3
Gray, Ann 8, 42, 98, 142–155, 162, 213n9
Green, Harry 119
Green, Henry 21
Greene, Hugh 115, 122–123
Gregory, Chris 38
Griffith, Moses 140
Griffiths, Trevor 29
Gripsrud, Jostein 206n7
Grisewood, Harman 208n7
Grove Family, The 208n17
Guerin, Sinéad 152

Hadlow, Janice 147, 148
Haigh, Peter 67, 76–78, 80
Hall, Adelaide 113
Hallam, Julia 7, 205n4
Hammond, Paul 214n8

Hancock's Half Hour 25
Hankey Committee 162, 214n6
Hankey, Lord Maurice 214n7
Hansel and Gretel 46
Hanson, Barry 85, 87
Happy Anniversary 216n29
Haralovich, Mary Beth 6, 97
Harding, Colin 161
Harlech Television 128
Harper, Sue 207n5
Harper, Sybil 210n8
Harris, Bimbi 108, 210n14
Harris, Leonard 173
Harrisson, Tom 165, 173, 215n19
Harry, Debbie 194
Hartley, John 47, 155
Hartmann, Maren 161
Heartbeat 18, 205n8
Hell Drivers 23
Henderson, Michael 99, 210n5
Henry, Victor 85
Herrnstein Smith, Barbara 59–60, 207n12
Heycock, Llewelyn 140
Hickethier, Knut 204n5
Hill, Annette 65, 214n6, 217n6
Hill, John 185, 187
Hillcoat, Christine 109
Hilmes, Michele 2, 11, 31, 56, 70
Himmelweit, Hilde T. 215n27
Hind, Chrissy 194
History of Britain, A 144, 146, 147–150, 152, 154–155, 213n4, 213n5, 213n10
Hobley, MacDonald 76, 79
Hobsbawm, Eric 103
Hoggart, Richard 21–22
Holder, Boscoe 116
Holland, Agnieszka 45
Hollyoaks 185, 187, 197, 206n2
Holmes, Su 7–8, 53, 65, 66, 67–81, 204n10, 208n17, 210n37, 214n12
Home, Anna 185, 193, 218n20, 218n24
Hood, Stuart 161
Hopcraft, Arthur 82, 85, 88, 93
Hopkins, John 85, 93
How Wars Begin 146
How Wars End 146
Howarth, Donald 85, 93

Hughes, Bettany 149–150
Hughes, Nathan 131, 138
Hull Arts Centre 85
'Humbug, Finger or Thumb?' 88, 93
Humphreys, Emyr 129
Hunkin, Oliver 122
Hunt, Tristram 145
Huxley, Julian 117

'If a Man Answers' 88, 93
Iggers, Georg G. 214n2
Imperial War Museum 200
Independent Broadcasting Authority (IBA) 185
Independent Television (ITV) 8, 15, 20, 37, 45, 53, 67, 69–71, 74–77, 79–81, 105, 107, 108, 127–128, 130–136, 139, 146–147, 162, 163, 186, 191, 195, 203n1, 203n2, 206n3, 208n3, 208n14, 208n17, 211n4, 214n12, 215n13, 215n16, 217n8
Independent Television Authority (ITA) 131, 133, 135, 136, 137, 138, 139–140, 147
Independent Television Commission (ITC) 192
Independent Television News Archive 200
In Search of Myths and Heroes 150, 154–155
Inspector Morse 29
International Association for Media and History (IAMHIST) 203n3
Irwin, John 146
Isaacs, Jeremy 145
ITV Wales Film and Television Archive 136, 137, 213n4
I Want to Marry Your Son 87, 93

Jacobs, Jason 1, 2, 6, 7, 8, 9, 11, 30, 53, 55–59, 66, 68, 69, 97, 127, 136, 203n5, 203n8, 206n6, 210n9
'Jack Flea's Birthday Celebration' 91, 94
Jackson, Michael 147
Jamaican Broadcasting Company 124
James, Allison 46
James, Clive 48
Jancovich, Mark 206n6
Jardine, Lisa 16
Jefferson, Thomas 40, 41, 43, 52
Jeffrey, Tom 215n18

Jeffries, Stuart 169
Jenkins, Geraint H. 128
Jenkins, Keith 5, 214n2
Jennings, Humphrey 165, 172
Jermyn, Deborah 65
Jewel in the Crown 52
Joffe, Roland 91
Johnson, Catherine 3, 7, 10, 12, 37, 53, 55–66, 130, 163, 206n5, 207n9
Johnson, Richard 2, 3, 8
Johnson-Smith, Jan 207n15
Jones, Aled 130, 213n2
Jones, Ken 185
Jones, Philip Henry 129
Jones, Tom 140
Judd, Denis 213n3

Karloff, Boris 39
Katz, Elihu 175–176, 183
Kavanagh, Jacqueline 69
Kelley, Peter 185
Kermode, Frank 16
Kerr, Paul 208n8
Kershaw, Ian 145–146
Kids 191
'King of the Castle' 88, 93
Kline, Steven 206n4
Kneale, Nigel 62, 207n9, 207n14
Knight Hopkins, Shirley 85
Kotcheff, Ted 20, 23
Kuehl, Jerry 143, 146
Kuhn, Annette 176

Lacey, Stephen 1, 5, 30, 36, 38, 39
Laing, Stewart 216n30
Landscape and Memory 148
Lanin, John 87
La Plante, Lynda 30
Latham, Stuart Harry 105
Lawrence, D.H. 49
Lawson, Mark 154
League of Coloured Peoples, 123
Leigh, Mike 82, 90–92, 94, 95
Lejeune, C.A. 72
Leman, Joy 6, 208n13, 210n7
'Lena, O My Lena' 20–23, 25, 26, 38
Leonard, Tom 214n5, 214n9

Let It Be 87
Lewis, Brian 161
Life on Earth 147
Lincoln, Andrew 48
Lindsay-Hogg, Michael 87, 91
Lingard, Joan 186, 194
Lion Television 149
Little, Kenneth 119
Little Bit of Madness, A 124
Littlewood, Yvonne 210n7, 210n14
Livings, Henry 85, 93
Livingstone, Douglas 41, 49, 51
Livingstone, Sonia 214n6
Loach, Ken 62, 209n11
London Weekend Show, The 217n19
London Weekend Television (LWT) 191
Longoria, Eva 18
Loren, Sophia 78
Lost 47
Lurie, Alison 46
Lury, Karen 185, 186
Luxford, Robin 107
Lyons, James 206n6

MacArthur, Colin 143
Macauley, Thomas 144
McCabe, Janet 206n6
McCall, Robert 121
McCarthy, Anna 7
McEnery, Peter 20, 41, 43, 47
McEwan, Ian 91, 94
McGivern, Cecil 74, 79–80, 106, 116, 208n11, 208n15, 208n16
MacGregor, Elizabeth 108, 109–110, 210n14
McGown, Alistair 185, 216n3
McGugan, Stuart 152
McLuskie, Peter 185, 186
MacMurraugh-Kavanagh, Madeleine 30
Madden, Cecil 74, 208n11
Madden, Paul 205n11
Madge, Charles 165, 172
Maggie 158, 186, 193–194, 197, 216n2, 216n3
Magic Rays of Light 209n2
Making a Living 191
Malcolm, Mary 103, 104
Mammon's Television – see *Teledu Mamon*
Mann, Denise 6, 8

Manpower Services Commission 185, 190, 192

Manvell, Roger 72

Marland, Michael 189

Marshall, Dulcie J. 123

Martin, David 120

Mass-Observation 157, 165–167, 171–183, 200, 215n18

Mast, Gerald 57

'Match of the Day' 89–90, 94

Mathieson, Muir 76

Mayhew, Christopher 116–117

Mead, Margaret 215n24

Medhurst, Jamie 4, 56, 97–98, 127–141, 203n9, 213n1

Media Archive of Central England (MACE) 200

'Medium, The' 88, 90, 93

Meehan, Eileen 7

Meet Mr Lucifer 216n29

Mercer, David 32, 87, 93

Middlemarch 49

Middleton, David 214n8

Midlands Television Research Group 185

Milland, Jeffrey 135

Miller, Daniel 174

Miller, Toby 38

Milligan, Spike 26

Millington, Bob 85, 90

Minelli, Vincente 23

Mirzoeff, Edward 146

Misztal, Barbara 214n8

Mitchell, Philip 130

Mittell, Jason 47

Mixed Marriages 122

Moores, Shaun 8, 161, 163, 171, 214n6

More O'Ferrall, George 103

Morgan-Russell, Simon 205n4

Morley, David 214n4, 214n6, 214n9, 215n14

Moscardo, Gianna 152–153, 155

Mosedale Horseshoe, The 88

Moseley, Rachel 7, 158, 184–197, 203n7, 204n10, 208n17, 216n1

Mourant, Arthur E. 117

Movie-go-Round 73

Movie Magazine 70

'Mrs Pool's Preserves' 93, 209n10

MTV 46

Munro, D.H. 106, 108

Music Makers 116

Nash, Robin 210n14

National Archives 137

National Film and Television Archive (NFTVA) 33, 43, 82, 95, 200, 216n2, 218n3

National Film Theatre 77

National Library of Wales 137

National Museum of Photography, Film and Television 43, 200, 215n17

National Screen and Sound Archive of Wales 200

Neighbours 34

Nelson, Robin 29–30, 85, 90

Newell, Mike 91

Newman, Sydney 20, 39, 83

Newsfilm Online 201

Newton, Darrell 4, 97, 113–126, 204n10, 211n3, 216n2

Nichols, Bill 149, 151, 153

Nicholson-Lord, David 102

Night in With the Girls, A 210n7

Noble, Peter 76, 79

Noordhof, George H. 116–117

Norden, Dennis 210n8

Northern Region Film and Television Archive 200

North West Film Archive 200

'No Trams to Lime Street' 20

Novick, Peter 150

Nowell-Smith, Geoffrey 23, 205n13

Nutley, Colin 185

NYPD Blue 30

O.C., The 187

O'Connell, Patrick 21

O'Day, Andrew 38, 205n4

Ofcom 204n7

Oh Boy! 186

Old Wives' Tale, The 44

Oliver, John 213n6

Oliver Twist 49

Olsson, Jan 4, 26

O'Malley, Mary 82

O'Malley, Tom 130
On a Clear Day You Can See Forever 23
Open the Box 215n16
Oppenheim, A.N. 215n24
Orlebar, Jeremy 34
Örnebring, Henrik 157, 170–183, 210n11, 215n18
Orr-Ewing, Ian 109, 210n14
O'Shea, Alan 162
O'Sullivan, Tim 7, 157, 158, 159–169, 170, 210n11, 214n3, 214n9
Oswell, David 163, 217n6
Our Friends in the North 30
Out of the Unknown 39
Out of This World 39
Owen, Alun 20, 23
Oxford Roadshow, The 217n19

Paine, Crispin 142–143
Parents' Day 191
Parry, Sir David Hughes 140
Parry, Thomas 140
Parry-Williams, Sir Thomas Herbert 140
Parsons, John 76, 79
Passerini, Luisa 103
Patten, Marguerite 208n17
Paulu, Burton 113
Peake, Lisa 136
People in Trouble 211n4
Peoples Century, The 215n16
Perks, Robert 101
'Permissive Society, The' 90–91, 94
Peters, Sylvia 108
Philips, R.E.K. 124
Piccini, Angela 150
Picture Parade 67–69, 71, 73–80, 208n1, 208n2
Pilkington Committee 75, 128, 133, 134–135, 139, 140, 162
Pines, Jim 115–116
Plaid Cymru (Welsh Nationalist Party) 128
Plater, Alan 82, 83, 85, 91, 93, 188, 189–190
Play For Today 82, 86, 91, 92 – see also individual episode titles
Political and Economic Planning 165, 214n10
Polygram 43, 45
Popular Television Association 146
Portelli, Alessandro 104

Porter, Gaby 155
Porter, Vincent 74, 207n5
Postma, Laurens 205n11
Potter, Dennis 23, 26, 30, 85
Potter, John 42, 44
Powell, Dilys 72
Poynton, Keith 42
Preger, Janey 82, 95
Prem, Tara 86, 88, 93
Prentice, Richard 152
Pride and Prejudice 43, 49
Professionals, The 217n4
Prout, Alan 46
Punie, Yves 161
Purvis, Tony 31

Quatermass and the Pit 207n9
Quatermass Experiment, The (1953) 59–60, 62–63, 207n9, 207n14
Quatermass Experiment, The (2005) 207n13
Quatermass II 62, 207n9
Question of Colour, A 120–121, 122
Quilley, Dennis 41, 47

Rabinowitz, Lauren 6, 97
Race and Colour: A Scientific Introduction to the Problem of Race Relations 116–118
Radio Caroline 83–84
Radio Essex 83–84
Radio London 83–84
Raleigh Yow, Valerie 210n13
Ranke, Leopold von 9
Rank, J. Arthur 214n7
Rank Organization 74
Reckord, Barry 92, 94
Redmond, Phil 158, 185, 187, 194, 195, 196–197, 206n2, 216n2, 216n3, 218n25, 218n26
Rees, Jasper 188
Rees, Philip Henry 129
Referees, The 83
Reid, Robert 119
Reith, Sir John 110, 113
Richards, Jeffery 165
Richardson, Miranda 45
Richman, Stella 41
Roberts, Emrys 140

Roberts, Graham 1, 4, 8, 143–144
Roberts, Rachel 85
Roberts, Wyn 137
Robertson, B.A. 194
Robertson, Denise 88, 90, 93, 94
Robeson, Paul 113, 121
Robottom, John 188
Robson, James 88, 93, 94, 95
Rolinson, David 205n4
Room at the Top 23
Rose, David 83, 84–86, 90, 92, 209n3, 209n5
Rosemary and Thyme 18, 205n8
Rosenthal, Jack 82, 85, 93
Ross, Duncan 106–107
'Rotten' 92, 95
Royal Court Theatre 85
Royal Television Society Library and Archive 200
Rudkin, David 82, 85, 91, 93
Rumpole of the Bailey 190
Russell, Willy 82, 88, 91, 93, 188, 217n10
Ryan, Michelle 130

'Said the Preacher' 85, 88, 93
Salter, Lionel 104, 109, 110, 210n14
Sandon, Emma 7, 97, 99–112, 204n11, 208n17, 209n1
Sandford, Jeremy 32
Sarris, Andrew 57
Saturday Night and Sunday Morning 21, 23, 168
Saturday Night Fever 197
Saville, Philip 89, 91, 92, 209n10
Scannell, Paddy 2, 47, 72, 101, 161, 170–171, 177, 183, 210n10
'Scarborough' 85–86, 93
Scene 186, 187–190, 192, 193
Schafer, Elizabeth 16
Schama, Simon 144, 145–146, 147–152, 154–155
Scher, Anna 194
Schools Broadcasting Council (SBC) 188, 192
Sconce, Jeffrey 213n3
Scottish Screen Archive 200
Scottish Television Film and Videotape Library 200
Scottish Youth Theatre 194
Scott of the Antarctic 205n15

Screen 1, 203n4, 208n17
Screen Education 32
Screenonline 20, 201, 205n10
Seaton, Jean 2, 4, 97
Second City Firsts 41, 53, 82, 86, 88–95, 209n10
– see also individual episode titles
Secret Garden, The (Audio Book) 45
Secret Garden, The (Film) 45, 50
Secret Garden, The (Stage Musical) 45
Secret Garden, The (TV) 11, 41–47, 49–50
Selby, Keith 34
Sendall, Bernard 7, 67, 71, 75, 77, 128, 133, 135
Sennett, Richard 147
Seven Ages of Britain 150
Shakespeare, William 16, 23, 26
Shand, Dave 77
Shelley, Winifrede 88
Shepherd, Jack 89, 94
Sheridan, Dorothy 165, 173, 215n18
Shils, Ed 175–176, 183
Shubik, Irene 39
Siegel, Mark 207n15
Signs of Trouble 191
Sillitoe, Alan 168
Silverstone, Roger 174
Silvey, Robert 162, 163, 165, 214n10
Simpson, Michael 190
Singer, Aubrey 147
Singing Detective, The 61
'Sin Shifter, The' 136
Six-Five Special 186, 187
Six O'Clock News, The 15
16 Up 217n19
Skutch, Ira 7, 97
Sky Plus 47
Slattery, Christine 209n2
Sloan, William David 2
Smashing Day 83
Smith, Anthony 9
Smith, Bonnie G. 150
Smith, Dai 133
Smith, Neville 89–90, 94, 209n11
Society for Cinema and Media Studies (SCMS) 1
Something Else 217n19
Song and Dance: A Little Show 115

Southern Television 185, 194, 195, 197
South West Film and Television Archive 200
Spartans, The 149
Special Enquiry No. 3: Has Britain a Colour Bar?
        118–120
Spiegel, Lynn 4, 6, 7, 8, 10, 26, 161, 175
Spotlight (1957) 122
Spotlight (1961–1967) 188
Stacey, Jackie 216n1
Starkey, David 145–146, 148, 150–151, 152
Starsky and Hutch 217n4
Startt, James D. 2
Stead, Robert 122
Steadman, Alison 89, 90
Stepney League of Coloured People, 123
Steptoe and Son 25
Stevenson, John 99
Stewart, John 209n1
Stokes, Jane 67, 71, 216n29
Stone, Peter 118
Stoppard, Tom 188
Street, Brian 173
Street, Sean 138
Sturcken, Frank 56
Sunday Night at the London Palladium 136
Sutcliffe, Thomas 188
Suzman, Janet 41, 47
Swallow, Norman 120–122
Sweeney, The 32

Talking to a Stranger 85
Taylor, A.J.P. 145–147, 213n6
Taylor, Laurie 191
Taylor, Philip M. 1, 4, 8, 143–144, 160
Teledu Cymru (aka Wales (West and North))
        97–98, 127–128, 130–138, 140, 213n1
Teledu Mamon (Mammon's Television) 128,
        133–134, 140
Television 209n2, 215n16
Television Act, (1954) 139
Television Newsreel 113
Television Wales and the West (TWW)
        127–128, 131, 132, 136, 139, 140
Television Wales Norwest 139
'Terry' 189–190
Terson, Peter 86
Thames Television 145

'That Quiet Earth' 85–86, 93, 209n4
That Was the Week That Was 25
Theatre Workshop 194
Thirty Minute Theatre 85–86, 88, 91–93,
        209n13 – see also individual episode titles
This Week 203n2
Thomas, Eric 140
Thomas, Howard 74–75
Thomas, James 175
Thomas, M. Wynn 129
Thomas, Sir Miles 141
Thomas, William 141
Thompson, John B. 160
Thompson, Robert J. 206n3
Thomson, Alistair 101, 103
Thornham, Sue 31
Thumim, Janet, 68, 79, 127, 138
Till Death Us Do Part 25–26
TiVo 47
Tonight 215n13
Tosh, John 10
Touch of Eastern Promise, A 86–88, 93
Traherne, Cennydd 140
Trevor, Jack 117
Tucker's Luck 185, 216n3
Tudor, David 141
Tulloch, John 29, 38, 205n4
Turnock, Rob 37, 56, 130, 163
TV Times Project 201, 203n2
Two People 191

UK Gold 25
Ulster Television Film Library 201
Undeb Cymru Fydd 137
'Under the Age' 85–86, 93
United Nations Educational, Scientific, and
        Cultural Organization (UNESCO) 124
Upstairs Downstairs 31–32, 42–43, 48, 60–61,
        206n3, 218n23
'Up the Junction' 62

Vahimagi, Tise 210n8
Vaughan, David 141
Vaughan, Peter 87
Vernon, John 210n14
Vesselo, Arthur 72
Victoria Theatre Company 90

Vince, Pamela 215n24
Voice of the Viewer and Listener 201
Voytek 39

Wales Television Association 131, 134, 139–140
Wales (West and North) – see Teledu Cymru
Ward, Bill 103–104, 105, 106–107, 108, 116, 210n14
Ward, Katie 161
Warwick, David 90
Waterman, Dennis 189
Watson, Francis 16–17, 204n2–3
Watt, Donald 143
We Bring You Live Pictures 209n2
Wednesday Play, The 82, 209n11 – see also individual episode titles
Welch, Elisabeth 113, 115–116
Weldon, Fay 188
Wells, Stanley 16
Wessex Film and Sound Archive 201
West African Rhythm Brothers 116
West Indian Students Union 123
Westward 132
What Now? 185, 216n3
Wheatley, Helen 7, 10, 31, 31–32, 38, 39, 42–43, 60–61, 203n7, 205n10, 206n3, 206n6, 207n10, 208n17, 218n23
White, Leonard 37–38, 39, 206n6
Whitehead, Ann 22
Whitehead, E.A. 85, 93
Whitelaw, Billie 20, 23

White Paper on Broadcasting (1952) 139
White Paper on Broadcasting (1953) 139
Williams, B. Haydn 128, 131, 140, 141
Williams, Gareth 205n12
Williams, P.O. 141
Williams, Raymond 2, 22, 216n30
Williams-Wynne, Colonel J.F. 141
Wind that Shakes the Barley 62
Winston, Brian 7
Woman in a Dressing Gown 23
Wood, Helen 203n7
Wood, Michael 148, 150, 154–155, 213n9
Wood, Nancy 101
Woolf, Virginia 49
World at War 145
Wright, Basil 72
Wyndham, John 39
Wyndham-Goldie, Grace 116, 215n13

Yes, Minister 29
Yorkshire Film Archive 201
You and Me and Him 87, 93
Young, Michael 175–176, 183
'You're Free' 85, 93
Youth Opportunities Programme (YOPS) 190
Ytreberg, Espen 147–148, 149

Z Cars 48, 83, 84–85, 190
Ziegler, Philip 173
Zola, Emile 49